FIVE VIEWS
ON
SANCTIFICATION

FIVE VIEWS
ON
SANCTIFICATION

Melvin E. Dieter
Anthony A. Hoekema
Stanley M. Horton
J. Robertson McQuilkin
John F. Walvoord

Academie
Books Grand Rapids,
Michigan
Zondervan Publishing House

FIVE VIEWS ON SANCTIFICATION

Copyright © 1987 by
The Zondervan Corporation
Grand Rapids, Michigan

ACADEMIE BOOKS
is an imprint of
Zondervan Publishing House
1415 Lake Drive S.E.
Grand Rapids, Michigan 49506

Library of Congress Cataloging in Publication Data

Five views on sanctification.

    Bibliography: p.
    Includes index.
    1. Sanctification.   I. Dieter, Melvin Easterday.

BT765.F58   1987   234'.8   86-28280

ISBN   0-310-41531-4

Printed in the United States of America

88 89 90 91 92 93 94 95 / AH / 10 9 8 7 6 5 4

CONTENTS

FOREWORD

The five authors of this volume describe the pathway to a holy, or sanctified, life. Each writes from an Evangelical perspective that views the Bible as authoritative and that considers a restored relationship to God through faith in Christ as an individual's greatest need and delight. This underlying unified perspective, however, encompasses various definitions of sanctification. The authors outline their own understanding of the doctrine and then address directly – and cordially – the views of their colleagues.

In spite of having theological backgrounds and convictions that diverge sharply in some areas, the authors stand together at several points in their understanding of sanctification. First, all agree that the Bible teaches a sanctification that is past, present, and future. It is past because it begins in a position of separation already gained in Christ's completed work. It is present in that it describes a process of cultivating a holy life. And sanctification has a future culmination at the return of Christ, when the effects of sin will be fully removed. Second, all agree that the process of sanctification requires believers to strive to express God's love in their experience. They must devote themselves to the traditional Christian disciplines and daily make the hard choices against evil and for God's ways of righteousness. Finally, all agree that the Bible promises success in this process of struggling against personal sin, through the power of the Holy Spirit.

But *how* does one achieve success in sanctification in this life? And *how much* success is possible? Is a crisis experience following one's conversion normal—or necessary? If so, what kind of experience, and how is it verified? As will be obvious, the authors disagree in their answers to these questions.

In evaluating the evident differences, the reader must note carefully the respective definitions of key biblical terms (especially *sin, old man/new man, perfect,* and the Spirit's *baptism*) as well as the Wesleyan term *entire sanctification.* In tracing the use of these concepts in the arguments and counterarguments, the student of sanctification must appreciate—as do all the authors—the need to preserve both divine sovereignty and human responsibility. Ideally, this discussion of sanctification will provide, not just stimulating theological divertissement, but encouragement to travel more thoughtfully the ancient and yet contemporary road to holiness, without which "no one will see the Lord" (Heb. 12:14).

The Publisher

Chapter 1

THE
WESLEYAN
PERSPECTIVE

Melvin E. Dieter

THE WESLEYAN PERSPECTIVE

Melvin E. Dieter

Almighty God, unto whom all hearts are open, all desires known, and from whom no secrets are hid: cleanse the thoughts of our hearts by the inspiration of Thy Holy Spirit, that we may perfectly love Thee, and worthily magnify Thy Holy Name; Through Christ, Our Lord. Amen. (*Book of Common Prayer*, 1695)

THE WESLEYAN WAY

A prayer for holiness and the perfect love of God has been a persistent petition of the church of Christ throughout its history. John Wesley, father of the Methodist family in the Christian world, regularly included this widely used collect of the Anglican church's *Book of Common Prayer* in his personal devotions and public ministry. For over two hundred years now, he and his followers have been known for their concern for an ethical faith. The Wesleyan doctrine of entire sanctification, or Christian perfection, expresses that concern most definitively.

Renewed and continuing interest in Wesley studies has helped to broaden some of the longstanding characterizations of John Wesley as a person and as a theologian within the larger Christian tradition. His distinctive contribution was his conviction that true biblical Christianity finds its highest expression and ultimate test of authenticity in the practical and ethical experience of the individual Christian and the church and only

11

secondarily in doctrinal and propositional definition. His persistence in pursuing that conviction throughout his ministry has often led historians to relegate his role in Christian history to that of the systematic practitioner rather than the informed theologian. Wesley's exceptional success in winning men and women to Christ and discipling them for service to God through his class meetings and other small groups has strongly shaped this popular and scholarly image of him—and justifiably so.[1]

It is becoming increasingly evident, however, that behind all his evangelistic passion and ministry of discipling lay a full-orbed theological understanding. Most of that understanding was built squarely upon the central doctrines of the Reformation and earlier Christian tradition as outlined in the *Articles* and prayer book of his Anglican faith. One emphasis, however, distinguished his interpretation of God's ways with men and women from that of the religion of his day, namely, the conviction that biblical Christianity must ultimately demonstrate its reality in "a faith that works by divine love" in the crucible of everyday life. This passion for seeing God's truth expressed in the experience and witness of faithful Christians was strongly fortified by his conviction that every person could respond positively or negatively to God's offer of salvation as they would. This freedom was of grace and not of nature. The realization that spiritual experience represented interaction between the sovereign grace of God and the freedom of humankind's response made Wesley a persistent observer of the spiritual experience of his followers. He believed that the knowledge of *how* God's truth translates itself into the experience of God's people by the Holy Spirit through the Word and the means of grace was critical for our proper understanding of the truth itself. Consequently not only the experience of Christians he knew but the whole experience of the church in the past engaged his attention.[2]

He was particularly interested in the life and witness of the early church fathers because he believed that their experiences of grace demonstrated best how men and women in the past had responded in wholehearted commitment and love to the will of God in their lives.[3] The new English translations of the Fathers that were appearing during his studies at Oxford University constituted one of the main sources of his understanding of Christian perfection and the nature of salvation. Such influences sometimes subtly, sometimes openly, distinguished his views from the prevailing mainline Reformed tradition and, together with the insights into relationships between holiness and love that he gleaned from writers like Thomas à Kempis, William Law, and Jeremy Taylor, became the heartbeat and life of his ministry and of the teaching that he adopted. The concept "faith working by love," as the ultimate hermeneutic for understanding God's entire plan of salvation, strongly shaped his teachings on sanctification. The "royal law of love" defined God's expectations for the life and witness of those who receive that salvation. When the implications of such emphases are incorporated into a theology of salvation, we can see why Wesley's theology differed at certain critical points from the accepted tradition of his time and today still stands as an alternative to the prevailing Reformed, Roman Catholic, or Orthodox teachings. It grounds itself mainly in the Reformed position but deviates from it by taking seriously certain key elements in each of the other two.[4]

Although Wesley used his observations of contemporary experience and his reflections on the lives of past Christians to shape his understanding of God's will, he nevertheless held God's Word as ultimate and authoritative. He refused to consider seriously any teaching unless it could stand its ground under the pure light of revelation. No Christian leader has ever been more faithful in bringing all observation, experience, and rational conclusions to the Scriptures for final judgment. "If by catholic principles," he said on one occasion, "you mean anything other than scriptural, they weigh nothing with me. I allow no other rule, whether of faith or practice, than the Holy Scriptures."[5] At the same time he insisted that God's truth was given to us to be translated into life and could be if it were received and believed. Therefore, to understand salvation fully, one must take into account the knowledge of God given to those who were honestly seeking His will and experiencing His grace; any valid test of true Christianity had to consider this evidence. Experience, he believed, could *confirm* a doctrine of Scripture, but it could not *establish* a doctrine of Scripture. Only the Bible itself could do that.[6]

Wesley's lifelong passion for Christian holiness was fired by his conviction that the Word of God teaches, by precept and by promise, that Christians should not be "content with any religion which does not imply the destruction of all the works of the devil, that is of all sin."[7] He never allowed that entirely sanctified Christians could become sinless in the sense that they could not fall again into sin through disobedience. He did teach that so long as men and women were the creatures of free will, they were able to respond obediently or disobediently to the grace of God. They would never be free from the *possibility* of deliberate, willful sinning in this life. They could, however, be delivered from the *necessity* of voluntary transgressions by living in moment-by-moment obedience to God's will. Whatever difficulty might arise in defining the theology, content, or means of attaining such a loving relationship with God, it could mean no less than freedom from the dominion of sin in this life. It did not, however, mean freedom from all the effects of sin in the deranged worldly order in which we experience even the most perfect of our present relationships under grace. Total freedom from the effects as well as the presence of all sin had to await the glory to come.[8]

Wesley believed that the promised present victory over sin was possible only through the Christ life implanted in believers by the Holy Spirit. Even those who enjoyed the closest walk with God, however, still had many imperfections in them as part and parcel of the fallen created order and had to depend daily on the atoning merits of Christ's blood and sincerely pray, "Forgive us our debts as we forgive our debtors." "For," he noted, "neither love nor 'the unction of the Holy One' makes us infallible: therefore . . . we cannot but mistake in many things."[9] In his well-known tract on Christian perfection, he maintained that "there is no *perfection of degrees*, as it is termed; none which does not admit of a continual increase. So that how much soever any man has attained, or in how high a degree soever he is perfect, he hath still need to 'grow in grace', and daily advance in the knowledge and love of God his Saviour."[10] In Wesleyan thought a person's full commitment to the relationship with God and neighbor in love is not a fixed superior state; it is, rather, a new stage, a new arena of ethical response to the divine will already inherent in the regeneration of new birth in Christ.

The Reformers' principles of *sola scriptura* and *sola gratia* were fixed stars in his constellation of theological principles as well. He also had their emphasis on personal faith. He departed from the Reformed tradition, however, in his teaching about the freedom from sin that believers could experience in this life.[11] "The doctrines of justification and sanctification are fused in a synthesis peculiar to Wesley, an amalgam of both Protestant and Catholic devotion." He "has transcended the principles of the Reformers, at any rate, has corrected a recognized limitation."[12] Wesley's synthesis combined the Reformed view of God's sovereign grace with the idea of saving faith as an active principle of holiness in the heart and life of a person. He joined the Reformed doctrine of an individual's total sinfulness and entire dependence on grace with the Arminian doctrine of human freedom, which made a person an acting subject with moral obligations.[13]

The abiding attention that Wesley paid to justification and sanctification is natural, therefore, and arose out of the practical and theological concerns that engaged him as he sought to understand the biblical view of salvation. His preaching and thinking were dominated by these and a few related doctrines that are reflected in Christian experience. He gave his major attention, however, to sanctification, a theme that weaves its way through the entire fabric of his preaching and theology.

SANCTIFICATION ACCORDING TO WESLEY

Wesley declared that the supreme and overruling purpose of God's plan of salvation is to renew men's and women's hearts in His own image. It is a teleological theme,[14] for he believed that all the grand currents of biblical salvation history moved toward this one end and had, in a restricted but definite manner, a fulfillment and perfection in this life. Wesley held that God had promised salvation from all willful sin, and he saw this promise in passages such as the following: Deuteronomy 30:6; Psalm 130:8; Ezekiel 36:25, 29; Matthew 5:48; 6:13; 22:37; John 3:8; 17:20–21, 23; Romans 8:3–4; 2 Corinthians 7:1; Ephesians 3:14–19; 5:25, 27; and 1 Thessalonians 5:23. He believed that such passages as Luke 1:69–75, Titus 2:11–14, and 1 John 4:17 indicated that this sanctification took place before death. By grace God would restore to us the holiness that had been lost in the Fall by our first parents.[15]

In a sermon representative of his lifelong beliefs on this doctrine, he declared,

> Ye know that all religion which does not answer this end, all that stops short of this, the renewal of our soul in the image of God, after the likeness of Him that created it, is no other than a poor farce, and a mere mockery of God, to the destruction of our own soul . . . . By nature ye are wholly corrupted. By grace ye shall be wholly renewed.[16]

The gracious element resides in God's good will to all, in that He is not willing that any should perish but that all should come to a saving knowledge of Himself. Only the merits of Christ's life and death bring us salvation, and His grace alone gives us the freedom to respond to His offer of forgiveness, cleansing, and a new relationship with Him in love. The grace of response is available to all persons; whosoever will may come. A subjective view of sanctification is firmly conjoined with the more prevalent objective view. Two apparently contradictory views come together; "freedom and dependence are joined."[17]

God first expressed this good will to humankind through His prevenient grace when He called Adam and Eve back to Himself after they had been corrupted in every part of their nature through their disobedience in Eden. And He has continued through all the ages since to call all their descendants—each one blighted by original sin and burdened by personal rebellion—back to Himself. His persistent purpose is to restore the divine moral image of love and purity of relationship with Him that had been lost because of their kinship with fallen Adam. "Real religion," he preached in 1758 from the text 1 John 3:8, is the restoration of human beings "by Him that bruises the serpent's head" to "all that the old serpent" deprived them of—not only to the favor of God, but to "likeness to the image of God"; not simply deliverance from sin but being filled with all the "fulness of God." Nothing short of this is true religion, he declared. The truth runs all through the Bible, he claimed, and he asked his readers not to "be . . . content with any religion which does not imply the destruction of the works of the devil, that is all sin." It is "faith that works by love."[18]

The agent of this call to justification and sanctification is the Holy Spirit, who gives us the faith by which both the objective and subjective elements of God's salvation in Jesus Christ become ours. The gracious work of the Spirit enables the sinful heart to respond in obedience to God's call to salvation. By this process we are gradually brought to the point of repentance and faith, by which we are born of God by the Spirit to new life in Jesus Christ. This new life in Christ not only brings us freedom from the objective guilt of sin through justification but through sanctification regenerates us and through the Spirit creates the subjective life of God and Christ in us.[19]

The Spirit's work of regeneration of the heart marks the

beginning point of sanctification. It means that we have been given that power over sin which is the birthright of every child of God as we seek to be conformed to His image. In regeneration the formation of the Christ life in us has begun; the call to holiness and divine love becomes the compelling motive of the new life under the power and inspiration of the Spirit, who has brought about our adoption as children of God. Every person who is born of God, from the moment of regeneration, has the promise of victory over sin and the devil and has the power of the Holy Spirit to realize that victory in everyday living.[20]

But Wesley, in conformity with all the Reformed traditions of his day as well as out of his own spiritual experience and understanding of Scripture, recognized that Christian believers, and especially those who were most serious in their desire to please God and forsake sin, experienced a continuing element of rebellion, a systemic illness, which weakened the will to holiness and love and divided their intention to love God and neighbor without reserve. "Indeed this grand point, that there are two contrary principles in believers—nature and grace, the flesh and the Spirit—runs through all the Epistles of St. Paul, yea through all the holy Scriptures," he taught.[21] Although other theological traditions of his day believed that this struggle against an innate, inward rebellion was a normal and even a necessary element of the Christian's quest for the holy life, Wesley believed that the whole gospel, in promise and command, indicated otherwise. He believed that there was freedom from the dominion of sin for every Christian, even under these unhappy inner struggles, and that God's grace was always moving the believer to a life of greater peace, happiness, and love. There was a remedy for the sickness of systemic sinfulness, namely, *entire sanctification*—a personal, definitive work of God's sanctifying grace by which the war within oneself might cease and the heart be fully released from rebellion into wholehearted love for God and others. This relationship of perfect love could be accomplished, not by excellence of any moral achievements, but by the same faith in the merits of Christ's sacrifice for sin that initially had brought justification and the new life in Christ. It was a "total death to sin and an entire renewal in the image of God."[22]

The theology of the Wesleyan revival movement is frequently expressed more clearly in its hymns than in its sermons and tracts. A hymn of Charles Wesley's expresses the faith of the Wesleyans at this point:

From all remaining filth within
Let me in Thee salvation have;
From actual and from inbred sin
My ransomed soul persist to save.

. . . .

Wash out my deep original stain—
Tell me no more it cannot be,
Demons or men! The Lamb was slain,
His blood was all poured out for me.[23]

The critical point of this purifying experience need not be chronologically distinct from justification and the new birth, but logically it is distinct from them in the continuum of salvation. However, the scriptural exhortation to believers to pursue perfection in love, as well as the struggles they commonly have with a divided heart, indicates that believers typically appropriate purity of love in a distinct crisis of faith sometime subsequent to justification. The new relationship of perfect love to God and others that results from this faith is not of a kind of love different from that which was experienced in justification but is, rather, the fulfillment of it. Negatively, entire sanctification is a cleansing of the heart, which brings healing of the remaining systemic hurts and bruises from Adam's sin. Positively, it is a freedom, a turning of the whole person toward God in love to seek and to know His will, which becomes the soul's delight. In his sermon "On Perfection," Wesley enumerated several features of this sanctification:

1. To love God with all one's heart and one's neighbour as oneself; 2. To have the mind that is in Christ; 3. To bear the fruit of the Spirit (in accordance with Gal. 5); 4. The restoration of the image of God in the soul, a recovery of man to the moral image of God, which consists of "righteousness and true holiness"; 5. Inward and outward righteousness, "holiness of life issuing from holiness of heart"; 6. God's sanctifying of the person in spirit, soul, and body; 7. The person's own perfect consecration to God; 8. A continuous presentation through Jesus of the individual's thoughts, words and actions as a sacrifice to God of praise and thanksgiving; 9. Salvation from all sin.[24]

These terse, biblically derived concepts constitute the critical mass of the concept of entire sanctification as it is understood in Wesleyan theology.

Such restoration of the image of God in love in the heart, although a crisis point in the quest for holiness, does not represent the final step in God's saving and sanctifying grace or the establishment of a fixed state of grace. Wesley allowed no stopping point in the Christian's quest for holiness–"no holiness of *degree*, no point of conclusion."[25] Quite to the contrary, every point of progress in grace renews one's zeal to realize more fully the immeasurable resources of God's grace and love toward those who trust and obey Him. To stop short of the crisis of faith by which we are restored through the Spirit to the love that we lost in the Fall was to ignore not only the privileges but the expectations of the finished work of Christ and the end point of the plan of salvation. To take that point of initial freedom in any way as a state of grace or a terminal victory was equally to ignore the promises and expectations of the salvation brought to us by Christ's work. Wesley believed that there are degrees of faith and of assurance of justifying faith as well as an infinite number of degrees in a person's experience of God. The idea of a gradual progression in sanctification is extended beyond the boundaries of this life, even though the basic relationship that nourishes such development is established in the crisis moment of entire sanctification.[26]

Wesley understood entire sanctification, or perfection in love, then, as a continuum of grace and response that leads persons from the guilt and despair of their sin to the knowledge of God and, by faith in His grace in Jesus Christ, to the crisis moment of the justification and the new birth.[27] The life of sanctification springs from the regenerated life created by the new birth and continues as the Holy Spirit through His gracious ministry calls them to moment-by-moment obedience to the will of God, which is the expression of His holiness and love. In this part of the Christian's progress in obeying the will of God and conforming to the mind of Christ, the remains of the rebellion and fallenness create conflict and often depression. The nature is still corrupted by a systemic illness that makes a free and ready response to the love of God a source of contention in the inner volitional being. The volitional powers have to be cleansed from the effects of the Fall, which remain even after justification, before persons can be wholly free to enjoy and express the pure love of God in all their relationships. His emphasis upon the importance of what God does "in us" through Christ, as well as upon what God does "for us" through Christ, constitutes Wesley's greatest contribution to the Christian church.

Wesley believed that the Bible clearly and persistently taught that God had wedded holy living and salvation by faith alone into one inseparable whole.[28] "If we believe the Bible, Who can deny it? Who can doubt of it?" he asked. "It runs through the Bible from the beginning to the end in one connected chain."[29] The proclamation of God's "great salvation," he contended, had been part of the tradition and experience of the primitive church[30] and had been experienced by earnest Christians in the subsequent history of the church whenever there was a genuine revival of biblical preaching and obedient discipleship. It had been largely neglected by the Protestant Reformers because of their abhorrence of the doctrines clustering around merit by works, which they saw as causing the failure of Evangelical doctrine in the medieval Catholic church. God had now entrusted to the Methodists the special responsibility to proclaim it again as the birthright of all Christians. In doing so they brought the Reformation principle of salvation by faith alone to its legitimate and logical conclusion.[31]

Wesley became convinced, even before his contacts with the Moravians, that this relationship of living before God in the perfection of love was the supreme end of Christianity. Not unlike Luther, his first efforts to know the truth for himself ended in frustration and despair. The disciplines and works of charity of his "Holy Club" were not enough.[32] Only after his own experience of personal faith in Christ, in what is now known as his "Aldersgate experience," did he see that one's relationship with God was established by the merit of Christ rather than the merit of personal good works.[33] Out of this new understanding of faith and grace, he saw that a clear call for Christian perfection by faith was the logical consequence of the Reformer's bold call for justification by faith. His formulation of sanctification as "faith working by love" began to define a concept of sanctification that Wesley felt was more biblical and closer to the tradition of the early Christian church than that which the Catholicism or Protestantism of his day were proclaiming. His view of faith as the means to love became his hermeneutic of grace and salvation; it places him, in the minds of some scholars, into the arena of Catholic devotion. But his refusal to forsake the Reformed principle of justification by faith, in the opinion of others, places him squarely in the camps of Calvin and Luther.[34]

For Wesley, God's sovereign grace through saving faith

becomes an active principle of holiness within the hearts of believing men and women. Out of his reflection of this mix of faith, life, reason, and the experience of the church, all judged and authenticated by the Word of God, Wesley's understanding of sanctification was fleshed out and placed at the center of his theological system. Thereafter, he stood by his conviction on the doctrine, in spite of the resistance he encountered from the lackluster deism so prevalent in his own Church of England and the rampant antinomianism in many of the nonestablished country churches. He and his followers set before their hearers the promise of a heart perfected in love, a personal restoration to the moral image of God, and the responsibility and power to express that love in relationship with God and neighbor. Through Christ and the indwelling Holy Spirit, the "bent to sinning" could be cleansed from the repentant, believing heart, and a "bent to loving obedience" could become the mainspring of one's life.

The belief that one can attain in this life a relationship with God and others that is characterized from moment to moment by divine love marks the dividing line of commitment for those who seek to be Wesleyan. This doctrine is so central to whole Wesleyan understanding of the plan of salvation that to leave Wesley at this point is to detour completely from the path he followed.[35]

THE THEOLOGICAL MILIEU

We are now ready to outline, in a more detailed but still necessarily limited scope, the particular biblical and theological themes that most directly inform the Wesleyan understanding of justification and sanctification summarized above.

Original Sin and Prevenient Grace

A central point in any theology is its accepted position on the nature of the human situation. One's doctrine of original sin is arguably as determinative a concept as any other for one's view of sanctification, and both in turn, depend on one's doctrine of grace. As we have noted, Wesleyans affirm the total corruption of the first man and woman through disobedience, in full agreement with the tradition of the Reformers and especially that of Calvin. They also affirm that fallen men and women can be restored to God's favor by the merits of Christ only and no other. In the *Minutes* of his 1745 conference, Wesley replied to the question as to where he came to the very edge of Calvinism by saying, "(1.) In ascribing all good to the free grace of God. (2.) In denying all natural free-will, and all power antecedent to grace. And, (3.) In excluding all merit from man; even for what he has or does by the grace of God."[36] Any understanding of the Wesleyan doctrine of salvation must take into account Wesleyans' full agreement with these three critical Evangelical teachings: beings are by nature totally corrupt; this corruption is the result of original sin; they can be justified only through God's grace in Christ. The Fall and its consequences are fundamental in the Wesleyan doctrines of justification and sanctification.[37]

Wesley's *Doctrine of Original Sin*, published in 1757, demonstrates how strongly his concepts of sin are rooted in that doctrine. Written in response to Dr. John Taylor's unitarianism, Wesley described the utter depravity created by the Fall in his most telling words on the subject.[38] In stark contrast with Taylor's idealistic view of the human condition, he maintained that this very doctrine of human corruption distinguishes Christianity from all false religion. "Is man by nature filled with all manner of evil? Is he void of all good? Is he wholly fallen? . . . Allow this and you are so far a Christian. Deny it and you are but a Heathen still."[39] This corruption is the source of all sin and corruption that subsequently follows in all the children of Adam and Eve:

> How wide do those parent-sins extend, from which all the rest derive their being;—that carnal mind which is enmity against God, pride of heart, self-will, and love of the world! Can we fix any bounds to them? Do they not diffuse themselves through all our thoughts, and mingle with all our tempers? Are they not the leaven which leavens, more or less, the whole mass of our affections? May we not, on a close and faithful examination of ourselves, perceive these roots of bitterness continually springing up, infecting all our words, and tainting all our actions?[40]

The real loss that Adam and Eve suffered in their rebellion against God was the loss of the *imago Dei*, which they had enjoyed. For Wesley, this consisted of three aspects: (1) *The natural image*, which gave men and women immortality, free will, and affections; (2) *The political image*, which gave them the authority to rule the natural realm; and, most important,

(3) *The moral image,* by which they were imbued with righteousness and true holiness and were like their Creator in love,
purity, and integrity. This third aspect of the divine image also
gave them their intellectual powers. The Fall affected all of
these dimensions, with the result that the *imago Dei* was lost.
Every part of humankind's nature was infected by sin. Love
and knowledge of God were replaced by alienation and loss of
desire to know Him. Free will rebelled against the divine will
in deliberate disobedience. The intellect was darkened and
dulled.[41]

In summary, then, Wesley defined original sin as a total
corruption of the whole of human nature.[42] In the sermon "The
Deceitfulness of Man's Heart," written in 1790, self-will, pride,
love of the world, independence of God, atheism, and idolatry
are specified as the origin of human evil.[43] Such views clearly
link Wesley's views of original sin and its consequences for the
race with those of Augustine: both interpret Paul's teaching on
it in a similar fashion, and both regard Adam as the first
ancestor and the representative of humankind.[44] Unlike Augustine, however, Wesley sees the Fall as the result of a lack of
love, not of concupiscence.

When Wesley discussed the loss of the image of God
through the Fall, however, he spoke in ultimate terms only of
the moral image, which he said was preeminent and alone
related to salvation. Human beings after the Fall did retain
vestiges of the natural and political images; people are self-
motivated, unlike the passive material creation, and still retain
a degree of lordship over the created order.[45] From this
understanding of the scriptural account of the Fall, Wesley saw
God's response as a plan of salvation that promised the
gracious restoration through faith of that relationship of perfect
love for God that the first man and woman enjoyed.[46] The
promise is to everyone who will believe on the sufficient
sacrifice of the Second Adam. The remedy for the imperfections
of the created order and for the loss of the natural and political
aspects of the divine image that Adam once enjoyed will have
to wait for the consummation of all things. Consequently,
Wesley believed, because we are imperfect persons in an
imperfect world, perfection "in love" is consistent with a
"thousand mistakes." But limited as we are by our own and the
world's imperfections, we may still enjoy a relationship in
which, through the power of the Holy Spirit, we can fulfill the
great and final commandment of loving God with our whole

heart and our neighbors as ourselves. Any lesser expectation falls short of the fullness of the "great salvation."[47]

This optimism, which springs up among the ruins of so drastic a reversal as the loss of the divine image, as described by Wesley and all Evangelical theologians of the Christian church, is an "optimism of grace." At this point Wesleyan theology diverges drastically from much of Reformation thought on how and to what degree God's grace overcomes and reverses the losses of the Fall. The optimism of grace, which leads to the belief in the promise (and therefore the possibility) of the full release from the effects of the loss of the spiritual relationship in the Garden of Eden and the full restoration of perfect love in the Christian's relationship with God and neighbor, rests in large measure on Wesley's understanding of the prevenience of grace and the freedom of human response. God is extending varying measures of grace to us all, and if we respond and receive it, "we *may* live," but if we choose not to, "we *will* die."[48] Wesleyans acknowledge that after the Fall persons have been infected by sin, pride, and a rebellious spirit in every part; by their own power and their own will they can choose nothing but sin.

Wesley held that there is neither natural knowledge of God nor natural conscience in men and women. When Paul speaks of these two sources of the knowledge of God, for which all are held accountable and because of which any who continue in their sin are condemned, he is speaking of the prevenient grace of God at work in drawing all persons to Himself. After the Fall, they possessed no natural ability by which they could know God or merit His salvation. Wesley summed up his view in this way:

> For allowing that all the souls of men are dead in sin by *nature*, this excuses none, seeing there is no man that is in a state of mere nature; there is no man, unless he has quenched the Spirit, that is wholly void of the grace of God. No man living is entirely destitute of what is vulgarly called *natural conscience*. But this is not natural: It is more properly termed, *preventing grace*. Every man has a greater or less measure of this, which waiteth not for the call of man. . . . So that no man sins because he has not grace, but because he does not use the grace which he hath.[49]

The "light that lighteth every man that cometh into the world" immediately began to make them aware of the need and the possibility of restoration in the midst of their ruin. God's immediate and unceasing effort to awaken and bring men and women to a consciousness of their need and to a trust in His grace is the dynamic force that carries along the continuum of grace, which leads them from grace to grace in a continuum of salvation. The critical end of this grace, which comes before saving grace, is love in the heart of every son and daughter of Adam and Eve so that they may serve God in "righteousness and true holiness" all of their days. Prevenient grace, then, is the beginning of the process by which God begins to lighten the darkness of the Fall for all men and women; it will bring those who faithfully receive it to saving grace, sanctifying grace, and grace for the life of love. When brought into dynamic interaction with all that Wesley says about the utter fallenness of man in any natural terms, it indicates that salvation comes to us only by the grace that flows from the atoning work of Jesus Christ, never because of any natural ability or achievement.

The Continuum of Law and Love

The second set of complementary doctrines that are integral to Wesley's understanding of sanctification is *law and love*. His studies of the Old and New Testament led him to the conclusion that persons who, under grace, fulfill the "royal law of love" as taught most simply and explicitly by Christ Himself in the Sermon on the Mount and subsequently by all of the New Testament writings are also fulfilling the moral intent of the Ten Commandments. Wesley thus relates the fulfillment of the law's moral obligations to the process and end of sanctification rather than to the more objective views of Reformation orthodoxy, which find the fulfillment and satisfaction of the moral law in the act of the believer's justification. There the emphasis is on our freedom from the moral obligations of the law because we are "clothed in the righteousness of Christ." Wesley, too, used such terminology,[50] but with a significant difference of application. The righteousness of Christ clothed us with God's forgiveness and favor; in this He maintained an objective stance toward the significance of our justification. But the fulfillment of Christ's work in atonement as it respects the law lies not so much in what He did on the cross "for us" as in what His work on the cross does "in us" as the life of Christ becomes ours in the new birth and sanctification.[51] As Lindström indicates, "This explains why sanctification in the sense of the fulfillment of the law occupies such an important place in his theology."[52]

Wesley always regarded the law as holy and good. There was not the strong law-versus-gospel tension that pervaded Luther's theology.[53] Wesley's understanding of the significance of the Sermon on the Mount became the heart of his understanding of the relationship between perfect love and the commandments of God as the royal law of love. Wesley declared that the Ten Commandments are renewed in the Sermon on the Mount in their sanctifying purity and spirituality and that they describe the life of practical Christian holiness, which is the end of faith and the commandments.[54] He concluded that to provide humankind with the grace to love God and to keep His commandments is the persistent promise that always attends the presentation of the law of God in the Old Testament. The subsequent promise of the gospel is in no sense contrary but fulfills the essential purposes of the moral law.[55]

The moral law, he said, "is an incorruptible picture of the High and Holy ONE that inhabiteth eternity. . . . It is the face of God unveiled; God manifested . . . to give, and not to destroy, life—that they may see God and live."[56] The law is good, therefore, and in itself is a revelation of the divine holiness, justice, and goodness. Although it unmasks us in our self-righteousness and is the severe taskmaster that brings us to Christ, behind all the apparent severity of the law is the love of God, driving and luring us to the life of love, which is the end of the law. The law in this sense becomes a gospel. But its fulfillment and the blessing that springs from obedience to it come only to those who participate in the life of Christ, who are partakers of the divine nature. The commandment and the promise are joined, and the royal law of love becomes the vision and delight only of those who are under grace.

Wesley rejected suggestions that this strong insistence on the importance of the law represented legalism, maintaining that the Bible nowhere condemned this understanding of what it meant to fulfill the law of God. He declared further that he rejected as well any purported liberty that was not "the liberty to love and to serve God," and he was fearful of no enslavement except "bondage to sin." Furthermore, Paul's declaration that God sent "His own Son in the likeness of sinful flesh . . . , that the righteousness of the law might be fulfilled in us" teaches us that the New Testament regards "the righteousness of the law" as "legal righteousness."[57] But Christians are absolved from "the curse of the moral law" and from its condemning power.[58] They are not even required to keep the moral law as a condition of their acceptance. They are always accepted only "in Christ."[59] But the Christian is under obligation to fulfill the law on the basis of faith. The fulfilling of the law therefore, is related to the act of sanctification rather than to the act of justification. The Christian's life is designed under grace to be a progressive movement from the new birth to entire sanctification and perfection in love. The end result of Christian perfection is not an inner spirituality but works of love. Saving faith is fulfilled in the outgoing life of holiness and self-giving in the love of Christ; otherwise, it is dead. By *salvation*, Wesley meant

> not barely, according to the vulgar notion, deliverance from hell, or going to heaven; but a present deliverance from sin, a restoration of the soul to its primitive health, its original purity; a recovery of the divine nature; the renewal of our souls after the image of God, in righteousness and true holiness, in justice, mercy, and truth.[60]

Faith is the means by which the law is established, and love is the fulfillment of the commandment. Love, not faith, becomes the final goal of the plan of salvation. Love is "the end of all the commandments of God," Wesley said. It is "the end, the sole end, of every dispensation of God, from the beginning of the world to the consummation of all things."[61] Faith in Christ is not to supersede but to produce holiness. Faith is only the "handmaid of love. . . . Biblical faith, for Wesley, is so entangled with love and obedience . . . that it does not exist without them."[62]

Since love cannot exist without the action of a moral being, the bent of Wesleyan theology is decidedly ethical; the essence of sanctification is love in action. True Christianity is to "have the mind of Christ," which is demonstrated in love for God and neighbor.[63] The real freedom of the Christian is not the freedom from guilt or release from the pangs of hell but the freedom to love with the love of God Himself shed abroad in the heart by the indwelling Holy Spirit.[64] In his *Plain Account*, Wesley summarized freedom as "nothing higher and nothing lower than this . . . love governing the heart and life, through all our tempers, words, and actions. . . . Christian perfection is purity of intention, dedicating all the life to God. It is giving God all our hearts."[65] "The saving Christ is not a proposition to be accepted, but a Person to be loved and obeyed," Wynkoop notes at this point of Wesley's teaching. The expression of faith is obedience and love.[66]

The Nature and Work of the Holy Spirit

The third essential element that contributes in a significant way to the Wesleyan understanding of sanctification is the work of the sanctifying Spirit. If the essence of the Divine is holy love, then His supreme desire is to communicate that holiness to His creatures whom He desires to share in His own image. The Holy Spirit is called *holy* not only because He is God but because, as the Scriptures reveal, He communicates God's own nature to His children. He imparts the life of love through the life of Jesus Christ who dwells in them by the Spirit's own presence and power. Holiness, in relation to God, Wesley understood as a verb as well as an adjective.[67] The Spirit is the Spirit of Christ. Wesley regarded this promise of the Holy Spirit as the one who will finally restore the true and wholehearted love of God in the hearts of all who will believe on Jesus Christ as one of the grand salvation themes of both the Old and the New Covenants. The "litany of biblical promises of purity of heart and perfect love"[68] that he recited repeatedly throughout his life usually began with God's promise to Moses in Deuteronomy 30 that He would "circumcise the hearts of the people" so they might love Him with all their hearts and keep His statutes. It moved on to the bold promises of Jeremiah 31 and Ezekiel 36, where God declares His purpose to restore His Spirit to His people in a New Covenant that will enable them to walk in His ways and obey Him because He will give them a new heart—a will to love rather than to disobey.

Wesley heard this theme of the centrality of the sanctifying Spirit resonating in Jesus' promise that those who seek after righteousness shall be filled. The theme was reiterated by Christ in the discourses with His disciples just before His death, as recorded by the apostle John. Charles Wesley's hymns on sanctification reinforced the Wesleyan belief that through the power of the indwelling Spirit the new people of God would be enabled to live in righteousness and true holiness all their lives. Inherent in the biblical command to be perfect is the promise of its fulfillment; the law, as we have noted, is also a gospel. God makes gracious provision for all that He asks of men and women. Wesley pointed out that a greater measure of the Holy Spirit is granted under the Christian dispensation than under the Jewish one, for the Christian's possibilities of salvation are much greater than anything that the previous dispensation could provide. Only after the glorification of Jesus Christ was the sanctifying grace of the Holy Spirit accorded to true believers in full measure.[69] Wesley found support for his doctrine of perfection in Christian experience as well as in the Scriptures. Through the Holy Spirit believers could have the assurance of his relationship with God in love, even as they had received the Spirit's witness to their new birth in Christ.

Although Wesley always advocated the zealous preaching of the pursuit of Christian perfection in his societies and all the church, he also advocated a pastoral approach in its presentation and application. Sincere, seeking persons should be "drawn" by hope, joy, and desire and should not be "driven" to the experience by slavish fear. Neither should they be overcome by anxiety, even because of the sin that remains in them. Their hope in Christ is always greater than their despair and should drive them all the more to the promises and the love of Christ, which will bring them the cleansing and freedom they desire.[70] Nor should they deprecate the grace they have already received through the Holy Spirit, who came to dwell in them when they first became a child of God. Wesley admonished his followers to "describe the blessings of a justified state as strongly as possible" whenever they testified to entire sanctification."[71]

THE BIBLICAL MILIEU

The doctrine of entire sanctification, or Christian perfection, which is at the heart of the Wesleyan "Theology of Love," has often been attacked as a purely perfectionist ideal—an attractive one, but unrealizable in this world of imperfection and sin. Wesleyans, however, have focused on that very ideal, which they regard as the reigning vision of the Scriptures themselves, set forth throughout as the essence of the gospel. To deny the expectation of its realization in some true measure when properly presented in its biblical balance and integrity is to fail to communicate the full riches of God's grace now available to His people for life and service. I cannot present here in full the arguments by which Wesley and his followers have sought to establish these biblical data. The brief review that follows, however, will amplify some of the biblical themes that were woven into the preceding theological summary and will introduce others that get to the heart of what Wesleyans see as the scriptural mandates and promises concerning the nature of Christian holiness.

It is critical to remember that Wesleyans do not come to their biblical understanding of sanctification by a system of logical deduction from certain proof texts or propositions. Their convictions on the possibilities of perfection in love in this life and a faith experience of heart cleansing subsequent to justification grow out of their attempt to see Scripture holistically. Wesleyans believe that lying behind the biblical and theological themes outlined above—the meaning of creation, the fall of men and women, the understanding of law and grace, and the ministry and work of the Holy Spirit—is the most prominent of all biblical themes, namely, the call to sanctification, or holiness, itself, with its ultimate end an ongoing relationship in love with God and all others. The life of holy love, therefore, should be the quest and expectation of everyone who is born of God. Christ's summation of the fulfillment of the law as the loving of God with all our heart, soul, and mind and our neighbor as our self (Matt. 22:37–39) is the basic biblical truth that sets the hermeneutical agenda for understanding God's purpose in all of His work of redemption in His Son Jesus Christ. Upon this command hangs all the law and the prophets. Expression of the holy love of God out of an undivided heart is the goal of the Christian life. All else is commentary.

The fundamental meaning of the word *sanctify* is "to set apart," or "to consecrate"; it is derived from the Hebrew *qādaš,* meaning "to separate" or "to divide." It means to remove persons or things from the realm of the profane and to set them apart to God. They become thereby "holy." Thus the entire nation of Israel was sanctified to the Lord (see Exod. 19:10). Peter declares that the church constitutes "a chosen people, . . . a holy nation, a people belonging to God" (1 Peter 2:9). In this sense all true Christians are sanctified and saints (see Acts 20:32; 26:18; Rom. 15:16; 1 Cor. 6:11; Eph. 5:26; Heb. 2:11; 10:10, 14; 13:12).

But the New Testament term carries a strong emphasis on another element—the ethical. The sanctified are to demonstrate the holiness and love, or character, of their God to whom they are consecrated. The concept is not absent from the Old

Testament, but it is certainly muted. In this context then, we see Peter applying to the church God's admonition to Israel, "I am the LORD your God; consecrate yourselves and be holy, because I am holy" (Lev. 11:44). He urges Christians, "Just as he who called you is holy, so be holy in all you do; for it is written: 'Be holy, because I am holy'" (1 Peter 1:15–16). Peter, of all persons, does not speak of some abstract concept of holiness. He admonishes believers, rather, that in contrast to their former wickedness, obedience and careful living should characterize their conduct. The context reveals that love is the test of holiness. In a similar manner Wesleyans would interpret Jesus' command in the Sermon on the Mount to "be perfect, therefore, as your heavenly Father is perfect" (Matt. 5:48). God insists that Christian holiness is more than an objective legality; it is also a subjective reality. "By their fruits ye shall know them" (Matt. 7:20 KJV). These words of Christ and the apostles cannot be taken as only ideals that become a new kind of legalism that entices us to do better but denies to us any real measure of experienced integrity and wholeness in our relationship with God in love.

God wants to have (indeed, needs to have) a holy people to have fellowship with—a theme that pervades Scripture. Consider, for example, Paul's prayer for the Christians at Thessalonica, "May God himself, the God of peace, sanctify you through and through. May your whole spirit, soul and body be kept blameless" (1 Thess. 5:23), and his declaration that "Christ loved the church and gave himself up for her to make her holy . . . to present her to himself as a radiant church, without stain or wrinkle or any other blemish, but holy and blameless" (Eph. 5:25–27). A more literal translation of the latter text shows its true implications more clearly: "Christ loved the assembly and gave up himself for it, in order that he might sanctify it, having already [or first] cleansed it by the washing of water by the Word." To prepare the church as His bride is the fundamental idea or goal. "Without stain or wrinkle" is another way of saying "holy and blameless"; both express the reality of the sanctification of the Christian and of the church and clearly carry moral connotations, as Paul expresses. Hebrews 13:12 expresses the same theme: "And so Jesus also suffered outside the city gate to make the people holy through his own blood." The central purpose of the cross was the sanctification of His people both corporately and individually.

The purpose of such sanctification is moral and ethical and not merely a Christian's claim to some special standing before God, as indicated in a study of the great prayer of Christ for His disciples in John 17. The Father has sanctified Him so that He might sanctify them and bring them into such a unity of love with the Father that their witness would convince the world. The world could know the reality of that unity only by concrete evidence of moral fitness issuing out of the divine love they were experiencing. The prayer was for the disciples and all who would believe on Christ through their word and their works, the "greater works" that they would do in the power of the Spirit (John 14:12 RSV). It is evident within this context that a purely positional standing in Christ or otherworldly experience of Him could never effect the witness in the world that Christ prayed for.

Mildred Wynkoop notes that John 17 parallels the Ephesians 4 passage remarkably:

> (1) Jesus had in mind a spiritually unified body of believers (2) that would bring glory to himself. (3) He died to sanctify them. All other elements of redemption were included but incidental to this. (4) Sanctification was in word and truth. This "word" obviously was not the Scripture primarily, but was found in living fellowship with the living Word, who is himself Truth. (5) The commission was accompanied by a moral fitness—for the unity of spirit indicated in both passages is moral clear through.[72]

All these passages sound the same note of divine intent: salvation centers on the practical sanctification of believers individually and as the people of God.

Adherents of this understanding recognize that there is no explicit exhortation to seek sanctification as such in the New Testament. Rather, there are admonitions to "let this mind be in you, which was also in Christ Jesus" (Phil. 2:5 KJV). Maturity of Christian life is to be found among those believers who have "put off . . . the old man" and have "put on the new man" (Eph. 4:22, 24 KJV). Christians are urged to cleanse themselves "from all filthiness of the flesh and spirit" (2 Cor. 7:1 KJV). "Every thought" is to be brought captive "to the obedience of Christ" (2 Cor. 10:5 KJV). We are to "lay aside every weight, and the sin which doth so easily beset us" (Heb. 12:1 KJV). Paul says that in the church at Corinth some believers were spiritual and some were carnal: "And I, brethren, could not speak unto you as unto spiritual, but as unto carnal, even as unto babes in Christ" (1 Cor. 3:1 KJV). In the previous chapter he speaks also of some as perfect—thereby implying that some are not perfect. Here, then (and in many similar texts), Christians are addressed and admonished who apparently have not yet experienced the spirituality, perfection, or freedom that should and could be theirs through the grace that is now available to them as children of God.

The call to such a life of freedom from the old rebellious nature and the concomitant call to the liberty to serve God and others wholeheartedly are central to apostolic work and preaching. Paul says:

> It was he who gave some to be apostles, some to be prophets, some to be evangelists, and some to be pastors and teachers, to prepare God's people for works of service, so that the body of Christ may be built up until we all reach unity in the faith and in the knowledge of the Son of God and become mature, attaining to the whole measure of the fullness of Christ. (Eph. 4:11–13)

These latter phrases all describe a wonderful ideal, or goal, in the Christian life, and the leader's primary task is to strive continually to bring all believers to that goal. Paul also says that the work of a minister of Christ is to "present everyone perfect in Christ (Col. 1:28). He speaks of himself as praying night and day "most earnestly" that he might "supply what is lacking in your faith" (1 Thess. 3:10). John indicates his own expectations for believers when he declares that "the blood of Jesus, his Son, purifies us from all sin" (1 John 1:7). His statement in 1 John 3:8 that "the reason the Son of God appeared was to destroy the devil's work" is basic to a biblical understanding of God's plan and purpose in salvation, especially in view of the moral, ethical, and existential connotations of the verses that surround this text. These and many other texts illustrate and enlarge on the words of Jesus: "I tell you the truth, everyone who sins is a slave to sin. . . . So if the Son sets you free, you will be free indeed" (John 8:34–36). The call to holiness and love as the expectation of the Christian life is a clarion call not left open to question; the ministry of the gospel must lead believers into the fullness of the biblical promise.

The biblical teaching on the creation of men and women in the "image" and "likeness" of God (Gen. 1:26–27) is another theme that reinforces and authenticates Wesleyans' concerns for this freedom from sin and the corresponding power to become wholehearted lovers of God. The concept of this image is not to be limited or even warped by identifying it with philosophical concepts of spirituality, rationality, and eternity; rather, it is to be expressed in terms of a loving interpersonal relationship that is marked by communion (1 John 1:3–4), responsibility (Gen. 2:15–17), and stewardship (Gen. 1:26–27). All these gifts were due to God's love, and men and women can never be fully redeemed without enjoying the freedom to serve God and each other in relationships of divine love from their whole hearts. This freedom and love is the goal of salvation. As we have already indicated, the Fall, then, was finally centered not in concupiscence but in a loss of love, of the divine image. It was a rebellion of free, willing agents acting out of selfishness. The antidote, according to Paul, is that in Christ we receive a "new nature, which is being renewed in knowledge after the image of its creator" (Col. 3:10 RSV). In "union with Christ," a new humanity is created. Wesleyans maintain that to allow any lesser standard than this restoration of the image of God to the souls of men and women is to diminish the fullness of atonement in Christ.

This "in Christ" life of believers is central to the Pauline understanding of the nature of salvation. Jesus Christ Himself introduces the theme, particularly in the intimate discourses with His apostles before His death, as recorded by John. "I am the vine; you are the branches. If a man remains in me and I in him, he will bear much fruit; apart from me you can do nothing" (John 15:5). Paul mentions that Christians are "in Christ," "in Him," or "in the Lord" in all but one of his letters—164 times in all. The total impact of such a biblical witness indicates to Wesleyans that a subjective, existential, and personal understanding of sin and salvation is necessary as well as one that is objective, or legal. The themes already represented are united when Paul exclaims, "If anyone is in Christ, he is a new creation; the old has gone, the new has come!" (2 Cor. 5:17; see also Rom. 8:1; 1 Cor. 15:22).

This incorporation into Christ involves justification, adoption, regeneration, and sanctification. The believer's righteousness, sanctification, and redemption are found in Him (1 Cor. 1:30). Wesleyans fully accept the persistent truth sounded by the Reformers that all of the merit that brings us salvation lies in the work of Christ alone and is appropriated by us through faith alone. It is all the gift of God (Eph. 2:8–9; cf. Acts 15:11;

Rom. 3:24; 5:15; 11:6; Titus 2:11; 3:7). Salvation is by grace. However, although the Reformation tradition frequently emphasizes justification and adoption, it often neglects regeneration and sanctification; a wholly *imputed* righteousness (objective salvation) comes to the fore, but *imparted* righteousness (subjective salvation) is neglected. Wesleyans would maintain that the biblical concept of salvation encompasses both and that both are found in the Pauline concept of being "in Christ," which constitutes the basic definition of a Christian in the New Testament.

Christ, however, is also in the Christian (Gal. 2:20). It is "the secret hidden for long ages and through many generations, but now disclosed to God's people. . . . The secret is this: Christ in you" (Col. 1:26–27 NEB; see also John 14:20; 17:23; Eph. 3:17; Rev. 3:20). Wholeness and restoration are found in union with Christ. It is not a union of identity but a relationship of freedom made possible by the qualities of Christ Jesus for "you have been brought to completion" (Col. 2:10 NEB).

Paul expresses this freedom when he says, "Therefore do not let sin reign in your mortal body. . . . For sin shall not be your master, because you are not under law, but under grace. . . . But now that you have been set free from sin and have become slaves to God, the benefit you reap leads to holiness, and the result is eternal life" (Rom. 6:12, 14, 22). The kingdom of God is within Christians (Luke 17:21), and the life of the kingdom (the Sermon on the Mount) is theirs. The life of Jesus is being revealed in their mortal bodies (2 Cor. 4:10). The resources for victory lie not in the individual but in Christ. Christians do not serve out of strength but out of yieldedness. God, through the grace of Christ and the power of the indwelling Spirit, sheds the love of God abroad in their hearts.

The presence of Christ and the freedom from the rebellious nature of the old Adam in the Christian's life in the Spirit, however, are not the final release from the presence and threat of sin. Its power and presence threaten and tempt us through our fallen bodies and minds as well as in all that surrounds us in a world that is yet to be redeemed. Paul plainly outlines this teaching in Romans 8, a chapter that is especially critical to a Wesleyan understanding of the life of holiness. After declaring freedom from the dominion and inner presence of sin in the life of the Spirit-filled Christian (vv. 1–17), he nevertheless acknowledges that we still live in a fallen, sinful world, even though we are the people of God who are already citizens of the new world order (vv. 18–30). Our minds and our bodies are subject to limitation (1 Cor. 13:12, Matt. 26:41). Completed redemption in these areas awaits the final consummation of all things. In the face of all the seeming contradictions that this truth presents, even to people who are already redeemed, the apostle says that we are kept in the love of God until the new order is established universally, (Rom. 8:18–30). "We eagerly await a Saviour . . . who . . . will transform our lowly bodies so that they will be like his glorious body (Phil. 3:20–21). God *will* save us from sin's power and dominion so that we may serve Him with a whole heart. He *may* save us from sickness and other realities of the time in which we now serve Him, as we trust ourselves to the goodness and wisdom of His divine lordship over time and all that He has created. Paul gives similar reassuring words to Titus. Christians are to live lives of holiness while they "wait for the blessed hope—the glorious appearing of our great God and Savior, Jesus Christ, who gave himself for us to redeem us from all wickedness and to purify for himself a people that are his very own, eager to do what is good" (Titus 2:13–14).

In the rich milieu of these and numerous other biblical patterns concerning the basic intent of the truths of salvation, Wesleyans interpret and understand the content of the life that is in Christ Jesus. With Wesley, they maintain that any doctrine of sanctification that stops short of these promises and potentials falls short of the full gospel. There have always been tensions of understanding as to how sanctification shall be entered into and maintained or how it may be expressed in all the vicissitudes of life. Differences have risen at times among Wesleyans themselves and at times with those who have a different understanding of sanctification. The objections of those who hold other opinions will be addressed in a limited way in the responses presented in this book. A brief survey of some of the tensions that have arisen in Wesleyanism itself in relation to the "Grand Depositum," as I have presented its classical-historical features here, is more appropriate to this essay.

SUBSEQUENT DEVELOPMENT OF THE DOCTRINE

The foremost proving ground for the full-fledged application of the Wesleyan understanding of Christian perfection, or entire sanctification, to the life of the church was the Wesleyan movement in America. More than twenty years before Wesley's death in 1791, lay men and women from his societies in England had already established similar centers of revival in New York City and Philadelphia. In his letters to these early lay evangelists, Wesley urged them to encourage new believers in Christ to press on to entire sanctification immediately upon their justification and new birth by the Spirit. Francis Asbury, who became the foremost leader of the Methodist Episcopal Church after its organization in 1784, also advocated the ardent preaching of the experience as one that every believer should expect immediately by faith. Wesley's sermons and tracts, especially his *Plain Account of Christian Perfection*, became the basic commentaries that aided Methodist circuit riders as they ranged through every nook and cranny of the new American nation, calling men and women to Christ and holiness.[73]

By the end of the famed post-Revolution revival known as the Second Great Awakening, a renewed interest in the experience of Christian perfection appeared within both the Methodist and Reformed wings of that movement. The doctrine was seen as the biblical answer to the instability and feeble witness that characterized so many of the revival's converts. Within their revivalistic Calvinist tradition, Charles G. Finney and his Oberlin College colleague, Asa Mahan, began to preach a message of Christian perfection and of a higher Christian life. They ardently espoused the doctrine in response to the need they sensed in their converts for a much clearer and more committed relationship with God. Within the framework of their New School Calvinism, their doctrine of entire sanctification closely paralleled that which was being preached in Methodism.[74] These variations and differing doctrinal contexts contributed to the later growth of the Keswick holiness movement and the often vigorous polemics that flowed back and forth between the Wesleyan holiness tradition and the more Calvinistically oriented movement.

At the same time, the ministry of a Methodist lay couple, Phoebe and Walter Palmer, became the catalytic agent of a revival of Wesley's doctrine of Christian perfection within their own church, a doctrine that many felt was being neglected in the midst of the exponential growth that had catapulted the Methodists to the front of the denominational world by 1840. The New School higher-life movement within American Calvinism and the holiness movement within Methodism quickly found a common ground, aided by the puritanism, pietism, and millennialism that permeated the warp and woof of American revivalism of the nineteenth century. They interpenetrated one another as they both promoted their concern for Christian holiness within almost all of American Protestantism—Wesleyan, Reformed, and Anabaptist. In this dynamic milieu the classical Wesleyan teachings on Christian perfection outlined above were proclaimed, tested, expanded, and, some believe, even altered, at least in tone and emphasis. A brief summary of these elements and the conflict that sometimes surrounded them within Methodism and the American holiness movement is necessary to understand the Wesleyan teaching on holiness as it came to be espoused in the new holiness churches that sprang up at the end of the nineteenth and beginning of the twentieth centuries in America and England.[75]

The preaching of the experience of sanctification was strongly colored by the fact that in America the doctrine developed within a revivalistic context. Revival preaching emphasized immediate and definable turning points in personal experience as essential to the Christian's life. Holiness preaching clustered the elements of Wesley's teaching on sanctification around the second crisis of faith, subsequent to justification, commonly called *entire sanctification*. This focusing of Wesley's message through the prism of the revivalists' direct call for immediate decision created conflict and criticism as the holiness revival blossomed within and beyond Methodism. Opponents claimed that the Wesleyan understanding that salvation was a continuum in which certain radical points of decision and infusions of justifying and sanctifying grace were set within a lifetime of process was being compromised. Proponents of the renewed emphasis on the crisis moment of entire sanctification—the Spirit's cleansing from all sin and freeing the soul to love—feared that their opponents' overemphasis on process and downplaying of crisis experience tended to destroy the hope of being entirely sanctified in this life. Such critics, they claimed, were departing from Wesley at the very point that made his view of sanctification unique in the first place. In this struggle to represent Wesley's views, which persisted within Methodism for most of the nineteenth century, the revivalist Wesleyans generally prevailed. According to their teaching, the Word of God called all Christians to receive entire sanctification as a work of grace subsequent to regeneration. The tensions within the prevailing church structures of the late nineteenth century, however, mainly those of Methodism, were such that those structures often could not contain the vigor (and sometimes the excessive zeal) of the holiness revival. Separation and new churches were the common result.[76]

After many adherents of the Methodist holiness movement either separated themselves or were separated by ecclesiastical pressure from the major branches of the church, North and South, they gathered themselves and the many converts that they had won outside of mainline Methodism into what we now know as the holiness churches. The new groups displayed disparate positions on a variety of issues, but their preaching of the centrality of entire sanctification as a second work of grace and the possibilities of living daily in obedience to God and love for others bound them together in a common identity. In the Church of the Nazarene, the Salvation Army, the Pilgrim Holiness Church, the Wesleyan Methodist Church (the latter two now merged into the Wesleyan Church), the Free Methodist church, the Church of God (Anderson, Indiana), and many related smaller religious bodies, the Wesleyan doctrine of sanctification found its major expression within the Methodist tradition after the turn of the nineteenth century.[77]

In the course of the doctrine's development in nineteenth-century Methodism and its subsequent creedalization as the formative doctrine of the holiness churches, certain emphases at times threatened the balance of the classical Wesleyan teaching. Phoebe Palmer's perception of the Wesleyan doctrine of entire sanctification became one of the first of these points of tension in its development in America. Her teachings on Christian holiness became a fixed element in the theology of the Methodist holiness movement because of her early prominence in the revival movement. Her simple, biblical exhortations to holiness were set in what is commonly known as her "altar terminology," and "shorter way." She believed strongly in the absolute authority of the Bible and, as is common in the revivalist tradition, applied it directly to preaching and life. Christ, she said, is the Christian's altar. Exodus 29:37 told her that whatever touched the altar would be holy; therefore, every Christian believer who was willing in faith to present himself or herself, without any reservation whatsoever, as a "living sacrifice" (Rom. 12:1) upon the altar provided by the finished work of Christ would be entirely sanctified and cleansed from all sin.

Mrs. Palmer taught that the clear promises of Scripture are

the voice of God because the Spirit is speaking them to us. Action upon a divine promise in faith constitutes the assurance that the promise is fulfilled in us. In this view, she seemed to be blending the act of faith and the assurance of faith into one. Her more theologically disciplined friends warned her of this tendency. She did believe, however, that the testimony of the inner witness of the Spirit, which Wesley strongly emphasized, would accompany the witness of God's faithfulness quickly, if not immediately, to those who cast themselves completely upon Christ for full salvation. The Bible also taught her that without holiness no one will see God and that our sanctification is His will for us; furthermore, "now" is always God's time for acceptance of His gracious offer of salvation. Therefore, the failure to act on these words of promise issues in unbelief, and unbelief issues in sin and disobedience. She also insisted that when persons experienced the blessing, it was their duty to confess it and zealously to seek to bring others into the same experience.[78]

Time will not allow us to consider all of the complex questions that are raised here, but we can sense that something has changed theologically. Although each of Mrs. Palmer's assumptions and statements can be documented with almost identical statements in Wesley himself, at the very least she has shifted the focus for understanding the tension between the Wesleyan polarities of growth and crisis as these relate to coming to perfection in love. It is obvious in her message that the "moment" of revivalist appeal, the immediacy of response anticipated (lest the hearer demonstrate unbelief and fall into condemnation by delay), and the entire cleansing in the moment of total consecration all tended to shift the point away from the balance that Wesley had maintained. For Mrs. Palmer, the experience of Christian perfection as the beginning of the life of growth in holiness rather than the culmination of its mature graces became the focal point of the Christian life. Her emphasis tended to revise the continuum of salvation within which Wesley had envisioned the experience.

"Altar terminology" when used as a formula for experiencing entire sanctification, as it sometimes was, was often abused under the assumption that it offered a kind of automatic operation of Scripture. When properly presented in the broader Wesleyan understanding, however, as she herself and many of her followers did, it became an effective means by which many people realized the life of love. The terminology is used prominently (indeed, almost universally) in holiness and higher-life teaching and preaching today.

The emphasis that teaching such as the above placed upon the moment of entire consecration and upon the crisis of complete moral adjustment of relationship tended to focus sanctification wholly on that single point of wholehearted commitment and to divorce it from the process of the gradual sanctification of the heart that began in regeneration and from the continuing growth in grace that follows the instant of death to self and perfection in love. Thus, the moment of the death to self and the birth to love readily became an end in itself—a goal rather than an essential element in the establishment of a dynamic new relationship of freedom and love in the hearts of believers as the Holy Spirit led them on from grace to grace in the will of God.[79]

Although Wesleyan holiness theology and its advocates never totally neglected the biblical and Wesleyan element of growth in grace before and after the event of entire sanctification, nevertheless the focus of many who testified to having received this second blessing centered more on the significance of the experience of the critical moment than on the nature of the ongoing relationship. Entire sanctification for Wesley was the moment of the believer's perfection in love, but only in a qualitative sense. Quantitatively, the lure of divine love was so immeasurable that the lifestyle of the sanctified believer was always that of a pilgrim and not that of a settler. There was no stopping place in the constant quest for personal spiritual growth and witness in love—in relationship with God and others.

Another emphasis widely disseminated, both in preaching and in some theological writings, implied that sin was some material-like substance that might be rooted out of the heart. Wesley himself contributed to this tendency by using terms such as "the circumcision of the heart" for the experience and by referring to the desires and tempers of the old nature of sin as a "root of bitterness" in the soul. On the whole, however, his concept of entire sanctification as a systemic cleansing of the person, of the experience as producing health and wholeness, tempered the concept of sanctification as an eradication of sin as though it were some unified entity that might be excised.[80]

The American revival context, especially as the movement grew, seemed to expedite the ease with which eradication could move from a simple analogy that was useful to describe the extent of the promised release from sin to become, rather, a concept in holiness teaching that created the impression for many hearers that sin was a substance that could be excised from the heart in the grace of the sanctifying moment. The use of eradication terminology became pervasive. It tended to narrow the focus of the popular theology of the movement and of the holiness churches, shaped as they were by the preaching of their evangelists, who presented sanctification teaching almost exclusively within special revivals or camp meetings held for the promotion of the doctrine. In concert with strong emphasis upon the critical nature of the moment of entire sanctification, their eradication theory further encouraged the development of an absolutist-static concept of grace within the Methodist tradition. The emphasis on eradication of the sinful nature among Wesleyan holiness advocates became more pronounced as the movement struggled with the Keswick higher-life movement over the question of whether the fullness of the Holy Spirit in the sanctified life freed one only from the dominion of sin or also from the presence of sin in the heart.[81]

Over the course of the last few decades, extensive biblical, theological, and historical reflection upon the Wesleyan doctrine of Christian holiness, much of it by the movement's own scholars, has turned its theology and preaching of sanctification more toward the post-justification process-crisis-process continuum that Wesley had described. Wesleyan holiness preaching has reemphasized also the cleansing and healing motifs of the redemption from all willful sin and thereby moderated the eradicationist terminology so that it is understood descriptively rather than prescriptively. Contemporary understanding also has commonly begun to express the believer's sanctification in Christ in terms of a perfect but dynamic relationship rather than a fixed state of experience. The experience is seen more holistically; the content and meaning of the second crisis has been enlarged, while its significance as an essential element in entering into perfection in love remains.[82]

The final emphasis in Wesleyan holiness preaching throughout the nineteenth and early twentieth centuries that has become a focal point of contemporary doctrinal debate is the use of Pentecostal, or "baptism with the Spirit," language to describe the dynamic of entire sanctification. The work of the Spirit is essential to any evangelical explication of the doctrine of sanctification. It is especially central in a Wesleyan understanding because of its historical emphasis upon Christian experience.

Although Wesley always acknowledged the Holy Spirit to be the active agent in the sanctification of believers, the texts that formed the biblical bases for the truth were largely drawn from Old Testament promise and prophesy as they were fulfilled in the New Testament words, work, and sacrifice of Jesus Christ. The Gospels and the Epistles furnished the major New Testament context of his teaching on Christian holiness.

The first and foremost of his classical defenders, his friend and confidant John Fletcher, however, interpreted and defended Wesley's doctrine of Christian perfection in a different manner. Drawing mainly on the Lukan and Johannine texts, he set his arguments for the Wesleyan teaching within the context of a Trinitarian-dispensationalist view of salvation history. He regarded the new age of the Spirit, which was ushered in on the day of Pentecost (following upon the ages of the Father and the Son), as the context that now prevails in God's gracious relationships with His people. The promise of the prophet Joel (that this age was coming) was fulfilled and continued to be fulfilled at and beyond the Pentecost experience, which had given birth to the new people of God. Pentecost represented the promise to every believer of the Holy Spirit's full blessing. Since Pentecost, he taught, every believer has received the Holy Spirit in measure when born of God, but the full potential of salvation from sin inherent in the promise of the Spirit is not realized until, in a subsequent moment of complete faith and obedience to the will of God, one becomes so filled with the Spirit that holiness and love become the habitual pattern of one's life. There could come the moment of entire sanctification in which God, because of the sanctification won for us by Christ on the cross, cleanses those who believe from every inclination contrary to the love of God and fills their hearts with the pure love of God and neighbor by the "baptism of the Holy Ghost" as promised by John the Baptist.[83]

Wesley and his brother Charles were fully aware of the new tack that Fletcher was following in his explication of the Methodist doctrine of Christian perfection. John Wesley did caution him on one occasion to guard against any use of the phrase "receiving the Spirit" in describing the second work of grace. He feared that if such language were employed it would imply that the Holy Spirit did not already live in those believers who had experienced the new birth but who had not yet been perfected in love. Consequently, he would appear to be denying the initiatory work of the Spirit in baptism into Christ.

It appears that otherwise the Wesleys, who edited and published Fletcher's work after his untimely death, gave assent to applying his Pentecostal and dispensational hermeneutic to their teaching on Christian perfection. Explicitly in sermon and letter and implicitly in his editing of some of Fletcher writings on these themes, John Wesley accepted, or at least showed no special concern for, the implications of Fletcher's methodology as he developed the first formal theology of Wesley's doctrine of Christian perfection.[84]

However, Fletcher's explicit use of Pentecostal language in his definition of the doctrine is only implicit in Wesley; it was not his primary emphasis, as we have noted above. Fletcher's works were widely read in Methodism as it established itself as the dominant movement in America in the nineteenth century. The Methodist holiness movement, reinforced by the perfectionist movement led by Charles G. Finney and Asa Mahan within New School Calvinism, adopted the same eschatological themes. Both revival movements were encouraged by the millennialism that has pervaded and shaped American history so significantly. By the end of the nineteenth century, the crisis of entire sanctification, or perfection in love, was commonly identified as "the baptism with the Holy Ghost." It was an expanding eschatological note in the whole of American revivalism.[85]

Subsequent use of "Spirit baptism" language within Pentecostal and charismatic movements and the publication of significant new studies of the meaning of the Pentecost event and the theology of the Holy Spirit have renewed the Wesley-Fletcher issues at this point again.[86] Current response within the Wesleyan movement to questions being raised about the movement's use of "the baptism of the Spirit" as the most apt understanding of the act of entire sanctification has been varied. On the one hand, some maintain that the predominant pattern and interpretive center of the sanctification experience is the Pentecost event. They continue to reject the exegesis of the passages in the Acts of the Apostles by James Dunn and others with similar exegetical understandings; they retain their strong support for the exegetical patterns established by late nineteenth-century holiness advocates.

Others acknowledge, with Wesley, that the texts in Acts certainly describe the initiatory reception of the Spirit in the new birth and baptism. They take seriously the validity of the recent exegetical questions being raised. They maintain, however, that interpretations of the Pentecostal texts by persons such as Dunn unduly restrict the full intent of these texts. They contend that the scope of the meaning inherent in "Spirit baptism" passages reaches much further than has been suggested by these exegetes. Therefore such language as used within the holiness tradition is still exegetically valid. The more restricted exegesis of the Pentecost texts, they believe, limits the expectations of the Old Testament promises that when the Spirit comes in His fullness, He will enable all the people of God to keep His commandments and walk before Him in a constancy of moral integrity. The use of these texts and terminology for the experience of the fullness of the Spirit, they maintain, is exegetically defensible and true to the plan of salvation as it is revealed in Old Testament type and in New Testament fulfillment.

Still others in the movement have tended to move away from the use of the Pentecostal hermeneutic and "Spirit baptism" motifs and to return to Wesley's basic terms of "death to sin," "circumcision of the heart," and the restoration of "the mind that was in Christ Jesus." The latter view moves more toward an interpretation of the experience that clusters around classical Christology and the sacrifice for sin on the cross; the former has an interpretation that clusters around pneumatology and the more eschatological-dispensationalist themes of the Spirit-empowered people who live in the Pentecostal age. Given the historical roots of the differences at this point of interpretation, it is likely that both understandings of the experience of entire sanctification will continue to exist in Wesleyanism.[87]

In spite of the variety of understandings and presentations of the doctrine of Christian holiness in the broad Wesleyan movement within contemporary Methodist, Holiness, and Pentecostal churches, all of them basically still find their understanding of "full salvation" in the succinct questions and responses John Wesley outlined at one point in his *Plain Account:*

Q. What is Christian Perfection?

A. The loving God with our heart, mind, soul, and strength. . . .

Q. Can any mistake flow from pure love?

A. I answer, (1) Many mistakes may consist with pure love. (2) Some may accidentally flow from it; I mean love itself may incline us to mistake. . . .

Q. How shall we avoid setting perfection too high or too low?

A. By keeping to the Bible, and setting it just as high as the Scripture does. It is nothing higher and nothing lower than this . . . love governing the heart and life, running through all our tempers, words, and actions. . . . [Christian] perfection . . . is purity of intention, dedicating all the life to God. It is the giving God all our heart; it is one desire and design ruling all our tempers. It is the devoting, not a part, but all our soul, body, and substance to God.[88]

BIBLIOGRAPHY

Fletcher, John. *Checks to Antinomianism*. Abr. ed. Kansas City: Beacon Hill, 1948.

Geiger, Kenneth E., ed. *The Word and the Doctrine: Studies in Contemporary Wesleyan-Arminian Theology*. Kansas City: Beacon Hill, 1965.

Lindström, Harald. *Wesley and Sanctification: A Study in the Doctrine of Salvation*. London: Epworth, 1950. Reprint. Grand Rapids: Zondervan, Francis Asbury Press, 1984.

Peck, Jesse. *The Central Idea of Christianity*. Boston: Degen, 1856.

Peters, John Leland. *Christian Perfection in American Methodism*. New York: Abingdon, 1956. Reprint. Grand Rapids: Zondervan, Francis Asbury Press, 1985.

Purkeiser, W. T., et al. *Exploring Christian Holiness*. 3 vols. Kansas City: Beacon Hill, 1986.

Turner, George Allen. *The More Excellent Way: The Scriptural Basis of the Wesleyan Message*. Winona Lake, Ind.: Light and Life, 1952.

Wesley, John. *A Plain Account of Christian Perfection*. London: Epworth, 1970.

———. *The Works of John Wesley*. Ed. Thomas Jackson. 14 vols. London: Wesley Conference Office, 1872. Reprint. Kansas City: Beacon Hill, 1978.

Wood, Laurence W. *Pentecostal Grace*. Grand Rapids: Zondervan, Francis Asbury Press, 1984.

Wynkoop, Mildred Bangs. *A Theology of Love: The Dynamic of Wesleyanism*. Kansas City: Beacon Hill, 1972.

Response to Dieter

With many of Melvin Dieter's points I agree wholeheartedly. I concur with his affirmation of the "total corruption" and
"utter depravity" of fallen humanity. I agree that Christ works
both for us and in us and that being in Christ brings both
justification and sanctification. I am grateful for his insistence
on continued growth in the Christian life. I appreciate especially the emphasis on holy living as the goal of salvation.

In connection with this last point, however, I should like to
make a correction. On page 35 Dieter says, "Although the
Reformation tradition frequently emphasizes justification and
adoption, it often neglects regeneration and sanctification." The
"Reformation tradition" obviously includes John Calvin. But
Calvin stressed the need for regeneration and sanctification as
much as the need for justification. As a matter of fact, in his
Institutes he deals at length with regeneration and sanctification
(including the Christian life, self-denial, and cross-bearing; see
book 3, chaps. 3–10) before he takes up justification (chaps.
11–16). Dieter also says that Wesley "relates the fulfillment of
the law's moral obligations to the process and end of sanctification rather than to the more objective views of Reformation
orthodoxy, which find the fulfillment and satisfaction of the
moral law in the act of the believer's justification" (p. 25).
Here again I must demur. To be sure, Calvin taught that Christ
kept the law for us so that we do not need to keep it to earn our
salvation. But Calvin also insisted that believers should keep

47

God's law as proof of their gratitude for the salvation they have received. In fact, he called this function of the law its "principal use."[1] Calvin also agrees with Wesley that holy living is the goal of salvation: "Since it is especially characteristic of his [God's] glory that he have no fellowship with wickedness and uncleanness, Scripture accordingly teaches that this [holiness] is the goal of our calling to which we must ever look if we would answer God when he calls."[2]

My major difficulty concerns the doctrine of "entire sanctification." Dieter presents this doctrine in three stages. First, the process of sanctification begins in regeneration (pp. 16–17, 19). Then, usually some time after regeneration, entire sanctification may occur "by the same faith . . . which initially had brought justification" (p. 17). Third, however, the believer must continue to grow in grace (p. 41). There must, in other words, be spiritual growth both before and after entire sanctification, the usual pattern being "process-crisis-process" (p. 42).

I conclude that, for Dieter, "entire sanctification" means the ability to live without sin during this present life. My evidence for this conclusion is the way he describes this stage in the Christian life: (1) in entire sanctification the "bent to sinning" is taken away (p. 21) and the "war within oneself" against "an innate inward rebellion" is over (p. 17); (2) entire sanctification is described as "an entire renewal in the image of God" (p. 17), "Christian perfection" (p. 36), "perfection in love" (p. 30), "perfect consecration to God" (p. 18), "perfect love to God and others" (p. 18; note that Webster's *New Collegiate Dictionary* defines *perfect* as "being entirely without fault or defect: flawless"), and "salvation from all sin" (p. 18). It should be noted that this salvation is qualified as meaning "salvation from all willful sin" (p. 15) and deliverance from "the necessity of voluntary transgressions" (p. 14).

To be sure, certain limitations to this "perfection" are suggested. Wesley, the author says on pages 13–14, "never allowed that entirely sanctified Christians could become sinless in the sense that they could not fall again into sin through disobedience." The word *again*, however, clearly implies that, during the time previous to such lapses, they were not falling

---

[1] John Calvin, *Institutes of the Christian Religion*, ed. John T. McNeill, trans. Ford Lewis Battles, 2 vols. (Philadelphia: Westminster, 1960), 2.7.12.
[2] Ibid., 3.6.2.

into sin. "Total freedom from the effects as well as the presence of all sin had [according to Wesley] to await the glory to come" (p. 14). But "effects of sin" seems to point only to the fact that these believers still live in a "deranged worldly order" (p. 14; cf. pp. 35–36), and the "presence of sin" that still remains is explained as something other than the "inner presence of sin in the life of the Spirit-filled Christian" (p. 35).

What Scripture evidence does Dieter offer to prove the possibility of living without willful sin in this life? Matthew 5:48 is quoted (p. 31)—"Be perfect, therefore, as your heavenly Father is perfect." Christ holds the ideal of perfection before us. But Jesus' words do not imply that we can attain this ideal in this life; the petition He taught us to pray daily, "Forgive us our debts" (6:12), rules out that possibility. The same comment can be made about Paul's aim to "present everyone perfect in Christ" (Col. 1:28, p. 33); the perfection here spoken of will not be realized until the time of Christ's return (cf. v. 22). The Bible nowhere teaches that the presentation of the church as "without stain or wrinkle or any other blemish" (Eph. 5:27, p. 31) or the attainment by believers "to the whole measure of the fullness of Christ" (4:13, p. 33) will occur before Christ's second coming. Paul's prayer for the Thessalonians (1 Thess. 5:23, p. 31) specifically mentions "the coming of our Lord Jesus Christ" as the point at which they will be totally blameless. The new nature, which, according to Colossians 3:10 (p. 34), we are said to have put on, is "being renewed . . . in the image of its Creator." If it is being renewed, it is not yet perfect.

I do not believe that the Bible allows for the possibility of living without sin, even without "willful sin," in this life, and therefore I do not accept Wesleyan teaching about entire sanctification (the doctrine set forth in this chapter). Since I have given the biblical evidence against this doctrine elsewhere in this volume, I will not repeat it here. On the question of the possibility of living sinlessly before our final glorification, the reader is referred to my chapter on the Reformed view of sanctification (pp. 75, 81, 83–85, 89–90). On the question of deliverance "from all willful sin" in this present life, the reader is referred to my response to McQuilkin (p. 188).

While I appreciate Dieter's insistence on continual spiritual growth, I must reject the possibility of sinless living on this side of glory. We are in Christ, to be sure, and we need to be more and more filled with the Spirit. But we are not yet perfect, either in love or in consecration. We are *genuinely* new but not yet *totally* new.

Response to Dieter

Stanley M. Horton

After a meeting of the Evangelical Theological Society, I was thanking Gordon H. Clark for some of the things I appreciated in his writings. When he found out I was Pentecostal, he immediately said, "That's experience, and experience can only lead you astray. All I want is the Word!" Probably, he would have given a similar response to John Wesley, due to Wesley's conviction (as Melvin Dieter states it) "that true biblical Christianity finds its highest expression and ultimate test of authenticity in the practical and ethical experience of the individual Christian and the church and only secondarily in doctrinal and propositional definition" (pp. 11–12). Pentecostals, however, make the Word primary. The first point in the Assemblies of God's "Statement of Fundamental Truths" is "The Scriptures Inspired," which states that they are "the infallible, authoritative rule of faith and conduct." Experience must be tested by the Word. But if we truly believe the Word, experience will follow. If it does not, then there is no reality to the faith that is professed.

The initial phase of the Pentecostal revival in the early 1900s was very much influenced by the Wesleyan holiness doctrine of a "second blessing" and came out of the same American revivalist context. A few went to the extreme of saying that this "second definite work" took out sin, "root and branch," to the point that individuals were not able to sin any more. Durham's "finished work of Calvary" teaching turned the Assemblies of God away from that type of teaching altogether. Most also recognized that, in their experience, neither the ability nor the tendency to sin was removed, even though they had previously claimed the experience.

Pentecostals remain highly influenced by Wesleyan theology, especially by Wesley's "passion for seeing God's truth expressed in the experience and witness of faithful Christians," and we too are fortified in this view by our conviction "that every person could respond positively or negatively to God's offer of salvation" (p. 12). We agree that, as creatures of free will, we are "able to respond obediently or disobediently to the grace of God." We would also agree that we can "be delivered from the *necessity* of voluntary transgressions by living in moment-by-moment obedience to God's will" (p. 14). We appreciate Wesley's emphasis on growth in grace but, from Scripture and experience, deny that there is an experience of "entire sanctification" that is a "total death to sin and an entire renewal in the image of God" (p. 17). We take it that the believer must continue to press on in faith and obedience and that we must still expect to be changed from "one degree of glory" to another while we are in this life. Rather than one experience of dedication or consecration, repeated—even daily—consecrations are necessary.

With respect to Wesley's "continuum of law and love," Pentecostals would also disagree with Reformation orthodoxy, which finds the fulfillment and satisfaction of the moral law in the act of the believer's justification. Rather than following the letter of the law, Pentecostals suggest that the Holy Spirit helps us to do the good things God really wanted when He gave the law.

Perhaps the key difference between Wesleyans and Pentecostals is the Wesleyan tendency (which was proposed by Fletcher, not Wesley) to identify entire sanctification with the baptism with the Holy Ghost. Pentecostals teach that the baptism in the Holy Spirit at Pentecost was an empowering experience, not an act of entire sanctification. It is interesting to note here that some Wesleyans have been influenced by James D. G. Dunn's exegesis of the Acts passages. I pointed out the weakness of some of Dunn's exegesis in my book *What the Bible Says About the Holy Spirit* (Springfield, Mo.: Gospel, 1976). Recently, Howard Ervin of Oral Roberts University has given a more thorough and detailed critique of Dunn in his book *Conversion-Initiation and the Baptism in the Holy Spirit* (Peabody,

Mass.: Hendrickson, 1984). We hold that the Bible teaches that the baptism in the Holy Spirit is a distinct experience given to those in the Book of Acts who were already believers and is still available to all believers today. We recognize the Holy Spirit as our Helper, through Whom we can live a life of victory. We too desire to be channels of Christ's love and seek to dedicate everything, "soul, body, and substance to God," as Wesley taught. It should be noted also that the Assemblies of God leaders and scholars are now able to talk more freely and cordially with those of Pentecostal holiness persuasion.

Response to Dieter

J. Robertson McQuilkin

Christians of all persuasions can be grateful to Melvin Dieter for summarizing the doctrine of sanctification as originally promoted by John Wesley, giving us a biblical exposition of selected themes that are central to that theology and tracing the subsequent historical development of holiness teaching, a development that has strongly conditioned present perceptions of Wesleyan teaching both externally and internally. Many will applaud the strong emphasis on practical, experiential sanctification, an emphasis often missing in theological expositions and even more often in Christian experience. We may also applaud the clear emphasis on a loving relationship with God as the ultimate purpose of law and grace, faith and holiness, and all else pertaining to our salvation.

Yet I am perplexed by certain ambiguities that seem to stem from a lack of careful biblical analysis of certain basic concepts: sin, holiness, perfection, and sanctification. Is *sin* to be defined as deliberate transgression of the known will of God, or is it any falling short of the glorious character of God in thought, word, or deed? The definition is perhaps the crucial issue in the debate on sanctification, but neither Wesley nor Dieter provides a biblical analysis of the term. Wesley seems to define sin as "voluntary transgressions" (p. 14). Any other failure to measure up to Godlikeness in moral character is a human error, "mistake," or "accident" (pp. 14, 23, 45). If the ability to refrain from sinning means merely the ability to refrain from deliberate rejection of God's known will, surely it is part of saving faith and available to any true child of God. But if sin includes any disposition or attitude that falls short of loving as Christ loves, of being as pure, contented, courageous, or self-controlled as He, who can claim to be sinless? So the definition of sin is crucial. It not only deserves recognition as a crucial issue, which I fail to find in the treatise, but it also deserves a thorough textual and theological analysis.

In the second place, what are we to understand by *holiness?* Does the Bible mention a holiness that is imputed, a standing based not on the believer's condition but on Christ's covenant with the Father? Dieter makes a strong case for a biblical use of *holy* as referring also to a condition that believers experience. But if Scripture uses the term in at least these two distinct ways, is it not imperative in key passages to demonstrate which meaning the biblical author intended? To use a passage intended to apply to all Israelites (or all Christians or the actual local assembly) as legally set apart for God's own possession, whether or not they behave that way, to prove a doctrine of experienced Godlikeness is to violate basic biblical hermeneutics.

The third crucial term demanding rigorous biblical definition is the elusive word *perfect.* Since the term is used in Scripture with a wide range of meaning, it is especially important when offering the possibility—indeed, the imperative—of "Christian perfection" to be sure of exactly what is offered and of whether such an offer is biblical. If Wesleyans mean by "Christian perfection" that it is possible for a believer, by the power of the Holy Spirit (or of the indwelling Christ), to obey God consistently in the conscious choices of life, I have no controversy, other than the practical problem that most people mean by *perfection* something different and thus may be confused or actually misled. The common understanding, both inside and outside perfectionist circles, is that *perfect* has an absolute sense of unfailing Godlikeness. I believe that neither Wesley nor Dieter teaches this view, but without precise definitions of *sin* and *perfect*, many will continue to aim for the absolute and may end up disappointed or self-deceived.

The final key term is a problem, not through any failure on the part of the author, but because of a basic ambiguity within Wesleyan and the broader holiness movement. Dieter analyzes the issue carefully and very helpfully. What does *entire sanctification* as an experience mean? The author clearly states that this experience, which enables a believer to love God with all one's being and to live a life of obedience, "need not be chronologically distinct from justification and the new birth" (p. 18). Even Wesley himself demonstrated some ambiguity (see pp. 18–19, 30, 43–44), which may be explained by the distinction between ideal (theoretical, logical, theological) sanctification, which occurs at regeneration, and the actual experiences of all Christians who do not continue on in "perfect love" and hence need a subsequent crisis experience. Dieter shows that developments in nineteenth-century American holiness teaching not only firmly set this second experience as theologically necessary but also increasingly identified it with the "baptism of the Spirit." My problem with believing in a theologically necessary second crisis experience is best expressed by Dieter himself: "Adherents of this understanding recognize that there is no explicit exhortation to seek sanctification [in the technical Wesleyan use of the word] as such in the New Testament" (p. 32).

It might be added that Scripture contains no exhortation to have nor teaching about a crisis experience subsequent to regeneration and necessary for sanctification. The consistent teaching of the New Testament on the problem of substandard Christian living is to point the believer back to the original event. Acts does report experiences with the Holy Spirit subsequent to regeneration, but nowhere are those events explained theologically or tied to the idea of experiential sanctification. Biblically uninterpreted history is not legitimate raw material from which to construct any doctrine, let alone so crucial a doctrine. It is more helpful to follow John Wesley in his original understanding that a second crisis encounter with God is not necessary theologically and ideally but is commonly needed by the believer. Reaffirmation of the original contract relationship may indeed be a crisis experience, and a necessary one for the drifting or rebellious believer.

Thus, if the ambiguous terms are defined in a particular way, classical Wesleyan teaching and the Keswick approach are quite compatible. If *sin* is any falling short of God's glorious character, no one is perfect. Yet, every Spirit-empowered believer may consistently refrain from deliberately violating God's known will. Believers receive this enabling at the time of conversion, when they are judicially sanctified, or set apart by the Spirit as God's possession. Should they fail to maintain this loving, obedient relationship, they no longer experience sanctification in the sense of spiritual growth, and they need a fresh encounter with God, a renewal that could be described as a second crisis experience.

Response to Dieter

Melvin Dieter is to be highly commended for a comprehensive, lucid, and accurate presentation of Wesleyan theology. The views expressed will be echoed by many others who seek, as John Wesley did, to have their lives in conformity to the holiness of God. John Wesley was a man of God who blazed a trail that not only influenced the lives of thousands in his generation but also affected the course of the church ever since. Today, as in the time of Wesley, there is so much need for cutting through the ritual, form, and theological debate that characterizes the church and for gaining a fresh glimpse of the holiness of God and the divine purpose to transform sinners into saints. Earnest Christians can certainly find much in the teachings and example of Wesley that accurately presents the Bible teaching on the subject of holiness.

Who can question Wesley's emphasis on the Scriptures as the only rule of faith and practice, the necessity of translating doctrine into life, the desire of God to bring holiness into the life of every Christian, and the marvelous grace of God as the cure for total depravity? Many admirers of John Wesley will echo these great truths. If there are problems in Wesleyan doctrine, often they spring from those who did not follow accurately the theological guidelines of the originator. The fact that some in the Wesleyan tradition have gone to extremes perhaps justifies suggestions for sharpening some of Wesley's definitions, which might have prevented these misapprehensions.

In Wesley's point of view, justification and sanctification occurred at the same time. But the distinction needs to be made that justification is a legal act of God that in itself is not experiential and that the original act of sanctification is a matter of position in Christ rather than a matter of experience. Both justification and positional sanctification occur when a person becomes a believer in Christ and are the grounds for progressive sanctification and spiritual experience. What needs to be emphasized is the teaching of Wesley that ultimate perfection is not to be achieved until the believer stands in the presence of God in heaven.

Wesley is right that, subsequent to the initial act of being born again and receiving salvation in Christ, there is normally a later act of the will in which individuals surrender their life to the will of God. In a sense, this step fulfills Romans 12:1–2, in which believers offer themselves as living sacrifices totally committed to God. While Wesley made clear that this initial act does not justify expectation of complete holiness in the days that follow, some of his admirers have implied that it puts the believer on a plateau of victorious life, a plateau that proves to be not permanent but transitory. Though Wesley did not believe that the sin nature could be eradicated in this life, some of his followers taught that the experience of personal commitment resulted in such a change in human nature.

Confusion also exists among the doctrines of the baptism of the Spirit, regeneration, and the filling of the Spirit. Regeneration and the baptism of the Spirit actually occur when a person believes on Christ and is born again and placed (baptized) into Christ (1 Cor. 12:13). The filling of the Spirit, however, is a repeated experience. Although it occurred at the same time as the baptism of the Spirit on the Day of Pentecost, subsequently it was distinguished from it and reoccurred. Baptism of the Spirit happens once for all at salvation; the filling of the Spirit may occur many times and is an important aspect of spiritual experience. This clarification would do much to prevent Pentecostal misuse of Wesleyan truth. While believers can be momentarily completely cleansed from sins committed, they cannot be cleansed from the sin nature, as Wesley himself would make clear. Wesley believed that the holy life is characterized by a moment-by-moment dependence upon God and upon the Holy Spirit and by the experience of the fruit of the Spirit (Gal. 5:22–23). Had the teachings of John Wesley been followed closely with caution, most of the proper grounds for criticism of Wesleyan theology would have been precluded.

Chapter 2

THE
REFORMED
PERSPECTIVE

Anthony A. Hoekema

THE REFORMED PERSPECTIVE

Anthony A. Hoekema

"Be holy because I, the LORD your God, am holy" (Lev. 19:2; quoted in 1 Peter 1:16). One of the outstanding qualities, or attributes, of God is His holiness. Not only is He holy, however; He also desires that we, whom He has created in His image, should be holy. The work of God by which He makes us holy we call *sanctification*.

DEFINITION

We may define sanctification as that gracious operation of the Holy Spirit, involving our responsible participation, by which He delivers us as justified sinners from the pollution of sin, renews our entire nature according to the image of God, and enables us to live lives that are pleasing to Him. I note first that sanctification is concerned with the *pollution* of sin. We commonly distinguish between the guilt and the pollution associated with sin. By *guilt* we mean the state of deserving condemnation or of being liable to punishment because God's law has been violated. In *justification*, which is a declarative act of God, the guilt of our sin is removed on the basis of the atoning work of Christ. By *pollution*, however, we mean the corruption of our nature, a corruption that is the result of sin and that, in turn, produces further sin. As a result of the Fall, we are all born in a state of corruption; the sins that we commit not only are products of that corruption but also add to it. In *sanctification* the pollution of sin is in the process of being removed (though it will not be totally removed until the life to come).

Sanctification, further, effects a renewal of our nature— that is, it brings about a change of direction rather than a change in substance. In sanctifying us, God does not equip us with powers or capacities that are totally different from those we had before; rather, He enables us to use the gifts He gave us in the right way instead of in sinful ways. Sanctification empowers us to think, will, and love in a way that glorifies God, namely, to think God's thoughts after Him and to do what is in harmony with His will.

Sanctification also means being enabled to live lives that are pleasing to God. It is commonly said that in sanctifying us God enables us to perform "good works." These good works must not be thought of as meritorious, and they cannot be done perfectly—that is, without flaw or blemish. Yet they are necessary. In Ephesians 2:10, in fact, good works are described as the fruit of our salvation: "For we are God's workmanship, created in Christ Jesus to do good works, which God prepared in advance for us to do." In other words, we are saved not *by* works but *for* works. Yet, since the expression *good works* might be interpreted somewhat atomistically (as suggesting, say, that we should do so many good works a day), I prefer to say that sanctification enables us to live lives that are pleasing to God.

THE BIBLICAL CONCEPT OF HOLINESS

Since the word *sanctify* means "to make holy" (from two Latin words, *sanctus*, holy, and *facere*, to make), we should look next at what the Bible teaches about holiness in human beings. The chief Old Testament word for *holy* is qāḏôš (its related verb being qāḏaš). The basic idea involved seems to be "separation from other things"—that is, something or someone placed into a realm or category separated from what is common or profane. In the earlier books of the Old Testament, the holiness of God's people is usually defined in ceremonial terms—describing the way in which priests were to be set apart for their special service or by which the people of Israel were to purify themselves through certain ritual observances. Later Old Testament books, however, particularly the Psalms and the Prophets, describe the holiness of God's people primarily in ethical terms—involving doing righteousness, speaking the truth, acting justly, loving mercy, and walking humbly with God (Ps. 15:1–2; Mic. 6:8). The basic meaning of *qādôš*, therefore, is that God's people are to be set apart for God's service and that they should avoid whatever displeases Him. The chief New Testament word for *holy* is *hagios* and its derivatives. Though used in various senses, this word often describes believers' sanctification, as in Ephesians 5:25–26 ("Christ loved the church and gave himself up for her, that he might sanctify her," RSV). In this sense, holiness in the New Testament means two things: (1) separation from the sinful practices of this present world and (2) consecration to God's service. Contrary to popular opinion, therefore, holiness means more than doing certain good things and not doing certain bad things; rather, it means being totally dedicated to God and separated from all that is sinful.[1]

We ask next what the Bible teaches about the way in which we are sanctified. We note first that we are sanctified *in union with Christ.* Paul teaches that we are made holy through being united with Christ in His death and resurrection. Certain opponents of Paul had been twisting his teachings about justification by faith so as to make them mean, Let's just go on sinning so that grace may increase (see Rom. 6:1). Paul replies, "By no means! We died to sin; how can we live in it any longer?" (v. 2). He goes on to show that we died to sin in union with Christ, who died for us on the cross: "We were therefore buried with him through baptism into death . . . . Our old self was crucified with him" (vv. 4, 6). Sanctification, therefore, must be understood as a dying to sin in Christ and with Christ, who also died to sin (v. 10).

In this same chapter, however, Paul also tells us that we are one with Christ in His resurrection. For he says,

> We were . . . buried with him . . . into death in order that, just as Christ was raised from the dead through the glory of the Father, we too may live a new life. If we have been united with him like this in his death, we will certainly also be united with him in his resurrection. (Rom. 6:4–5)

We are now called to live a new life because we arose with Christ and share His resurrection life with Him. Colossians 3:1 mentions the same result: "Since, then, you have been raised with Christ, set your hearts on things above, where Christ is seated at the right hand of God" (see also Eph. 2:4–6). Passages of this sort remind us that we should not only say that Christ died for us and arose for us but also confess that we died and arose with Christ—died with Him to sin and arose with Him to new life.

We are being sanctified through growing into a fuller and richer union with Christ. Paul tells us that God's plan for us is that "speaking the truth in love, we will in all things grow up into him who is the Head, that is, Christ" (Eph. 4:15). He goes on to make clear that sanctification involves not simply individuals in isolation from each other but the entire community of God's people: "From him [Christ] the whole body . . . grows and builds itself up in love, as each part does its work" (v. 16). As we grow closer to Christ, we grow closer to each other. We are sanctified through fellowship with those who are in Christ with us.

Our sanctification in union with Christ is masterfully summed up in 1 Corinthians 1:30 ("It is because of him that you are in Christ Jesus, who has become for us wisdom from God—that is, our righteousness, holiness and redemption"). The word here rendered "holiness" is *hagiasmos*, translated "sanctification" in other versions (KJV, ASV, NASB, RSV). Paul catches us here by surprise. Christ, he says, has not only brought about our sanctification; He *is* our sanctification. If we are one with Christ, we are being sanctified; and the only way we can be sanctified is through being one with Christ. Calvin has put it well: "As long as Christ remains outside of us, and we are separated from him, all that he has suffered and done for the salvation of the human race remains useless and of no value for us."[2]

We are also sanctified by means of *the truth*. In his so-called High Priestly Prayer, Jesus prays for His disciples, "Sanctify them by [or, according to some versions, in] the truth" (John 17:17). Christ, who came to bear witness to the saving truth of God, prays that the Father may keep His disciples in the sphere of this redemptive truth. Once Christ was no longer on the earth this truth would be found in God's Word. He therefore adds, "Your word is truth." We must grow in sanctification through the Bible, which is God's Word. That the Bible is one of the chief means whereby God sanctifies His people is clearly taught in 2 Timothy 3:16–17 ("All Scripture is God-breathed and is useful for teaching, rebuking, correcting and training in righteousness, so that the man of God may be thoroughly equipped for every good work"). Later in this chapter I discuss separately the role of the law of God in our sanctification.

The Bible also teaches that we are sanctified *by faith*. One of the central truths proclaimed in the Protestant Reformation is that we are justified by faith. It is equally true, however, that we are sanctified by faith. Paul, recounting Jesus' words spoken to him on the way to Damascus, says that Christ sent him to the Gentiles to "turn them from darkness to light . . . so that they may receive . . . a place among those who are sanctified by faith in me" (Acts 26:18). According to Herman Bavinck, "Faith is the outstanding means of sanctification."[3]

How is faith a means of sanctification? First, by faith we continue to grasp our union with Christ, which is the heart of sanctification. In regeneration, which is totally a work of God, we are made one with Christ and enabled to believe in Him; but we continue to live in union with Christ through the exercise of that faith. We learn, for example, from Ephesians 3:17 that Christ dwells in our hearts through faith. Paul expresses this truth graphically in Galatians 2:20 ("I have been crucified with Christ and I no longer live, but Christ lives in me. The life I live in the body, I live by faith in the Son of God, who loved me and gave himself for me").

Second, by faith we accept the fact that in Christ sin no longer has the mastery over us. Believers must not only recognize intellectually but embrace in full belief the truth that "our old self was crucified with him [Christ] so that the body of sin might be rendered powerless, that we should no longer be slaves to sin" (Rom. 6:6) and that sin is no longer our master because we are not under law but under grace (v. 14).

Third, by faith we grasp the power of the Holy Spirit, which enables us to overcome sin and live for God. Through faith we must appropriate the encouraging truth that by the Spirit we are able to put to death the misdeeds of the body (Rom. 8:13) and that if we live by the Spirit we will receive strength to cease gratifying the desires of the sinful nature and to bring forth the Spirit's fruit (Gal. 5:16, 22–23). Faith, in fact, is the shield with which we "can extinguish all the flaming arrows of the evil one" (Eph. 6:16).

Finally, faith is not only a receptive organ but also an operative power. True faith by its very nature produces spiritual fruit. "In Christ Jesus," affirms Paul, "neither circumcision nor uncircumcision has any value. The only thing that counts is faith expressing itself [literally, "energizing" itself, from Gk. *energeō*] through love" (Gal. 5:6). Faith produces work (1 Thess. 1:3); the goal of God's command to us is love, "which comes from a pure heart and a good conscience and a sincere faith" (1 Tim. 1:5). In words that are often quoted, James declares "As the body without the spirit is dead, so faith without deeds is dead" (James 2:26). The Heidelberg Catechism, one of the best-known Reformed creeds, expresses this truth as follows: "It is impossible for those grafted into Christ by true faith not to produce fruits of gratitude" (Answer 64).

We should therefore speak not only of justification by faith as a cardinal Reformational teaching but also of sanctification by faith. The apostle John sums up the significance of faith: "This is the victory that has overcome the world, even our faith" (1 John 5:4).

THE PATTERN OF SANCTIFICATION

The pattern of sanctification is likeness to God. Since Christ, however, is the perfect image of God (2 Cor. 4:4; Col. 1:15; John 14:8–9; Heb. 1:3), we may also say that the pattern of sanctification is likeness to Christ.

God originally created us in His image and likeness (Gen. 1:26–27). Through the fall into sin, however, the image of God in humankind became perverted. In the process of redemption, particularly in regeneration and sanctification, that image is being renewed.[4]

As we continue to think about sanctification, we now concern ourselves with the third phase of the history of the image of God, namely, with the renewal of the image. Sanctification means that we are being renewed in accordance with the image of God—that, in other words, we are becoming more like God, or like Christ, who is the perfect image of God. Our renewal in the image of God, however, may be viewed from two angles: as the work of God in us and as a process in which we are actively engaged.

First, then, Scripture teaches that God Himself, in sanctifying us, is renewing us in His likeness by making us more like Christ. From Romans 8:29, in fact, we learn that conformity to the image of Christ is the purpose for which God chose us: "For those God foreknew he also predestined to be conformed to the likeness of his Son, that he might be the firstborn among many brothers." God foreknew (in the sense of "foreloved") His chosen people before they came into existence. Those who were so foreknown by Him, He foreordained, or predestined, to be made like His Son. Since the Son perfectly reflects the

Father, "the likeness of His Son" is equivalent to "the likeness of Himself." God's goal in election, therefore, is to make us an innumerable company of Christ's brothers and sisters who are fully like His Son and thus fully like Himself.

Perhaps the most vivid description of this aspect of our sanctification is found in 2 Corinthians 3:18 ("And we, who with unveiled faces all reflect the Lord's glory, are being transformed into his likeness with ever-increasing glory, which comes from the Lord, who is the Spirit"). We who are God's people today, Paul is here saying, are continually reflecting the glory of the Lord, or the glory of Christ, with unveiled faces. Since each of us is "a letter from Christ . . . written not with ink but with the Spirit of the living God" (v. 3), people should be seeing something of the glory of Christ when they look at us. As we are reflecting that glory, however, we are also being transformed into the same image—that is, into the likeness of Christ—from one degree of glory to another. As we continually reflect the glory of Christ, we are continually being transformed into His image. This transformation, furthermore, is brought about in us by the Lord, who is also the Spirit.

Secondly, however, we also have a responsibility in this matter, namely, to seek to become more like Christ by following His example. Renewal in the image of God, in other words, is not just an indicative; it is also an imperative.

Jesus Himself taught us that we should follow His example. After He had washed the disciples' feet—a menial task that none of the disciples had offered to do—Jesus said to them, "Now that I, your Lord and Teacher, have washed your feet, you also should wash one another's feet. I have set you an example that you should do as I have done for you" (John 13:14–15). When Jesus said these words, He was not instituting a ritual of ecclesiastical footwashing. But he was directing his disciples, and thus all believers, to follow His example of lowly service (cf. Luke 22:25–27).

Though Paul laid great stress on the work of Christ as our Savior from sin, he also taught that we must follow Christ's example. In Ephesians 5:1, for example, he writes, "Be imitators of God, therefore, as dearly loved children." Though God is indeed transforming us more and more into His likeness, we who are His people must also keep on trying to imitate God. There are, of course, many ways in which we cannot be like God: for instance, in His omniscience, omnipresence, or omnipotence. But there are ways in which we can and should be like God. One of these ways is described in the immediately preceding verse: "Be kind and compassionate to one another, forgiving each other, just as in Christ God forgave you" (4:32). We must follow God's example in forgiving others. Another way of imitating God is to "live a life of love, just as Christ loved us" (5:2). Not only must we love others; we must love others as Christ loved us.

In 1 Corinthians 11:1 Paul writes, "Be imitators of me, as I am of Christ" (RSV). One is amazed at Paul's willingness to hold himself up as an example. But Paul, in turn, was trying to pattern his life after that of Christ, who is our ultimate example.

Another way in which Paul teaches the imitation of Christ is in the well-known "mind of Christ" passage (Phil. 2:5–11). Paul urges his readers to "have this mind among yourselves, which you have in Christ Jesus" (v. 5 RSV). He goes on to describe this mind of Christ as an attitude of humble service like that exemplified by Jesus when He was on earth.

Peter makes a similar point: "To this you were called, because Christ suffered for you, leaving you an example, that you should follow in his steps" (1 Peter 2:21). It is clear, therefore, that following Christ's example is not an incidental but an essential aspect of the Christian life.[5] It is also clear that likeness to God and to Christ is the pattern of sanctification.

GOD AND HIS PEOPLE IN SANCTIFICATION

Whose work is sanctification? In looking at the pattern of sanctification, we have observed that sanctification is both the work of God and the responsibility of His people.

Scripture plainly teaches that God is the author of sanctification. The work of sanctification, however, is ascribed to all three persons of the Trinity. Jesus prays to the Father, "Sanctify them by the truth" (John 17:17), thereby ascribing sanctification to the Father. The author of Hebrews makes a similar point: "Our fathers disciplined us for a little while as they thought best; but God disciplines us for our good, that we may share in his holiness" (Heb. 12:10). "Disciplines" (Gk. *paideuō*, literally, "child training") suggests such things as suffering, adversity, persecution, and the like. Since the purpose of this discipline is that we may share in God's holiness, we conclude that the process here described is what we have been calling *sanctification* and that God may use such things as suffering and pain as means of sanctification. God is identified in the previous verse as "the Father of our spirits" and here as one who disciplines.

Sanctification, however, is also ascribed to the Son, as we learn from Ephesians 5:25–27. Here Paul tells his readers that husbands should love their wives

> just as Christ loved the church and gave himself up for her to make her holy [or to sanctify her, RSV], cleansing her by the washing with water through the word, and to present her to himself as a radiant church, without stain or wrinkle or any other blemish, but holy and blameless.

Christ, the Second Person of the Trinity, is here identified as the agent of sanctification, cleansing the church "by the washing with water through the word." Most commentators understand the first part of this expression as referring to the sacrament of baptism; the passage thus suggests that the sacraments (baptism and the Lord's Supper) are also means of sanctification. The expression "through the word" should be connected with the verb "cleansing." Christ cleanses His church from sin by means of the Word of God, or the Scriptures. It is exciting to note that, according to this passage, the final goal of sanctification is that the holiness of the church will be perfect, "without stain or wrinkle or any other blemish."

Though the word *sanctification* is not used in Titus 2:14, this passage also sees Christ as the author of our sanctification for He "gave himself for us to redeem us from all wickedness and to purify for himself a people that are his very own, eager to do what is good." In 1 Corinthians 1:30, as noted above, Christ is said to have become our holiness, or sanctification.

Sanctification is also commonly ascribed to the Holy Spirit. Peter says that God's people "have been chosen according to the foreknowledge of God the Father, through the sanctifying work of the Spirit, for obedience to Jesus Christ" (1 Peter 1:2). Paul tells us in Romans 15:16 that he was sent to proclaim the gospel "so that the Gentiles might become an offering acceptable to God, sanctified by the Holy Spirit." He also thanks God that He chose the Thessalonians "to be saved through the sanctifying work of the Spirit and through belief in the truth" (2 Thess. 2:13). And Titus 3:5 states that God saved us "through the washing of rebirth and renewal by the Holy Spirit."

The work of the Trinity, however, cannot be divided. It is not surprising, therefore, that we also find sanctification ascribed to the triune God without any designation of persons ("May God himself, the God of peace, sanctify you through and through," 1 Thess. 5:23).

It is most important for us to realize that sanctification is not something that we do by ourselves, with our own efforts and in our own strength. Sanctification is not a human activity but a divine gift.

The Bible, however, also describes sanctification as a process that involves our responsible participation. To the members of the church at Corinth, designated in an earlier epistle as "those sanctified in Christ Jesus" (1 Cor. 1:2), Paul says, "Since we have these promises, dear friends, let us purify ourselves from everything that contaminates body and spirit, perfecting holiness out of reverence for God" (2 Cor. 7:1). The promises are those mentioned in the preceding verses, embodying particularly the great covenant promise: "I will be their God and they will be my people" (6:16). Since we are God's covenant people, Paul is saying, we have a solemn responsibility. We must fight against sin, both of the body and of the mind. The Greek word *epitelountes*, translated "perfecting," has in it the root of the word for "goal" (*telos*) and means "progressively bringing to its goal." What we usually think of as God's work is here vividly described as the believer's task, namely, to bring holiness to its goal.

> I urge you, brothers, in view of God's mercy, to offer your bodies as living sacrifices, holy and pleasing to God—this is your spiritual act of worship. Do not conform any longer to the pattern of this world, but be transformed by the renewing of your mind. (Rom. 12:1–2)

Paul here appeals to his readers to show their gratitude for God's mercy by offering themselves to God as living sacrifices, in contrast to the dead sacrifices offered in Old Testament times. Think of your bodies, Paul is saying, as belonging to God as totally and irrevocably as did the bulls and goats offered by Old Testament priests. Stop conforming yourselves outwardly to the pattern of this evil age, but rather continue to be transformed within through the renewal of your total attitude toward life. Though it is God who brings about our inner transformation (cf. 2 Cor. 3:18), we must yield our hearts, minds, and wills to the Holy Spirit, who is remaking us.

The author of Hebrews puts it this way: "Pursue peace with all men, and the sanctification [or holiness, Gk. *hagiasmos*] without which no one will see the Lord" (Heb. 12:14 NASB). Sanctification is here pictured as something that we must continually pursue. According to Scripture, therefore, though sanctification is primarily God's work in us, it is not a process in which we remain passive but one in which we must be continually active.

These two aspects of sanctification are mentioned together in a remarkable passage: "Therefore, my dear friends, as you have always obeyed . . . continue to work out your salvation with fear and trembling, for it is God who works in you to will and to act according to his good purpose" (Phil. 2:12–13). Since Paul is addressing "saints in Christ Jesus" (1:1), the command "work out your salvation" must be understood not as an evangelistic appeal to the unsaved but as a word to believers. Paul is asking his readers to continue to "work out" what God in His grace has "worked in." The word *katergazesthe,* translated "work out," is commonly used in the papyri (short Greek manuscripts dating from 200 B.C. to A.D. 200, which illustrate the usage of New Testament words) to describe the cultivation of land by farmers.[6] We could therefore paraphrase Paul's words as follows: Keep on cultivating the salvation God has given you. Believers must continually seek to apply the salvation they have received to every area of life and to make it evident in every activity. Verse 12, in other words, must be understood as describing the believer's responsibility to advance his or her sanctification.

The basis for this exhortation, as given in verse 13, is not that this working out of our salvation depends entirely on us. Instead, surprisingly, Paul states, "For it is God who works in you to will and to act." God works in us the entire process of our sanctification—both the willing of it and the doing of it. The harder we work, the more sure we may be that God is working in us.

How, then, shall we describe the relationship between God's working and our working? Should we say, as some have done,[7] that sanctification is a work of God in which believers cooperate? This way of stating the doctrine, however, wrongly implies that God and we each do part of the work of sanctification. According to John Murray,

> God's working in us is not suspended because we work, nor our working suspended because God works. Neither is the relation strictly one of cooperation as if God did his part

and we did ours . . . . God works in us and we also work. But the relation is that *because* God works we work.[8]

Summing up, we may say that sanctification is a supernatural work of God in which the believer is active. The more active we are in sanctification, the more sure we may be that the energizing power that enables us to be active is God's power.

DEFINITIVE AND PROGRESSIVE SANCTIFICATION

Reformed theologians commonly assert that sanctification continues throughout a believer's life, in distinction from justification, which is a definitive act of God, occurring once for all.[9] Though the New Testament often describes sanctification as a lifelong process, there is also an important sense in which Scripture depicts it as an act of God that is definitive—that is, that occurs at a point in time rather than along a timeline.[10] John Murray, in fact, observes: "It is a fact too frequently overlooked that in the New Testament the most characteristic terms that refer to sanctification are used, not of a process, but of a once-for-all definitive act."[11]

Passages that describe sanctification in the definitive sense include 1 Corinthians 1:2. Paul here addresses the believers in Corinth as "those sanctified in Christ Jesus"; the Greek verb is in the perfect tense, which describes completed action with continuing result. Protestant theologians usually understand justification to be a declarative act of God by which He pronounces the believing sinner righteous in Christ—an act, therefore, which is not continuing or progressive but once for all. In 1 Corinthians 6:11, however, sanctification is coordinated with justification as a definitive act of God: "But you were washed, you were sanctified, you were justified in the name of the Lord Jesus Christ and by the Spirit of our God." In the Greek text the three verbs are in the aorist tense, which usually describes instantaneous action (sometimes called "snapshot" action). Just as these believers have been justified once for all at a certain point in time, so, Paul says here, there is also a sense in which they have been sanctified once for all. Furthermore, both Acts 20:32 and 26:18 speak of believers as "those who are sanctified"; in both cases the verb is in the perfect tense.

The definitive aspect of sanctification is expressed most vividly and sharply in Romans 6. When Paul says in verse 2 of

this chapter, "We died to sin," he is expressing in unambigu-
ous language the truth that the person who is in Christ has
made "a definitive and irreversible breach with the realm in
which sin reigns."[12] Paul further underscores this decisive,
once-for-all break with sin by telling us that if we are in Christ,
our old self has been crucified with him (v. 6, the aorist tense
again suggesting definitive action), sin shall no longer lord it
over us, because we are now under the reign of grace (v. 14),
and we now obey from the heart the pattern of Christian
teaching to which we have been made subject (v. 17). The main
thrust of this entire chapter is to show that the believer has
been placed into a new relationship—one that can never be
undone. Murray summarizes this position: "This means that
there is a decisive and definitive breach with the power and
service of sin in the case of everyone who has come under the
control of the provisions of grace."[13]

Not only does Paul teach that believers have died to sin, he
also affirms that they have been decisively and definitively
raised with Christ. Using verb tenses that describe instantaneous, or snapshot, action, Paul asserts that "God . . . made us
alive with Christ even when we were dead in transgressions
. . . . And God raised us up with Christ" (Eph. 2:4–6). Though
we were by nature dead in sin, God mercifully made us who
are believers one with the risen Christ, thus raising us up with
Him; this "raising" is described here not as a long process but
as something that happened at a certain point in time. The
Colossians, furthermore, are not told that they must progressively be raised with Christ; they are told, "Since, then, you
have been raised [aorist tense] with Christ, set your hearts on
things above, where Christ is seated at the right hand of God"
(Col. 3:1). In the light of these texts, we conclude that one's
sanctification means not only a decisive break with the enslav-
ing power of sin but also a decisive and irreversible union with
Christ in His resurrection, a union by means of which the
believer is enabled to live in newness of life (Rom. 6:4) and
because of which he or she has now become a new creature
(2 Cor. 5:17). As a result of our definitive sanctification,
therefore, we who are in Christ must now count ourselves
"dead to sin but alive to God in Christ Jesus" (Rom. 6:11).

Clearly, therefore, the New Testament teaches definitive
sanctification. We must ask now, when did believers die to sin
and arise with Christ? To this question no simple answer can be
given; there is both an objective and a subjective side to this

matter. In the objective sense, believers died with Christ when He died on the cross and were raised with Christ when He arose from the dead in Joseph's garden. Since believers were chosen in Christ before the creation of the world, they were, at least in one sense, in Christ when He died and arose. Christ must never be thought of apart from His people, nor His people apart from Him. When Christ died, He made the decisive break with sin, a break that accrues to our benefit; and when Christ arose, He brought into existence the new life into which we may enter by faith.

But we must not disregard the subjective aspect of our oneness with Christ in His death and resurrection. Paul says that God made us alive with Christ when we were dead in transgressions (Eph. 2:5), and that we died to sin when we were baptized into Christ Jesus (Rom. 6:2–3). In our own experience we arose with Christ when we became one with the risen Lord (Col. 3:1). Paul reminds the Colossians that at a certain point in their lives (presumably, the time of their conversion) they voluntarily put off their old selves and put on their new selves (3:9–10). To do full justice to biblical teaching, therefore, we must stress both aspects of this question: the past historical and the present experiential. In one sense we died to sin and arose to new life when Christ died and arose; in another sense, however, we died to sin and arose to new life when by faith we grasped our oneness with Christ in His death and resurrection.[14]

Biblical teaching on definitive sanctification suggests that believers should look upon themselves and each other as those who have died to sin and are now new persons in Christ. To be sure, the newness that believers have in Christ is not equivalent to sinless perfection; as long as they are in this present life, they must struggle against sin, and they will sometimes fall into sin. Believers, therefore, should see themselves and each other as persons who are *genuinely* new, though not yet *totally* new. But the doctrine of definitive sanctification helps us to see that those who are in Christ have made a decisive and irreversible break with sin. Murray expresses this truth eloquently:

> As we cannot allow for any reversal or repetition of the resurrection [of Christ], so we cannot allow for any compromise on the doctrine that every believer is a new man, that the old man has been crucified, that the body of sin has been destroyed, and that, as a new man in Christ Jesus, he serves God in the newness which is none other than that of the

Holy Spirit of whom he has become the habitation and his body the temple.[15]

It should be added that definitive sanctification as described above does not refer to an experience separate from or subsequent to justification, as a kind of "second blessing." In its experiential sense, definitive sanctification is simultaneous with justification, as an aspect of union with Christ.

As I have mentioned, however, the Bible teaches that there is also a sense in which sanctification is a lifelong process and is therefore progressive. Rather than nullifying what Paul says about definitive sanctification, this teaching supplements it.

The progressive sense of sanctification is evident, first of all, from biblical statements that assert that sin is still present in the believer. We may think of Old Testament passages like 1 Kings 8:46; Psalm 19:12; Psalm 143:2; Proverbs 20:9; and Isaiah 64:6. The New Testament also is quite clear on this point. When discussing our need to be justified by faith, Paul vividly describes the universal sinfulness of humankind: "There is no difference, for all have sinned and fall short of the glory of God" (Rom. 3:22–23). "The glory of God" here can perhaps best be understood as meaning "glorifying God"; since the verb "fall short" is in the present tense in Greek, we may render the second half of the verse as "and continue to fall short of glorifying God." In an incidental but revealing statement, James, writing to believers, says, "We all stumble in many ways" (James 3:2). Probably the clearest New Testament statement of the point under discussion is found in 1 John 1:8. Addressing those who claim to have fellowship with God, John writes, "If we claim to be without sin [literally, if we say that we have no sin], we deceive ourselves and the truth is not in us." The conclusion is inevitable: because sin continues to be present in those who are in Christ, the sanctification of believers must be a continuing process.

Scripture discusses directly both a negative and a positive aspect of progressive sanctification, involving both the putting to death of sinful practices and the growth of the new self. In Romans 6, as we have seen, Paul vividly sets forth the definitive aspect of sanctification. In Romans 8:13, however, he points out that sanctification must also be progressive: "For if you live according to the sinful nature, you will die; but if by the Spirit you put to death [literally, keep on putting to death] the misdeeds of the body, you will live." Believers, whom he has previously described as having died to sin, he now enjoins to keep on killing the sinful actions to which they might still be inclined. Paul's readers have definitively broken with sin as the realm in which they live, move, and have their being; yet they must still continue to fight against sin as long as they live. Since they can do so only through the strength of the Spirit, this struggle against sin must be understood as an aspect of their sanctification.

Paul tells the Colossians that they have both died with Christ (Col. 3:3) and been raised with Christ (v. 1); that is, they have definitively and irreversibly entered into new life in fellowship with Christ. Yet in verse 5 of this chapter he enjoins them: "Put to death, therefore, whatever belongs to your earthly nature: sexual immorality, impurity, lust, evil desires and greed, which is idolatry." Though they have died to sin, they must still put sin to death; as he often does, Paul here combines the indicative and the imperative. The putting to death of these sinful practices, which can only be done through the strength of the Spirit, involves the strenuous and lifelong activity of the believer.

From 2 Corinthians 7:1, quoted above, we learned that believers must still contend with and seek to purify themselves from defilements of body and spirit. A similar injunction is found in 1 John 3:3. After having affirmed that when Christ appears we shall be like him, John goes on to say, "Everyone who has this hope in him purifies [literally, continues to purify] himself, just as he is pure." Christians are not simply to sit back and wait for the time when they will be totally like Christ; they must be constantly and energetically active in the struggle to overcome evil with good. Continuing purification implies continuing sanctification.

The progressive nature of sanctification is also shown in passages dealing with its positive aspect: the growth of the new self. In Colossians 3:9–10 Paul, as we saw, reminds his readers that they have taken off the old self and have put on the new self; the new self that they have put on, however, is described as one "which is being renewed in knowledge in the image of its Creator" (v. 10). Since the new self is here said to need renewal, it obviously does not yet exist in a state of sinless perfection. The participle *anakainoumenon*, translated "being renewed," is in the present tense, indicating that this renewal of the new self is a lifelong process. Interestingly, this passage presents both facets of sanctification: once and for all, believers have taken off the old self and put on the new self (definitive sanctification), but the new self that they have put on must be continually renewed (progressive sanctification).

The most striking description of the progressive nature of sanctification is in 2 Corinthians 3:18, "We, who with unveiled faces all reflect the Lord's glory, are being transformed into his likeness with ever-increasing glory, which comes from the Lord, who is the Spirit." As believers reflect the glory of the Lord, they are being continually and progressively transformed into the likeness of Christ by the Lord Himself, who is also the Spirit (v. 17). The word *metamorphoumetha,* here rendered "we are being transformed," describes a change not just of outward form but of inner essence. Both the present tense of this verb and the words "from one degree of glory to another" (RSV) indicate that this transformation is not instantaneous but progressive.

Whereas some of the passages just cited stress the divine authorship of our sanctification, other texts underscore the participation of believers in this process. In Romans 12:2 believers are urged to stop being conformed to this present age and, instead, to be transformed continually by the renewing of their minds; in the last part of 2 Corinthians 7:1 we are directed to continue perfecting holiness out of reverence for God. In Ephesians 4:15 sanctification is described as progressive growth into Christ: "Speaking the truth in love, we are to grow up in every way into him who is the head, into Christ" (RSV). Peter also uses the metaphor of growth to describe the Christian life: "But grow [or keep on growing] in the grace and knowledge of our Lord and Savior Jesus Christ" (2 Peter 3:18).

Sanctification, therefore, must be understood as being both definitive and progressive. In its definitive sense, it means that work of the Spirit whereby He causes us to die to sin, to be raised with Christ, and to be made new creatures. In its progressive sense, it must be understood as that work of the Spirit whereby He continually renews and transforms us into the likeness of Christ, enabling us to keep on growing in grace and to keep on perfecting our holiness. One could think of definitive sanctification as the beginning of the process and of progressive sanctification as the continual maturing of the new person who was created by definitive sanctification. While sanctification in its totality is the work of God from beginning to end, particularly in its progressive phase the active participation of the believer is required.

IS THE BELIEVER BOTH AN "OLD SELF" AND A "NEW SELF"?

We turn next to another problem involved in our sanctification, namely, the question of the relation between our so-called old self and our new self (or old person and new person). These expressions are found only in the writings of Paul. The term *old self* is found in Romans 6:6; Colossians 3:9; and Ephesians 4:22.[16] The term *new self* is found in Colossians 3:10 (where Gk. *neos* is used for "new") and Ephesians 4:24 (where Gk. *kainos* is used for "new").[17]

In these passages Paul contrasts the old self associated with the life of sin with the new self that we have put on, now that we are in Christ. On the question of the relation between these two selves, Reformed theologians differ. Most of them, particularly those who taught and wrote some years ago, hold that the old self and the new self are distinguishable aspects of the believer. Before conversion believers had an old self; at the time of conversion, however, they put on the new self—but without totally losing the old self. The Christian, on this view, is understood to be partly a new self and partly an old self—something like a Dr. Jekyll and Mr. Hyde. At times the old self is in control, but at other times the new self is in the saddle; the struggle of life, according to this view, is the struggle between these two aspects of the believer's being.

By way of example, consider how one of the ablest proponents of this view describes the fight against sin in believers:

> The struggle [in the Christian life] . . . is between the inner man of the heart, which has been created to be like God in true righteousness and holiness, and the old man who, though driven out of the center, still wants to maintain his existence, and who fights all the more fiercely the more territory he loses. . . . This is a struggle between two people in the same person. . . . In every deliberation and deed of the believer, therefore, good and evil are as it were mingled together; . . . in all his thoughts and actions something of the old and something of the new man is present.[18]

John Murray, however, who for many years taught systematic theology at Westminster Seminary, takes vigorous exception to this understanding of the old and the new self:

The contrast between the old man and the new man has frequently been interpreted as the contrast between that which is new in the believer and that which is old . . . . Hence the antithesis which exists in the believer between holiness and sin . . . is the antithesis between the new man and the old man in him. The believer is both old man and new man; when he does well he is acting in terms of the new man which he is; when he sins he is acting in terms of the old man which he also still is. This interpretation does not find support in Paul's teaching.[19]

I believe that Murray is correct here. Let us turn to some Scripture passages that teach that the person who is in Christ is no longer an old man or old self, but is now a new self.

We begin with Romans 6:6, "For we know that our old self was crucified with him so that the body of sin might be rendered powerless, that we should no longer be slaves to sin." What does Paul mean here by the "old self"? Murray suggests that this expression designates "the person in his unity as dominated by the flesh and sin."[20] In other words, Paul is here talking about a totality: the total person enslaved by sin—what we all are by nature. That "person enslaved by sin," he is saying, was crucified with Christ. When Christ died on the cross, He dealt a deathblow to the old self we once were. Given the meaning of "crucified," Romans 6:6 states with unmistakable clarity that we who are in Christ, who are one with Him in His death, are no longer the old selves we once were.

Other passages in Paul's epistles confirm this understanding of the death of the old self. Colossians 3:9–10, for example, considered above in connection with definitive sanctification, teaches us also about the old and the new self: "Do not lie to each other, since you have taken off your old self with its practices and have put on the new self, which is being renewed in knowledge in the image of its Creator." Paul here tells the Colossian believers not that they now (or daily) *should* take off the old self and put on the new self, but that they *have already done so!* They made this change when, at the time of their conversion, they appropriated by faith what Christ had done for them when He died and arose again.

The Greek participles *apekdusamenoi* and *endusamenoi*, rendered "taken off" and "put on," are in the aorist tense, which describes snapshot action; Paul is referring to something these believers have done in the past. You ought not to lie, he says, nor to lust, be sinfully angry, or slander, *because* you have taken

off your old self and *because* you have put on your new self.[21]
You must stop committing these sins because such conduct is
obviously inconsistent with your having put on the new self.
And the very figure Paul uses strengthens this thought: one
does not wear two sets of clothes at the same time—one takes
off one set and puts on another. Paul here pictures believers as
people who are now clothed with the new self and no longer
with the old.

Ephesians 4:20–24 is closely parallel but seems to offer
some difficulty:

> You, however, did not come to know Christ that way.
> Surely you heard of him and were taught in him in
> accordance with the truth that is in Jesus. You were taught,
> with regard to your former way of life, to put off your old
> self, which is being corrupted by its deceitful desires; to be
> made new in the attitude of your minds; and to put on the
> new self, created to be like God in true righteousness and
> holiness.

The Greek text of verses 22–24 has three main infinitives
(*apothesthai, ananeousthai,* and *endusasthai*), which mean "to put
off," "to be made new," and "to put on," and which in many
versions are translated as imperatives, as if Paul were telling the
believers in Ephesus what they should now do (cf. "put off . . .
be renewed . . . put on," RSV). Following this rendering, the
passage would convey a command, which would indeed be
inconsistent with the position just defended (that believers
have already taken off the old self and put on the new).

Though the translation found in the Revised Standard
Version is not grammatically incorrect, there is another possibility. These infinitives can also be understood as so-called
"explanatory infinitives," that is, as simply giving the content
of the teaching referred to in verses 20–21. In this analysis, Paul
is assuming that his readers have done what they were taught
to do. This understanding of the text makes its teaching parallel
to that of the similar passage considered above from Colossians, which is commonly considered a twin epistle to Ephesians. The rendering found in the New International Version is
therefore to be preferred to that of the Revised Standard
Version. So interpreted, Ephesians 4:22–24 tells the believers in
Ephesus that they should not continue to live as the unconverted Gentiles do (vv. 17–19), since, as they were taught, they
have put off the old self and have put on the new self. The new

self that they have put on has, in fact, been created like God in true righteousness and holiness.[22]

From the passages just considered, therefore, it is clear that, according to the New Testament and consistent with its teaching on the definitive aspect of sanctification, believers are no longer the old selves they once were. They are not, as has often been taught, both old selves and new selves but are indeed new selves in Christ. Paul highlights this important point in the stirring words of 2 Corinthians 5:17 ("Therefore, if anyone is in Christ, he is a new creation; the old has gone, the new has come!"). We must not minimize the importance of this teaching and of its bearing on our sanctification. John Murray again says it well:

> The old man is the unregenerate man; the new man is the regenerate man created in Christ Jesus unto good works. It is no more feasible to call the believer a new man and an old man, than it is to call him a regenerate man and an unregenerate. And neither is it warranted to speak of the believer as having in him the old man and the new man. This kind of terminology is without warrant and it is but another method of doing prejudice to the doctrine which Paul was so jealous to establish when he said, "Our old man has been crucified."[23]

Though believers are new persons, however, they have not yet attained sinless perfection; they must still struggle against sin. In Colossians 3:10 the new self that believers have put on is described as a self that is being renewed; this renewal, as we saw, is a lifelong process. In Ephesians 4:23 Paul reminds his readers that, although they have put off the old self and put on the new, they are being made new in the attitude of their minds. The infinitive *ananeousthai*, rendered "made new," is in the present tense, suggesting a continuing process. Believers who have become new creatures in Christ are still told to put to death the misdeeds of the body (Rom. 8:13), to kill whatever is sinful in them (Col. 3:5), to rid themselves of such sins as lust, greed, rage, malice, and filthy language (vv. 5, 8), and to purify themselves from everything that contaminates body and spirit (2 Cor. 7:1).[24]

The new self described in the New Testament, therefore, is not equivalent to sinless perfection; it is *genuinely* new, though not yet *totally* new. The newness of the new self is not static but dynamic, needing continual renewal, growth, and transformation. A believer deeply conscious of his or her shortcomings does not need to say, Because I am still a sinner, I cannot consider myself a new person. Rather, he or she should say, I am a new person, but I still have a lot of growing to do.

The New Testament often describes the Christian life as a constant battle against sin. Believers are enjoined to put on the full armor of God so that they may be victorious in their struggle against evil powers (Eph. 6:11–13), to fight the good fight of the faith (1 Tim. 6:12; cf. 2 Tim. 4:7), not to gratify evil desires (Gal. 5:16), and to resist sin to the point of shedding their blood (Heb. 12:4). In 1 Corinthians 9:26–27, Paul describes his own fierce struggle against sin as if he were a boxer: "I do not fight like a man beating the air. No, I beat my body and make it my slave so that after I have preached to others, I myself will not be disqualified for the prize."[25]

Yet, though the struggle against sin is very real, believers are no longer enslaved to sin. The crucifixion of the old self with Christ, Paul teaches, implies that we have been freed from the slavery of sin (Rom. 6:6); because we are not under law but under grace, sin shall no longer be our master (v. 14). "The sin which still inheres in the believer and the sin he commits does not have dominion over him."[26]

Summing up, we may say that believers are no longer old persons but new persons who are being progressively renewed. They must still battle against sin and will sometimes fall into sin, but they are no longer its slaves. In the strength of the Spirit they are now able to resist sin, since for every temptation God will provide a way of escape (1 Cor. 10:13).

One important implication of this teaching is that believers should have positive images of themselves. The basis for such a self-image is not sinful pride in our own achievements or virtues but seeing ourselves in the light of God's redemptive work in our lives. Christianity not only means believing something about Christ; it also means believing something about ourselves, namely, that we are indeed new creatures in Christ.[27]

THE QUESTION OF PERFECTIONISM

Some Christian groups hold that it is possible for a believer to live without sin during this present life. John Wesley taught that there is a second work of grace subsequent to justification called *entire sanctification*, or the possibility of living in such perfect love for God that one feels no sin.[28] According to Wesley, this possibility lies within the reach of every believer, and every believer should try to attain it. A number of churches and groups in the Wesleyan tradition similarly teach entire sanctification as a "second blessing" after justification.

This view teaches that entire sanctification is (1) a distinct experience, separate from and subsequent to justification, and (2) an instantaneous experience, involving the removal of inbred sin, or the root of sin, and the destruction of the "carnal nature."[29] Sin is defined as being a "voluntary transgression of a known law."[30] Finally, the perfection that it is said believers can attain is always qualified: it is not Adamic, angelic, or resurrection perfection, and it is not the same as the perfection of Christ. One writer, in fact, describes the experience attainable as "imperfect perfection."[31]

Against this teaching the following considerations may be advanced: First, perfectionists (as those holding this teaching are commonly called) weaken the definition of sin by limiting it only to deliberate sin. But how easy it is not to recognize sin as sin! Does the perfectionist view harmonize with David's confession and prayer in Psalm 19:12 ("Who can discern his errors? Forgive my hidden faults")?

Second, perfectionism lowers the standard of perfection. If this "perfection" is neither like that of Adam before the Fall nor like that of resurrected believers, why call it *perfection?* Does it make sense to speak of "imperfect perfection"?

Third, this teaching makes sanctification a "second work of grace," separate from justification. But the New Testament keeps these two together. In 1 Corinthians 1:30 Christ is said to have been made "our righteousness and sanctification and redemption" (RSV); we cannot, in other words, have Christ as our justification without at the same time having Him as our sanctification (cf. also 1 Cor. 6:11). Though our definitive sanctification occurs at a point in time, it is not an experience separate from or subsequent to our justification; the two are simultaneous.[32] Progressive sanctification, as we saw, continues throughout life. We are therefore to look not for a specific, dated "second blessing" but for continued renewal and growth (Rom. 12:2; Col. 3:10; Eph. 4:23; 2 Peter 3:18).

Fourth, the Scriptures do not teach that it is possible for believers to live without sin in this life. As mentioned above, the Bible teaches that no one can claim to be free from sin: "If we claim to be without sin, we deceive ourselves and the truth is not in us" (1 John 1:8). The Scriptures also suggest regular confession of sin and prayer for forgiveness, as the very next verse teaches: "If we confess our sins, he is faithful and just and will forgive us our sins and purify us from all unrighteousness" (v. 9). See also the fifth petition of the Lord's Prayer: "Forgive us our debts, as we also have forgiven our debtors" (Matt. 6:12). Since Jesus here teaches us to pray for our *daily* bread, He obviously desires us to ask God daily to forgive us our sins.

The Bible also teaches that believers must continually fight against sin as long as they are in this life. Earlier in this chapter I summarized the scriptural evidence for this teaching; here we look more closely at Galatians 5:16–17 (NASB):

> But I say, walk [literally, keep on walking] by the Spirit, and you will not carry out the desire of the flesh. For the flesh sets its desire [literally, lusts] against the Spirit, and the Spirit against the flesh; for these are in opposition to one another, so that you may not do the things that you please.[33]

What does Paul mean here by *flesh*? Though the word *flesh* as used in the New Testament may have various meanings, here it means the tendency within human beings to disobey God in every area of life. We must not restrict the meaning of this word so that it refers only to what we commonly call fleshly sins, or sins of the body; we must understand *flesh* as designating sins committed by the whole person. In the list of "deeds of the flesh" (vv. 19–21), only five out of fifteen describe what we usually call bodily sins; the rest are "sins of the spirit" (hatred, discord, jealousy, and the like).

We learn from Romans 8:9 that believers are not in the flesh but in the Spirit; that is, believers are no longer enslaved to the flesh but are now being ruled by the Spirit. Nevertheless, Galatians 5:16–17 implies that believers must still fight against sinful impulses coming from the flesh, for the desires of the flesh are opposed to the desires of the Spirit. Scripture therefore promises that if we keep on walking by the Spirit, we will not carry out or fulfill the desire of the flesh (v. 16). But it is clear that believers must continue to battle against evil tendencies within them until their final breath.

To be sure, Galatians 5:24 teaches that believers have crucified the flesh. Yet they must continue to struggle against the desires of the flesh (vv. 16–17). Similarly, believers are dead to sin (Rom. 6:2, 11) but must still put to death the misdeeds of the body (Rom. 8:13); they have been crucified to the world

(Gal. 6:14) but yet must no longer be conformed to the pattern of this world (Rom. 12:2); they are without the yeast of sin but yet must get rid of the old yeast (1 Cor. 5:7). Passages of this sort illustrate the tension Paul saw in himself and in his fellow believers. The presence of this tension rules out the claim that believers can attain sinless perfection in this present life.[34]

We conclude that the Bible does not picture the believer now as having had all sinful impulses eradicated, as no longer needing to fight against evil desires, or as able to live totally without sin. Though we do not agree with the teachings of perfectionists, however, we must admire and seek to emulate their passion for holy living.

SANCTIFICATION AND THE LAW

Many Christians claim that when a person becomes a believer, he or she has nothing more to do with the law. "Free from the law—O blessed condition!" would seem to describe their attitude toward God's law in all its functions.

In one sense, to be sure, the believer is free from the law. Romans 6:14 says plainly, "For sin shall not be your master, because you are not under law, but under grace." "Not under law" here means that we are no longer under condemnation because of our failure to keep the law. Paul points out in Galatians 3:10 that all who fail to do everything that is written in the book of God's law are under a curse—the curse of everlasting punishment. But he goes on to say that "Christ redeemed us from the curse of the law by becoming a curse for us, for it is written: 'Cursed is everyone who is hung on a tree.' He redeemed us in order that the blessing given to Abraham might come to the Gentiles through Christ Jesus" (vv. 13–14). Christ, that is, bore the "curse of the law" for us so completely that He became a curse for us—by suffering the results of the curse throughout His life, particularly on the cross. The blessing of Abraham (that is, the blessing of justification by faith; see v. 8) has therefore become ours. In the sense that believers no longer need to keep the law as a way of earning their salvation, they indeed have been delivered from it.

In another sense, however, believers are not free from the law. They should be deeply concerned about keeping God's law as a way of expressing their gratitude to Him for the gift of salvation. Calvin identified this use of the law as its third and chief function in the lives of believers:

> The third and principal use [of the law], which pertains more closely to the proper purpose of the law, finds its place among believers in whose hearts the Spirit of God already lives and reigns. . . . Here is the best instrument for them to learn more thoroughly each day the nature of the Lord's will to which they aspire . . . . Again, because we need not only teaching but also exhortation, the servant of God will also avail himself of this benefit of the law.[35]

The Bible definitely teaches this "third and principal" use of the law. For example, at the very beginning of the Sinaitic law, God said, "I am the LORD your God, who brought you out of Egypt, out of the land of slavery" (Exod. 20:2), thereby reminding His people of His gracious act of delivering them from Egypt—that deliverance to which they owed their existence as a nation. "Now keep these commandments," God was saying, "in thankfulness for all My mercies shown to you."

The law was to be kept out of gratitude to God, which explains the delight that Old Testament saints had in God's law. So, for example, after speaking of the blessedness of the man who does not walk in the counsel of the wicked, the author of Psalm 1 goes on to say, "But his delight is in the law of the LORD, and on his law he meditates day and night" (v. 2). Here *law* means the precepts of God, given not only in the Ten Commandments but in other parts of His written revelation as well—precepts that give guidance for the believer's life. The same delight is expressed in Psalm 19:7–8:

> The law of the LORD is perfect, reviving the soul.
> The statutes of the LORD are trustworthy, making wise the simple.
> The precepts of the LORD are right, giving joy to the heart.
> The commands of the LORD are radiant, giving light to the eyes.

All of Psalm 119, the longest psalm in the Bible, is a paean of praise to the beauty and sweetness of God's law and to the joy the Psalmist finds in keeping it: "Direct me in the path of your commands, for there I find delight" (v. 35).

The New Testament, which further amplifies Old Testament teaching, similarly urges believers to keep God's law in gratitude for blessings received. We find this directive first of all in the words of Jesus. In His Sermon on the Mount He said, "Anyone who breaks one of the least of these commandments [those found in the Law or the Prophets] and teaches others to do the same will be called least in the kingdom of heaven, but whoever practices and teaches these commands will be called great in the kingdom of heaven" (Matt. 5:19). On another occasion Jesus told His disciples, "If you obey my commands, you will remain in my love, just as I have obeyed my Father's commands and remain in his love" (John 15:10). Jesus' command, however, is not different from what the Ten Commandments require, for He went on to say, "My command is this: Love each other as I have loved you" (v. 12); at another time He taught that the entire content of the last six commandments of the Decalogue is "Love your neighbor as yourself" (Matt. 22:39). It is clear that New Testament believers must still keep the Ten Commandments; they have, however, the example of Christ as a kind of "visual aid" (cf. "as I have loved you," John 13:34).

Paul, often cited as one who puts law and grace into sharp contrast, also considers the law (in Calvin's third use) still binding on Christians. In Romans 8:3–4 he indicates that the purpose of Christ's incarnation was to enable His people to fulfill the law:

> For God has done what the law, weakened by the flesh, could not do: sending his own Son in the likeness of sinful flesh and for sin, he condemned sin in the flesh, in order that the just requirement of the law might be fulfilled in us, who walk not according to the flesh but according to the Spirit. (RSV)

Some Christians see a sharp contrast between lawkeeping and living by the Spirit. According to this passage, however, these two expressions describe the same thing: Spirit-led believers are precisely the ones doing their best to keep God's law.

The thought that the believer has nothing more to do with the law is furthest from Paul's mind. He describes love for one's neighbor as a debt that we continually owe to one another, indicating that such love is the fulfillment of the law:

> Let no debt remain outstanding, except the continuing debt to love one another, for he who loves his fellowman has fulfilled the law. The commandments, "Do not commit adultery," "Do not murder," "Do not steal," "Do not covet," and whatever other commandment there may be, are summed up in this one rule: "Love your neighbor as yourself." Love does no harm to its neighbor. Therefore love is the fulfillment of the law. (Rom. 13:8–10)

Paul here not only instructs believers to continue to fulfill the law; he also implies that, contrary to the opinion of some, there is no conflict between lawkeeping and love.

In 1 Corinthians 9:20–21 Paul discusses his missionary approach as well as his relation to the law: "To the Jews I became like a Jew, to win the Jews. . . . To those not having the law [the Gentiles] I became like one not having the law (though I am not free from God's law but am under Christ's law)." Paul here clearly sees himself as always subject to the law of Christ—as always "under law to Christ" (ASV).

Similar statements are found in the Catholic Epistles. James teaches that lawkeeping, rather than holding us in bondage, brings true freedom: "But the man who looks intently into the perfect law that gives freedom, and continues to do this . . . , will be blessed in what he does" (James 1:25). John connects the law with knowing God and experiencing the fullness of his love: "We know that we have come to know him if we obey his commands. The man who says, 'I know him,' but does not do what he commands is a liar, and the truth is not in him. But if anyone obeys his word, God's love is truly made complete in him" (1 John 2:3–5).

The Christian life, we conclude, must be a law-formed life. Though believers must not try to keep God's law as a means of earning their salvation, they are nevertheless enjoined to do their best to keep this law as a means of showing their thankfulness to God for the salvation they have received as a gift of grace. For believers, lawkeeping is an expression of Christian love and the way to Christian freedom; it is equivalent to walking by the Spirit. Since the law mirrors God, living in obedience to God's law is living as image-bearers of God. The law, therefore, is one of the most important means whereby God sanctifies us.[36]

THE GOAL OF SANCTIFICATION

The goal of sanctification may be viewed from two perspectives: its final and its proximate goal. The final goal of sanctification can be nothing other than the glory of God. As we think about this gracious divine activity, we should consider primarily not our own future happiness but the glory of our wonderful God.

The Bible indicates that the glory of God is the final end of our sanctification. After having written in Ephesians 1:4–5 that

God has chosen us in Christ before the foundation of the world and that He has predestined us to be adopted as His children, Paul adds, "to the praise of his glorious grace" (v. 6)—an idea that is repeated in verses 12 and 14 ("for the praise of his glory" and "to the praise of his glory," respectively). Elsewhere Paul prays that the love of his fellow Christians may abound more and more, so that they may be pure and blameless, filled with the fruit of righteousness, "to the glory and praise of God" (Phil. 1:9–11). Why did God raise us up with Christ and seat us with Him in the heavenly realms? "In order that in the coming ages he [God] might show the incomparable riches of his grace, expressed in his kindness to us in Christ Jesus" (Eph. 2:7). In other words, all the amazing blessings of our salvation, including our sanctification, have as their final goal the praise of the glory of God. Nothing in all of history will reveal the fullness of God's perfections as brilliantly as will the completed glorification of His people.

In the Book of Revelation the apostle John pulls aside the curtain of mystery and gives us a glimpse into heaven. He hears voices—the voices of the redeemed—singing, "To him who sits on the throne and to the Lamb be praise and honor and glory and power, for ever and ever!" (Rev. 5:13). The ultimate goal of all of God's wondrous works, including the sanctification of His people, is that He shall be given praise, honor, and glory forevermore.

The proximate goal of sanctification is the perfection of God's people. This perfection will be the final stage in the history of the image of God, for in the life to come, God's people will perfectly image Him and Christ, who is "the exact representation of his being" (Heb. 1:3). Paul says in 1 Corinthians 15:49, "Just as we have borne the likeness of the earthly man, so shall we bear the likeness of the man from heaven." This "man from heaven" is obviously Jesus Christ, whose glorified image, Paul is here saying, we shall fully bear and reveal in the resurrection.

John says something similar in 1 John 3:2. Though it has not yet been made known, John affirms, what we who are God's children will be in the future, "We know that when he [Christ] appears, we shall be like him, for we shall see him as he is." The goal of our sanctification, as here described, is perfect and total likeness to Christ, and therefore to God. This total likeness will not entail the loss of personal identity, since we shall retain our individuality; it will, however, mean a completely sinless existence (see also Eph. 5:27; Heb. 12:23; Rev. 22:14–15).

Such future perfection is the purpose for which God has predestined us: "For those God foreknew he also predestined to be conformed to the likeness of his Son" (Rom. 8:29). God's purpose for us, in other words, is not just future happiness or a guaranteed entrance into heaven but perfect likeness to Christ and therefore to Himself. God could not, in fact, have designed a higher destiny for His people than that they should be completely like His only Son, in whom He delights.

The future perfection of God's people will be a sharing of the final glorification of Christ. We are not only heirs of God, Paul tells us in Romans 8:17, but fellow heirs with Christ, "provided we suffer with him in order that we may also be glorified with him" (RSV). As has often been said, we must never think of Christ apart from His people nor of Christ's people apart from Him. So it will be in the life to come: the glorification of Christ's people will occur together with the final glorification of Christ. When our sanctification has been completed, we shall be totally like Christ even in His glorification. Then, in a perfect and sinless way, we shall continually magnify and exalt the unfathomable riches of the grace of God, world without end.

BIBLIOGRAPHY

Bavinck, Herman. *Gereformeerde Dogmatiek*. 3d ed. 4 vols. Kampen: Kok, 1918.

Berkhof, Louis. *Systematic Theology*. Rev. and enl. ed. Grand Rapids: Eerdmans, 1941.

Berkouwer, G. C. *Faith and Sanctification*. Trans. John Vriend. Grand Rapids: Eerdmans, 1952.

———. *Man: The Image of God*. Trans. Dirk W. Jellema. Grand Rapids: Eerdmans, 1962

Hoekema, Anthony A. *The Christian Looks at Himself*. 2d ed. Grand Rapids: Eerdmans, 1977.

———. *Created in God's Image*. Grand Rapids: Eerdmans, 1986.

Murray, John. *Collected Writings of John Murray*. 2 vols. Carlisle, Pa.: Banner of Truth Trust, 1977.

———. *Redemption—Accomplished and Applied*. Grand Rapids: Eerdmans, 1955.

Response to Hoekema

Melvin E. Dieter

The definition of sanctification with which Anthony Hoekema begins his article is both precise and concise. It expresses beautifully the goal of salvation and of the Christian life. I believe that I am not unfair in noting, however, that throughout the entire explication of his Reformed position, the sharp edges of the implications of classical Calvinism for the doctrine of sanctification seem to be significantly modified by the influence of American pietism and revivalism, both of which tend toward a more Arminian understanding of the nature of sanctification and human responsibility. Throughout the whole discussion, Hoekema reveals little of the pessimism for the human condition or for the prospects for practical sanctification that is inherent and often explicit in traditional Calvinism. But there is still the fear of any use of perfectionist categories so typical of all Reformed dialogue with Wesleyan-Arminian views. We should note that Wesleyanism is not perfectionism (which implies a Pelagianism), and it certainly does not imply sinless perfection; it is probably more misrepresented at this point than at any other. It believes in Christian perfection—the measure of wholeness in love that God's grace makes possible for His children at any point in their relationship with Him.

But in spite of these tensions and the actual points of difference between the Reformed and Wesleyan views, I again rejoice in the similarity of biblical understanding that marks them at so many points. When Hoekema outlines the means of sanctification through union with Christ, through the truth, and through faith, with the result that "sin no longer has the mastery over us" (pp. 65, 82), he speaks eloquently for all Bible-believing Christians, regardless of the means to the end or the terms that are used to develop these teachings. Christlikeness and faith working through love are all that really matter; the interaction and dialogue between our different points of view teach us at least this much.

But the nuances of the basic differences between Hoekema's definition as understood in a Reformed context and the dynamics of sanctification as they are understood by some of the other positions in this volume begin to show up immediately as he defines the key terms used in the definition. For example, when Hoekema says that the corruption of sin produces other sins, which add to the sinful nature of the individual (pp. 84–85), it immediately suggests some kind of irresistible force of sin in us that inevitably must cause us to continue to sin. This view fits a Reformed understanding of fallen humanity much more accurately than does the Wesleyan one, which is outlined in my essay. Furthermore, when he states that this pollution is always only in the process of being removed and can not be totally removed in this life, we encounter one of the key differences between the Calvinist and Wesleyan definitions of sanctification. A Wesleyan has no problem saying that there is a certain corruption of sin as a part of our life in a fallen natural order, a corruption that denies us final and complete freedom from the results of the Fall and the subsequent sins of humankind. That level of freedom will not be provided until the glorification of the body and the restoration of God's rule in all creation. But is the freedom from that kind of corruption of sin the kind of freedom that the grace of Jesus Christ provides for us in this life? Obviously not.

The distinction between the two is clearly shown in Romans 7 and 8. Despite the differing interpretations of Romans 7, a passage so central to the sanctification theme, one thing is obvious: the real dilemma that must be overcome is one of the ability, as Kierkegaard says, "to will one will." This point is confirmed in Romans 8, where the freedom from that devastating frustration in fulfilling the law of God found in Romans 7 is declared to be found in the law of the Spirit of life in Jesus Christ. The fulfillment of the law is wholehearted love of God and neighbor, and the call and promise of such relationships is found in Romans 12.

Romans 8, besides celebrating the kind of freedom from sin that Hoekema allows as the expectation of the sanctified life, speaks also of the fact that believers continue to groan under the limitations of their own fallen bodies and of the unredeemed world system in which they live. It seems that the confusion of the latter life under the limitations of natural imperfections with the former life of freedom from sin in our relationship with God in Christ through the Spirit causes much of the misunderstanding, which results in Reformed theologians charging Wesleyans and Pentecostals with perfectionism, or claims of sinlessness. We can be freed to love God with our whole hearts by faith and the continued relationship of grace and loving response. We can never be freed from the struggles with the corruption of our bodies and the world. If sanctification includes the former, we can be entirely sanctified in the sense that higher-life theology maintains. If it comprehends perfection of the latter state, it is never completed in this life.

The freedom to love is the heart of Christian perfection. The corruption of the "bent to sinning," which always threatens the obedience of the believer before his or her entrance into the full life of wholehearted love, is the only corruption from which God's Word promises us deliverance in this life. With, Wesley, we hold that any doctrine of sanctification that offers a lesser possibility for the normal Christian life through grace and faith falls short of the whole purpose of the redemption from sin that lies at the heart of the gospel of Jesus Christ and the coming of the Holy Spirit.

In short, Hoekema is correct in his statement that absolute perfection will not be totally achieved until the "life to come" (pp. 89–90). If the question at hand is, Can we daily live so perfectly that we will not fall short of absolute perfection of response to God and neighbor in all of our actions? the answer is surely no. Our sins of omission, brought on by the weakness of our fallen bodies, minds, and affectional nature, are so many that we must daily pray, "Forgive us our sins, as we forgive those who sin against us." The real issue in sanctification, however, is whether we can be free from our willful inclination to resist God and the good so that we can be inclined to love and obedience in our daily walk by the indwelling, cleansing power of the Holy Spirit. The Spirit came to provide God's people with obedient hearts to do His will and keep His statutes (Ezek. 36:27).

This distinction has always been at the heart of the conflict between Calvinist and Wesleyan views of sanctification. It is inherent in the varying understanding of God's relationship with humankind and the differences in the understanding of election, prevenient grace, and freedom of the will. Very simply, one might say that the points at which different theologians stop along the line of tension spanning the gap between divine sovereignty and genuine human freedom, within parameters set by that sovereignty, mark the hairline distinctions that in their extended development seem to create such great divides between us. The very fact that these two systems can continue to appeal to Scripture with a great deal of support and integrity merely proves the reality of the tension and may itself be one of the greatest witnesses to the freedom that God grants us in the face of the overawing reality of His absolute lordship.

Response to Hoekema

Stanley M. Horton

There is much that I appreciate in Anthony Hoekema's presentation of the Reformed position. He is clear in his discussion of the distinction between definitive and progressive sanctification. He also gives much more emphasis to the importance of treating progressive sanctification as a lifelong process than I expected from the Reformed position.

Too often in our part of the Midwest I hear from members of Calvinistic churches such things as, "We must expect to sin a little every day," or "It is better not to live too holy a life lest you begin to trust in your good works for your salvation," or "Once you are saved you can live and die in gross sin and still go to heaven." These statements do not come from theologians, yet I am sure none of them would ever be said if the people had the kind of teaching given by Hoekema in his treatment of the Reformed position.

I appreciate also his beginning the definition of sanctification by referring to "that gracious operation of the Holy Spirit" and his stating further that "by faith we grasp the power of the Holy Spirit, which enables us to overcome sin and live for God. . . . by the Spirit we are able to put to death the misdeeds of the body" (p. 65). It is true that the entire Trinity is involved in the work of sanctification, a fact that Hoekema brings out very clearly, yet too often the work of the Holy Spirit has been ignored. The New Testament reflects a realization that the believers knew they needed the constant help of the Spirit.

Unfortunately, a good deal of church history shows a neglect of the third person of the Trinity. Very few books were written about the Spirit in the 1700s and 1800s. Many of the writers of systematic theologies had very little to say about Him. A few decades ago, it was very uncommon in most denominations to hear a sermon on the Holy Spirit. The situation has changed now, which is partly due, I believe, to the faithful witness of the Pentecostal movement.

It should be noted, however, that the Reformed position still gives considerably less attention to the Holy Spirit than do the other positions discussed in this book. Hoekema mentions Him in only two or three other places, and then only briefly. He gives a great deal more attention to the place of the law, and saying that Spirit-led believers do their best to keep God's law. This view could lead some to suppose that they must follow the letter of the law. Rather, the Holy Spirit gives the believer the help and power to live in the kind of God-pleasing way that God wanted to see in Israel when He gave the law. The basic meaning of law is "instruction," and we need the Holy Spirit to illuminate the instruction of the Old Testament in the light of the New. I would agree, however, that the conflict in Romans is between the law and sin, rather than between the law and grace, for love is indeed still the fulfilling of the Law.

I feel, however, that "to fall short of glorifying God" (p. 75) is only part of what Romans 3:23 means. The glory of God is the full weight of what He is in all His holiness, righteousness, mercy, grace, and love. Sin, in the sense of falling short of the mark or deviating to one side or the other, still keeps us falling short of the glory of God in this life, a fact we realize more the closer we walk with the Lord. But the Holy Spirit does help us in the matter of glorifying God. My observation of Pentecostal churches is that the Spirit brings a new desire to give praise to God and glorify Jesus in both worship and daily life. Though we still fall short, we press on.

We differ, of course, with respect to the matter of election. The election of Israel, as well as the New Testament passages and the many warnings in the Bible, shows that the election is of the body and is an election to God's purposes, rather than an election of individuals. Even children of the kingdom can be cast out. Robert Shank, a Baptist, in his book *Elect in the Son* (Springfield, Mo.: Westcott, 1970), presents evidence for this view, a view most Pentecostals would accept.

Hoekema's discussion of the question of perfectionism is

excellent, as is his discussion of both the ultimate and proximate goals of sanctification. Actually, most in the Assemblies of God would agree more than disagree with what Hoekema says about sanctification. But we would give more attention to the help of the Holy Spirit and to the baptism in the Holy Spirit as the empowering experience that is still available today.

Response to Hoekema

J. Robertson McQuilkin

I substantially agree with every major point enunciated by Anthony Hoekema. The case for the Reformed perspective on sanctification is argued with clarity, force, and, usually, careful biblical exegesis. I do wish, however, that he had made a more definite distinction between subjective/experiential sanctification and objective/transactional, or positional, sanctification. Again, I wish he had defined theologically the "old self" and the "new self" and explained the nature of the continuity between the old and new in the same person. But these matters are not of the essence of his argument.

My problem, then, is not with what was said but with what was left unsaid. And for practical success in the Christian life, that omission may be critical. Is there a substantive difference among Christians, or are they all more or less on an inevitable continuum from regeneration to glorification, differing only in their degree of growth toward the image restored? If there is such a thing as a Christian behaving like an unconverted person, consistently failing to bear the fruit of the Spirit, spiritually weak and ineffective, we learn nothing of it in Hoekema's treatise.

Paul and Peter clearly identified this variety of Christian and did not present such a condition as normative or acceptable. Reformed doctrine cannot make room for Wesleyan or Pentecostal prescriptions for solving this problem, but should not Reformed theologians set forth an alternative solution, more biblical and more effective? Yet many Reformed theologians ignore the problem of the defeated Christian or even deny the existence of any such class of believer. Since the condition of a Christian who, because of ignorance, unbelief, or disobedience, is not living under the controlling influence of the Holy Spirit is not even recognized, the second great omission is any reference to a solution to the problem.

If both Scripture and Christian experience testify that there is a quality of life that is subnormal, and if many godly and biblically learned people testify that there is a solution to such a problem—a solution offered in Scripture and experienced by Christians—the issue must at least be addressed. If there is such a life and such a solution, it is a tragic loss to fail to proclaim it.

In summary, it might be said that there is no basic conflict between Hoekema's presentation of Reformed teaching on sanctification and the Keswick approach. But for those Calvinists who deny the existence of an unacceptable, qualitatively distinct way of life experienced by some Christians, a way that can and must be corrected by a renewal of the original faith-commitment to God, a conflict does exist.

Response to Hoekema

John F. Walvoord

The presentation of sanctification from the Reformed perspective by Anthony A. Hoekema is a model of lucid theological discussion and presents an admirable survey not only of the Reformed position but of its contrast to other theological perspectives. With few exceptions the author's views correspond to the traditional Augustinian-dispensational perspective. Accordingly, the Reformed position correctly interprets sanctification both as a definitive act that is decisive and irreversible and as a process that goes on through life and has its climax in heaven in the perfect sanctification of believers. Practically all of his discussion will be most helpful in enabling the reader to comprehend biblical revelation on the subject of sanctification.

There are some surprising variations from the Augustinian-dispensational perspective, as well as variations from the traditional historic Reformed perspective. In his discussion, Hoekema does not clearly delineate the existence of the old nature and the new nature in a Christian and reverts to the concept, as found in the New International Version, of the "old self" and "new self." This position reflects an apparent change in viewpoint on his part from his article in the *Bulletin of the Evangelical Theological Society* (Spring 1962), in which he accepted the concept of the old and new natures in regenerated persons.

There is some confusion with the terms "old man" and

"new man" where Hoekema contrasts John Murray's view (which he follows) and the older Calvinistic position as set forth by Hodge. This problem can be resolved if it is understood that "old man" and "new man" are references not to the old or new nature, or self, but rather to the old manner of life, which is an expression of the old nature, and to the new manner of life, which is an expression of the new nature. The NIV's translation of "old man" as "old self" in Colossians 3:9 can be questioned. As the subsequent context of this verse indicates, Paul is talking about our manner of life after being saved rather than our essential nature.

In his discussion of the commandments, Hoekema implies that Christians are under the Ten Commandments. (It should be noted that nine of the ten are repeated in the New Testament as applicable to the Christian. The one commandment omitted is that of keeping the Sabbath.) The word *law* (Gk. *nomos*) has many variations in its usage in the New Testament and does not necessarily refer to the Ten Commandments, but in general all can agree that Christians are under moral law, as indicated clearly in the New Testament. While moral law condemns, it also demonstrates the holiness of God and provides a standard for the Christian life.

One surprising variation in Hoekema is his statement in his footnote (p. 243, n. 25) that he considers Romans 7:13–25 a picture of the unregenerate person. This position is contrary to historic Calvinistic teaching stemming from Augustine. It is not demonstrable that an unbeliever has two inner, contending natures, and the traditional Reformed position that this struggle is within a regenerated person is preferable.

Hoekema strangely omits any reference to or discussion of either the filling of the Spirit or the baptism of the Spirit. In the Augustinian-dispensational perspective, the filling of the Spirit is the secret of sanctification. The filling is obtained through confession of sin, yieldedness to God, and appropriation of God's provision for walking by the Spirit. The struggle of regenerated individuals to achieve sanctification in their life is best clarified by explaining this process of being filled by the Spirit. Taken as a whole, however, Hoekema's discussion is remarkable for its clarity and comprehensive treatment and, in most respects, presents the doctrine of sanctification in a way that will help the reader.

Chapter 3

THE
PENTECOSTAL
PERSPECTIVE

Stanley M. Horton

THE PENTECOSTAL PERSPECTIVE

Stanley M. Horton

ROOTS OF THE PENTECOSTAL MOVEMENT

The present Pentecostal movement had its beginning in Bethel Bible College of Topeka, Kansas, on January 1, 1901. There students, as they searched the Scriptures, came to the conclusion that speaking in tongues as recorded in Acts 2:4 is the initial outward evidence that a person has been baptized in the Holy Spirit as an empowering experience for Christian service.[1] A revival began that spread to Missouri and Texas but initially showed no great results.

Then in 1906, W. J. Seymour, a black holiness preacher, accepted this teaching in Texas, found a response among some of the holiness people, and was invited to California. He soon secured a former Methodist church at 312 Azusa Street in Los Angeles. This became a center where both whites and blacks gathered. Soon people were coming from all over the United States and Canada, even from overseas.[2] Seymour kept a low profile, and the services were full of praise and worship to Jesus. From this beginning numerous Pentecostal churches sprang up.

In 1906, my grandfather, Elmer K. Fisher, who had been influenced by Reuben A. Torrey at Moody Bible Institute in Chicago, was pastor of the First Baptist Church of Glendale, California. After much prayer, he began a series of sermons on the Holy Spirit as our Source of spiritual power. The deacons approached him to say that he could preach on courage or on Daniel but they did not like the excitement his sermons on the Holy Spirit were causing. As a result, my grandfather resigned from that pastorate.

Shortly before this incident, Dr. Smale, the pastor of the First Baptist Church of Los Angeles, returned from a visit to the Evan Roberts revival in Wales. His heart was filled with a great desire to see a similar revival in his own church. Because he met resistance, he left his church and, with some of his deacons, started the New Testament Church in downtown Los Angeles. My grandfather joined him there.

On Easter Sunday, Mrs. Seymour and others came to the New Testament Church and told how the Holy Spirit was being outpoured in the Azusa Street Mission just as He had been at Pentecost (Acts 2:4). Immediately a number of people, including my grandfather, responded and received the Pentecostal baptism in the Holy Spirit.

He then took my grandmother to the Azusa Street Mission. When she saw and heard what was happening, she said, "I already have this." They responded by saying, "You couldn't have; you're a Baptist." Because of their Wesleyan holiness background, they were teaching that it was necessary to receive a sanctification experience first, as a preparation for receiving the baptism in the Holy Spirit. Sanctification, they said, was "a second definite work of grace" that would cleanse believers from "inbred sin" and make them a clean vessel for the Holy Spirit to fill. My grandmother, however, the daughter of Professor Heman Howes Sanford of Syracuse University, had had an unusual experience about 1880, when she was speaking to a group of Baptist women near Erie, Pennsylvania. She felt an unusual anointing of the Holy Spirit and began to speak in a language she had never learned. Then the Holy Spirit gave her an interpretation that was all Scripture and fitted together to form a message. After that experience, when she was alone in earnest prayer, the Holy Spirit would often give her edification and refreshing through this language. But she kept it private and personal, not identifying it with the Book of Acts until she came to Azusa Street Mission.

There she did not argue but began to pray to be sanctified. In a very few minutes she was speaking in tongues again, this time in Danish, as she found out from a visitor from Denmark. My mother also was there, and she too began to pray to be sanctified. In less than ten minutes she started speaking in tongues in French, as a French-speaking woman who was present told her.

The early Pentecostals continued to teach sanctification as a second definite work of grace, believing that the baptism in the Holy Spirit represented a third experience. Many, however, especially among those of Baptist or Reformed background, had scriptural questions about this teaching. Many others, like my mother, could not distinguish a second definite work in their own experience.

In 1910, William H. Durham, a Chicago holiness preacher who had received the baptism in the Holy Spirit, began to preach what he called the "finished work of Calvary." Durham taught that the faith that justifies a person brings that one into Christ. In Christ the believer is complete with regard to sanctification and all else that is part of or related to salvation. The conversion experience includes Christ's cleansing of the soul so that the believer becomes a "new creature" and needs no subsequent work of grace for sanctification. He or she needs only to abide in Christ, receive and walk in the Spirit, and grow in grace and the knowledge of God and Christ. The sinful nature, however, is not removed but is crucified with Christ, and the righteousness of Christ is imputed. As long as a faith relationship with Christ is maintained, that righteousness will bear fruit in practical, daily living. By sinning, people indicate that they have broken their relationship with Christ and that the old, sinful nature has asserted itself and needs to be crucified by faith in the cross. Durham also called for people to grow in grace in order to perfect the inward work as they abide in Christ, to "desire the sincere milk of the Word," and to progress toward maturity.

Durham, a magnetic preacher, affected thousands in the Chicago area. Then in 1911, he decided to go to Los Angeles. By this time, my grandfather Fisher had established what was then the largest Pentecostal church in the city, called the Upper Room Mission, and had come to believe in a second definite work, simply because this view had been taught at Azusa Street. At first, he invited Durham to preach at his church, but when he heard what Durham was preaching, he canceled the meetings. Durham then went to the Azusa Street Mission, where hundreds crowded to hear him. But when Seymour returned from an evangelistic tour, he locked him out, at which point Durham started his own church in Los Angeles.

Durham's preaching immediately brought sharp controversy. Charles Parham, a holiness Pentecostal preacher who had done much to popularize the new movement, prayed that God would take Durham's life if the doctrine of a second definite work was true. Durham actually died six months later, an event that Parham considered a vindication of holiness doctrine. Durham's death, however, did not lessen the controversy.

Actually, much of the teaching in the Azusa Street Mission had prepared people to accept Durham's message. Although holiness Pentecostals have typically discussed sanctification in terms of the Holy Spirit, in Azusa Street there was great emphasis on the work of Christ and a tremendous exaltation of the blood of Christ and the Cross. Though they encouraged believers to be filled with the Spirit and to demonstrate this filling by speaking in other tongues, the worship was definitely Christ centered. Thus it was not hard for many to accept Durham's claim that their faith should be in Christ rather than in an experience of sanctification.

The holiness Pentecostals recognized rightly that much of Durham's teaching was like that of Count Nickolaus von Zinzendorf, who taught that Christian perfection is imputed and is by faith in the blood of Christ, so that the moment a person is justified, sanctification is complete. They relied heavily on Wesley's arguments against positions similar to those held by Zinzendorf in their attempts to refute Durham's teaching.

There were extremes on both sides. Some holiness Pentecostals declared that at conversion God pardoned sinners but left them so full of sin and corruption that it took "a second work of grace" to keep them from going to hell. Some of Durham's followers taught that, since the work of Christ was fully accomplished on the cross, it was finished and complete in us the moment we believe, so that we are immediately and totally righteous and are secure in this position no matter how much we sin. Durham himself, however, was careful to emphasize his belief in holiness, sanctification, and growth in grace. His followers continued to maintain that sanctification as a second definite work of grace did not properly recognize the power of the blood of Christ.[3]

Durham's teaching brought a division in the Pentecostal movement, a division that continues to this day. Holiness Pentecostal groups (such as the Church of God of Cleveland, Tennessee, and the Pentecostal Holiness Church) still teach a crisis experience of sanctification as a second definite work of grace that is prerequisite to the baptism in the Holy Spirit. Those groups influenced by Durham may call for heart purity but in general see faith and the cleansing of the blood of Christ as the only prerequisite for baptism in the Spirit. The Assemblies of God, with over fifteen million adherents worldwide, is the largest such group.

THE ASSEMBLIES OF GOD AND DEBATE OVER HOLINESS

The Assemblies of God began as the result of a call by Eudorus N. Bell in *Word and Witness* magazine for a conference of Pentecostal believers, which took place in 1914 at Hot Springs, Arkansas.[4] About three hundred persons attended, and the General Council of the Assemblies of God was formed as "a voluntary, cooperative fellowship." By 1918 its headquarters were established in Springfield, Missouri, where its international headquarters remain.

Shortly after its founding, however, a controversy over the nature of the Trinity caused some to leave the young fellowship. The dissidents took their non-Wesleyan, christocentric "finished work of Calvary" doctrine to an extreme. They focused everything on Jesus and propounded a "revelation" of a modal view of the Trinity that made Jesus the one Person in the Godhead. They demanded that those who had been baptized in the name of the Father, the Son, and the Holy Ghost be rebaptized in the name of Jesus only, basing their views on the apostolic pattern in the Book of Acts. Their claim that *Jesus* is "the name" of the Father, Son, and Holy Spirit in Matthew 28:19 became the hallmark of Pentecostal unitarianism, the so-called Oneness, or Jesus Only, movement. Frank Ewart, its leading exponent, argued that, since all the fullness of the Godhead dwells bodily in Jesus (Col. 2:9), He must be the totality of the Godhead. Ewart's followers came to my mother and told her that she would lose her salvation if she did not "get baptized over again in Jesus' name." She was a sensitive person, and her first reaction was, "How can this be, since my salvation is so precious to me?" Then she began to feel incensed that anyone would thus question Christ's work in her, which led her in turn to observe, "I'm getting angry. I must be losing my salvation." So she went to be rebaptized. Later, from her own study of Scripture, she returned to a belief in the Trinity and eventually joined the Assemblies of God. Many, including several early leaders of the Assemblies of God, were swept into this rebaptism on the grounds that it was honoring to Jesus. However, many of these also returned.

The controversy over this issue of God's oneness caused the Assemblies of God to adopt a sixteen-point "Statement of Fundamental Truths" to provide a basis for continued fellowship. This statement, as it was first adopted in 1916, gave detailed attention to the nature of the Trinity as "the Adorable Godhead," with three distinct Persons in the one Being. Other doctrines were stated only briefly.

Point 9 of this statement was entitled "Entire Sanctification" and reads as follows:

> The Scriptures teach a life of holiness without which no man shall see the Lord. By the power of the Holy Ghost we are able to obey the command, "Be ye holy, for I am holy." Entire sanctification is the will of God for all believers, and should be earnestly pursued by walking in obedience to God's Word. Heb. 12:14; 1 Peter 1:15–16; 1 Thess. 5:23, 24; 1 John 2:6.[5]

This statement treats sanctification as the work of the Holy Spirit with the cooperation of the believer. The term *entire sanctification* is not defined, possibly because some did not want to rule out completely the possibility of a second definite work, while others may have held the view that it was "entire" on the cross. However, the statement does present sanctification as a goal to be pursued. The followers of Durham at this period were not theologically oriented and preached a simple, Christ-centered gospel. Most of those who came together to form the Assemblies of God agreed that there was no second definite work and that holiness was important. They therefore had little trouble adopting this statement.

The early writings and Sunday school materials of the Assemblies of God (published by its subsidiary, the Gospel Publishing House) continued to stress a Christ-centered holiness and opposed the idea of a second definite work of sanctification. At first glance, Myer Pearlman, a most influential Assemblies of God writer, seems to be an exception. He states:

> It must be acknowledged that progress in sanctification often involves a crisis experience almost as definite as that of conversion. By one means or another the believer receives a revelation of the holiness of God and the possibility of a

closer walk with Him, and this is followed by a consciousness of defilement. Compare Isaiah 6. He has come to a crossroad in his Christian experience where he must decided either to go back or go forward with God. Confessing past failures, he makes a reconsecration and as a result receives a new accession of peace, joy, and victory, and also the witness that God has accepted his consecration. Some have called this experience a second work of grace.[6]

Pearlman, however is simply trying to help people who come into the Assemblies of God from one of the holiness churches. He wants them to see that what they call a "second definite work" could well be a real experience, but one that must be reinterpreted in the light of what the Bible teaches.

Pearlman also makes it clear that he rejects any teaching that proposes that a person might be "saved or justified without being sanctified." He suggests further that another explanation of experiences thought to be a second definite work of grace might be rather the awakening of believers to the position that they already have in Christ. In other places, Pearlman treats eradication of inbred sin as contrary to both Scripture and experience.[7] Clearly, he has no place for a sanctification experience as the Pentecostals had taught it at the turn of the century. His influence as a Bible institute teacher, writer, and camp-meeting speaker had been strongly felt throughout the Assemblies of God.

In the local churches two aspects of sanctification were repeatedly emphasized. There were frequent calls for consecration and reconsecration to the service and worship of the Lord. There was also a great emphasis on the necessity for separation from the world. A favorite text was "Wherefore come out from among them, and be ye separate, saith the Lord, and touch not the unclean thing" (2 Cor. 6:17 KJV). The "unclean thing" was usually interpreted to include alcoholic beverages, tobacco in any form, social dancing, card games, gambling, and theater, especially the moving-picture theater. For the women it also included facial make-up, short hair, and short dresses. In local situations other things might be added. (For example, a convention I attended in northern California in the late 1930s added circuses and carnivals to the list.)

World War II brought a dislocation of many people, due in large part to employment opportunities. There was some confusion as individuals began to find that not all our churches held exactly the same standards of external holiness. There was also an observable trend away from what was called "clothes line" preaching to a greater emphasis on positive devotion to God and His service and on a cooperation with God in the matter of sanctification. About that time, however, the general superintendent of the Assemblies of God, Ernest Swing Williams, wrote, "I feel that the weakness in our movement when it comes to preaching sanctification, is that the doctrine is taught so vaguely that many fail to get sight of something definite which they may have in their own lives."[8]

This vagueness continued to be felt, not only with regard to sanctification, but also with regard to some of the other brief sections in the "Statement of Fundamental Truths." The ministers and delegates to the general council in session voted to appoint a committee to bring a proposal for its revision. All of us who were on that committee were especially concerned over point 9, "Entire Sanctification." We felt that the word *entire* was ambiguous because we were using it with a different meaning than that promoted by holiness Pentecostals, who taught a second definite work.

The revised statement was presented to the General Council of the Assemblies of God convened at Portland, Oregon, August 23–29, 1961. After two days of discussion, it was accepted unanimously. In point 9, the word *entire* was dropped. The section is now headed simply "Sanctification" and states:

> Sanctification is an act of separation from that which is evil, and of dedication unto God. (Rom 12:1–2; 1 Thess. 5:23; Heb. 13:12). The Scriptures teach a life of "holiness without which no man shall see the Lord" (Heb. 12:14). By the power of the Holy Ghost we are able to obey the command: "Be ye holy, for I am holy" (1 Peter 1:15–16).

> Sanctification is realized in the believer by recognizing his identification with Christ in His death and resurrection, and by faith reckoning daily upon the fact of that union, and by offering every faculty continually to the dominion of the Holy Ghost (Rom. 6:1–11, 13; 8:1–2, 13; Gal. 2:20; Phil. 2:12; 1 Peter 1:5).[9]

The definitions given by earlier Assemblies of God writers show that this revised statement does agree with what had been taught. Myer Pearlman, in a textbook used by a number of early Pentecostal Bible institutes, defines sanctification as including (1) separation from sin and the world and

(2) dedication, or consecration, to the fellowship and service of God through Christ. He identifies *sanctified* and *holy* as synonymous and adds that, "while the primary meaning of holy is that of separation unto service, the idea of purification is also involved."[10] He recognizes cleanliness also as a condition of holiness, but not the holiness or sanctification itself, "which is primarily separation and dedication."

The founder of the Southwestern Assemblies of God College, P. C. Nelson, says that sanctification exhibits the fruit of right relationship with God in a life separated from a sinful world and dedicated to God.[11] He emphasizes that it is not enough to be separated from evil. Devotion to the use and service of God is necessary. E. S. Williams agrees but puts a heavier emphasis on separation, where "the believer cuts loose from the world and sin, being made pure through the atoning work of Christ and by the power of the Holy Spirit."[12] He states further that the purpose of sanctification is "to enable the soul to live above sin, living for God instead." The general superintendent of the Assemblies of God in 1986, G. Raymond Carlson, concurs. He states that "sanctification involves two great truths. The first is consecration," which he identifies as including separation from sin and dedication to God. For him the second truth is purification.[13] The leadership in the Assemblies of God, thus, has continued to maintain that sanctification involves being dedicated, purified, and enabled to live a holy life.

The early Assemblies of God writers agree also that sanctification is twofold. In one aspect it is positional and instantaneous, and in another, practical and progressive. Nelson, Pearlman, and Williams all draw attention to Paul's addressing the Corinthian believers as saints and as already sanctified in Christ (1 Cor. 1:2; 6:11). Yet, at the same time, they were far from perfect; many were not walking worthy of their high calling, and some were even involved in open sin.

Nelson draws attention to 1 Corinthians 6:11, "But you were washed, you were sanctified, you were justified in the name of the Lord Jesus Christ and by the Spirit of our God." He also quotes from Hebrews 10:10, 14 and goes on to say:

> When we believe on the Lord Jesus Christ and accept Him as our Savior, we are justified by faith in Him and stand before God without any condemnation on our souls: we are regenerated, that is, born again through the operation of the

Holy Spirit and the Word of God, and have become new creatures. We are also separated from sin and cleansed and purged by the blood of Jesus (1 John 1:7), and by our own will we set ourselves apart to the service of God, and Christ is now our "wisdom, and righteousness, and sanctification, and redemption" (1 Cor. 1:30).[14]

Pearlman also emphasizes that sanctification is simultaneous in this sense with justification, and Williams says, "Each believer in Christ is sanctified positionally when he accepts Christ. This is a truth that needs to be seen if a person desires to live a sanctified life."[15]

The above writers all stress even more strongly that sanctification is also a progressive work. Even though all believers are separated to God in Christ, this relation only begins a life process whereby His holiness is made actual in our lives. It calls for a daily separation as the believer seeks to become more and more conformed to the image of Christ. The fact that this is a process and is not instantaneous is further confirmed by such passages as 2 Corinthians 3:18 ("And we, who with unveiled faces all reflect the Lord's glory, are being transformed into his likeness with ever-increasing glory [from one degree of glory to another], which comes from the Lord, who is the Spirit").

Peter further exhorts us to "grow in the grace and knowledge of our Lord and Savior Jesus Christ" (2 Peter 3:18). Hebrews 12 indicates that this process may involve many experiences, including discipline and punishment, and then comments that this discipline is not only for our good but specifically, "that we may share in his holiness" (v. 10). Pearlman at this point emphasizes that "this does not mean that we grow into sanctification, but that we progress in sanctification."[16] As Hebrews 12:14 says, "Make every effort . . . to be holy; without holiness no one will see the Lord." All these early Assemblies of God writers also agree that sanctification involves crucifying "the sinful nature with its passions and desires" (Gal. 5:24) and at the same time receiving the "quickening grace of Christ which brings forth the fruit of righteousness"; and they recognize that "when a person leaves holiness and begins to walk after the flesh, he has lost his sanctification."[17]

SANCTIFICATION IN ASSEMBLIES OF GOD TEACHING

With this history in mind, we can now consider what the Assemblies of God teaches about sanctification today. Current writers show the influence of those of the former generation and often refer to them. There is continuity in the theology, but in some cases there have been changes in application and practice. Writers still speak of sanctification as including instantaneous sanctification, progressive sanctification, and entire sanctification. Among some local assemblies, however, there is not as much emphasis on the external aspects of holiness nor on the standards inherited from the holiness movement of the nineteenth century.

Instantaneous Sanctification

The first aspect is simply stated by Ralph W. Harris, former editor of church school literature for the Assemblies of God and now editor of the *Complete Biblical Library*. He says, "Sanctification is instantaneous, for the moment a person believes in Christ he is separated from sin and unto God."[18] In my own writings for the *Adult Teacher* of the Assemblies of God Gospel Publishing House, I have repeatedly spoken of our being sanctified, or made holy, by faith in Christ. In discussing the question, Who are the saints today? I wrote:

> There is a progressive aspect to sanctification whereby we grow in grace (2 Peter 1:4–8; 3:18). But there is also an instantaneous aspect to sanctification whereby at the time we are born again we are set apart from the world to follow Jesus and are saints in this sense. Unfortunately, some of the formal churches have set certain men and women on a pedestal and called them saints. But the New Testament calls all believers saints, even those who are far from perfect. If we are Christians at all, we are consecrated and dedicated to follow Jesus. All are saints if they are headed in the right direction, even though they may have just started on the way. It is sad that the word *saint* has been spoiled for us by those who use it as a title for their heroes.[19]

We recognize also that water baptism declares our union with Christ in His death and resurrection. "In him you were also circumcised [as the sign of the covenant and promise], in the putting off of the sinful nature [or the flesh], not with a circumcision done by the hands of men but with the circumcision done by Christ, having been buried with him in baptism and raised with him through your faith in the power [or working] of God, who raised him from the dead" (Col. 2:11–12). Thus, Paul testifies, "I have been crucified with Christ and I no longer live, but Christ lives in me. The life I live in the body, I live by faith in the Son of God, who loved me and gave himself for me" (Gal. 2:20; cf. Eph. 2:4–6).

We are thus united with Christ in a new kind of life that we live unto God. This new life is made possible only by the work of Christ and our union with Him. "It is because of him that you are in Christ Jesus, who has become for us wisdom from God—that is, our righteousness, holiness [sanctification, KJV] and redemption" (1 Cor. 1:30, a reference used in the "Statement of Fundamental Truths").

It is clear from these verses that our life of holiness is possible only because of Christ's work and that this initial sanctification, or positional sanctification, is necessary before we can begin to live a sanctified life. As Hebrews 10:10 says, "And by that will [the will of God accomplished by Christ], we have been made holy [sanctified, KJV] through the sacrifice of the body of Jesus Christ once for all." That is, God's will and purpose through Christ's sacrifice of Himself was and is, not only our redemption, but our sanctification. By Christ's sacrifice, sinful persons are put into perfect relationship with God. We are sanctified, dedicated, consecrated, set apart for God and for His worship and service. As we walk with Jesus in simple faith, we are thus made partakers of the fruits of His obedience. We are set free to do God's will.

The cross is thus the key to our positional sanctification. We have this position because of what Christ has done. Assemblies of God writers continue to speak of "the finished work of Calvary."[20] Without recognizing Christ's finished work we cannot properly understand the progressive work of sanctification in our own lives.

Progressive Sanctification

The need for progressive sanctification is indicated when Paul addresses the Corinthians not as spiritual but as "worldly [carnal, fleshly, the result of human weakness]—mere infants in Christ" (1 Cor. 3:1). That is, their condition was not measuring up to the position they had in Christ. He also warns them that if they remain worldly, their carnality will be judged, and they will forfeit reward at the judgment (1 Cor. 3:13–14). This teaching fits in with Paul's exhortations to "grow in grace." You are sanctified positionally, he says, but "it is God's will that you should be holy . . . that each of you should learn to control his own body" (1 Thess. 4:3–4). We are dead to sin through our identification with Christ (Col. 3:3). But that is not enough. You yourselves, Paul says, must take responsibility to "put to death . . . whatever belongs to your earthly nature: sexual immortality, impurity, lust, evil desires and greed, which is idolatry. . . . You used to walk in these ways, in the life you once lived. But now you must rid yourselves of all such things as these: anger, rage, malice, slander, and filthy language from your lips. Do not lie to each other, since you have taken off your old self with its practices and have put on the new self, which is being renewed in knowledge in the image of its Creator" (Col. 3:5–10). As Ephesians indicates, you have been "taught, with regard to your former way of life, to put off your old self, which is being corrupted by its deceitful desires; to be made new in the attitude of your minds; and to put on the new self, created to be like God in true righteousness and holiness" (Eph. 4:22–24).

These verses do not mean that the whole responsibility for progressive sanctification is put on the believer. We have our part, but God also has His part. He has appointed means to provide for both external and internal sanctification in our daily lives. These means are the blood of Christ, the Holy Spirit, and the inspired Word of God, the sixty-six books of the Bible.

The blood of Christ is effective in giving us positional sanctification, in which we are identified with Christ (Heb. 2:10–11). But there is also a continuous aspect, whereby the blood of Christ continues to cleanse and sanctify us. "But if we walk [keep walking] in the light, as he is in the light, we have [keep on having] fellowship with one another [between us and God], and the blood of Jesus, his Son, purifies [keeps on cleansing, purifying] us from every sin" (1 John 1:7).

Apparently, there were some who did not understand this provision for the continual cleansing by the blood of Christ, for John goes on to say, "If we claim we have not sinned, we make him [God] out to be a liar and his word has no place in our lives" (v. 10). Here the phrase "have not sinned" is in the Greek perfect tense, which normally refers to an action or event in the past that has continuing results in the present. In other words, if we say we have had a sanctification experience that guarantees that we no longer have sin in our lives or that we do not or cannot sin any more, then we are making God out to be a liar and we are not giving His Word any place in our daily lives. In such a case, we are saying that we do not need the continued cleansing of the blood. But God has just said in 1 John 1:7 that we do need that continued cleansing of the blood, so we are making Him a liar. Furthermore, the Bible is full of exhortations to help us have victory over sin. Therefore, if we say that we do not or cannot sin any more, we are saying that we do not need to pay attention to God's Word or give it its proper place in our lives. The same conclusions apply to those who say that because they have absolute positional sanctification through the blood of the cross, they do not need the continuous cleansing of the blood.

Actually, the closer we walk with the Lord, the more we realize our need for the continued cleansing and purifying by the blood of Christ. When Isaiah caught a vision of the glory and holiness of God, he suddenly became conscious of his own need for cleansing (Isa. 6:5). But "If we confess our sins, he is faithful and just and will forgive us our sins and purify us from all unrighteousness" (1 John 1:9). He, through the blood of His eternal sacrifice, removes every barrier to fellowship with Himself.

Progressive sanctification must involve the whole person. But the Bible teaches that the external effects and evidences of sanctification must be the result of an internal work. The Holy Spirit here is the agent, and His work is the most important means of our progressive sanctification. He, as E. S. Williams puts it, does a work "in the soul, strengthening the holy qualities which are born into man through regeneration and bringing about their increase. While God employs means, and man is expected to cooperate with God, sanctifying himself, the work is a work of God" (1 Thess. 5:23; Heb. 13:20–21).[21]

The Holy Spirit is involved in the initial work of sanctification, as 1 Corinthians 6:11 indicates: "But you were washed, you were sanctified, you were justified in the name of the Lord Jesus Christ and by the Spirit of our God." Again, 2 Thessalonians 2:13 speaks of salvation (probably meaning our future salvation and inheritance) "through the sanctifying work of the Spirit and through belief in the truth." Romans 15:16 and 1 Peter 1:1–2 also speak of this sanctifying work of the Spirit. These passages also imply progress in sanctification through the work of the Holy Spirit.

In my book *What the Bible Says About the Holy Spirit*, I point out:

The Holy Spirit is also a witness to us that God has accepted Christ's sacrifice and "hath perfected forever them that are sanctified" [has made perfect forever those who are being made holy, NIV] (Heb. 10:14). This is further confirmed by Jeremiah's prophecy (Heb. 10:16; Jer. 31:33), even though Jeremiah himself did not mention the Holy Spirit. In this context, the "perfecting" was accomplished in the sacrifice of Christ on Calvary. "Forever" means either continuously or for all time and refers to the fact that His sacrifice was "once for all" (Heb. 9:28). "Sanctified" [being made holy, NIV] is in a continuous form of the verb, "those who are being sanctified [made holy] or consecrated, dedicated to God and His service."[22]

The Holy Spirit through whom we have sanctification, or consecration (1 Peter 1:2), also enables us to cooperate with this work by purifying our souls in obedience to the truth, resulting in a sincere brotherly love (1 Peter 1:22).

This may involve partaking of Christ's sufferings. But if it brings reproach for His name's sake, we are happy, for the Spirit of glory and of God rests on us (1 Peter 4:14). In the [realm of the] natural, self-preservation is the first law of human nature. The world emphasizes self-interest, taking care of "number one." Competition leads to a desire to dominate others and play the tyrant. But Jesus was among us as a Servant of all. The greatest among us is to be the servant (slave) of all (Luke 22:27; Matt. 20:25–28; 23:11). It is only possible for us to overcome our natural drives through the power of the Spirit as Christ lives in us and His nature is being formed in us. Then, the supply of God's grace will make it possible even to die for our Lord. What a contrast there is between the death of Stephen and the death of Herod Agrippa I. Stephen, full of the Holy Spirit, looked into heaven, saw the glory of God, and was able to forgive his murderers (Acts 7:55–60). Herod in self-exaltation took glory to himself that belonged to God and died in agony under God's judgment (Acts 12:21–23).[23]

The work of the Spirit in sanctification thus brings growth in grace and brings about the development of the fruit of the Spirit. This process was and is made possible through Christ, who sanctified us through His blood (Heb. 13:12). But it was made personal to us by the Holy Spirit, who sanctified us by separating us from evil and dedicating us to God when He gave us new life and placed us into the body of Christ (1 Cor. 6:11; 12:13). But Paul prays that this initial aspect of sanctification will be continued as God sanctifies us wholly, through and through (1 Thess. 5:23).

We must cooperate with the Holy Spirit in this work by presenting ourselves to God (Rom. 12:1–2), by seeking the Holy Spirit's help as we pursue holiness, dedicating ourselves to God in right relationships to God and man, for without such holiness no one will see the Lord (Heb. 12:14). That holiness is like His, which the Holy Spirit helps us to achieve (1 Peter 1:15–16).

Actually, the work of the Spirit that receives by far the greatest attention in the New Testament is the whole work of sanctification.

> It takes precedence over witnessing, evangelism, giving and every other form of Christian service. God wants us to be something, not just to do something. For only as we become like Jesus can what we do be effective and bring glory to Him. Our worship also, as it is guided by the Spirit and prompted by the Spirit in every aspect encourages us in this very thing.[24]

The third means of sanctification is the Word of God. In Jesus' High Priestly Prayer for His disciples, He said, "Sanctify them by the truth; your word is truth" (John 17:17). This means is not unrelated to the work of the Holy Spirit, however, nor is it even in addition to it. The sword of the Spirit is the Word of God (Eph. 6:17). In fact, the Word is His primary tool for accomplishing His work in the hearts and lives of individuals. The people He uses are His willing agents, but the means of doing the work is the Word.

The Word is indeed effective only as it is made alive through the Holy Spirit. Paul said, God "has made us competent [qualified, and therefore effective] as ministers of a new covenant—not of the letter, but of the Spirit; for the letter kills [and leaves in condemnation], but the Spirit gives life" (2 Cor. 3:6). He goes on to show that this ministry is much more glorious than that which caused Moses' face to shine.

Moses hid that glory by putting a veil over his face. But as Paul further points out, another veil was over the minds of the unbelieving Jews of his day, and it was keeping them from seeing a greater glory—the glory of Christ. Not until the Jews turn to the Lord is this veil taken away from their minds. But when it is, the Lord they see is not the Lord Moses saw; yet it is, for the Lord they see is Christ revealed by the Spirit.

Where the Spirit of the Lord is, then, the veil is gone and there is liberty (freedom) from the bondage of the Law that put the veil over their minds. (See also John 8:31–32). Then we all, both Jews and Gentiles, with open (unveiled) faces now do behold by the Spirit, the glory of the Lord . . . . As we continue to behold the glory of the Lord, even though as in a glass (an imperfect mirror, therefore imperfectly seeing Him, not because of any lack on the part of the Spirit, but because of our inability), we are changed from glory to glory (from one degree of glory to another) even as by the Spirit of the Lord (2 Cor. 3:18). That is, Moses was the only one who saw the glory at Sinai. Then, he only had the one experience and had to veil the glory. But through the Spirit, the glorified Christ who is our Mediator at God's right hand is continually revealed to us all (2 Cor. 3:18), and we keep on being changed.[25]

Thus God sees our potential for improvement and makes provision for it through the Spirit and the Word.

God's purpose in sanctification is to bring us to maturity, not (at least in this life) to absolute or final perfection. To accomplish this goal, Paul in Ephesians 4 tells us that Christ took captives and thus made them His slaves. Then he gave them as gifts to the church, "some to be apostles, some to be prophets, some to be evangelists, and some to be pastors and teachers, to prepare God's people for works of service, so that the body of Christ may be built up until we all reach unity in the faith and in the knowledge of the Son of God and become mature, attaining to the whole measure of the fullness of Christ" (vv. 7–13).

Though Paul does not mention the Spirit or the Word here, both are clearly involved in bringing us to maturity. The ministries of apostle, prophet, evangelist, and pastor-teacher are gifted by the Holy Spirit, as 1 Corinthians 12–14 indicates. Then Paul goes on to show the need for the truth of the Word by saying that these ministries will bring us to a maturity in which "we will no longer be infants, tossed back and forth by the waves, and blown here and there by every wind of teaching and by the cunning and craftiness of men in their deceitful scheming. Instead, speaking the truth in love, we will in all things grow up into him who is the Head, that is, Christ" (Eph.

4:14–15). In this passage and many others false teachers are seen to be a hindrance to sanctification and spiritual growth. In contrast to them, the apostle Paul proclaimed Christ, "admonishing and teaching everyone with all wisdom, so that we may present everyone perfect in Christ. To this end I labor, struggling with all his energy, which so powerfully works in me" (Col. 1:28–29).

The Word is important also because along with growth in grace there must be growth in knowledge. Paul continually prayed for the Colossians that God would fill them with the knowledge of His will through all spiritual wisdom and understanding, so that they might "live a life worthy of the Lord and may please him in every way: bearing fruit in every good work, growing in the knowledge of God, being strengthened with all power according to his glorious might so that [they might] have great endurance and patience" (Col. 1:10–11). Here again there is cooperation between the Word and the Spirit. Note also the following: the Holy Spirit is a teacher (John 14:26); He is the Spirit of truth (14:17; 15:26; 16:13; 1 John 4:6); the truth is what Jesus proclaims from God (John 1:17; 8:40, 45–46; 18:37); Jesus is the truth (14:6); God's Word is the truth (17:17); the Holy Spirit guides us into all the truth (16:13); and the Spirit is also the truth (1 John 5:6).

John 1:14 and 18 indicate that Jesus came to declare, explain, reveal, interpret, make known and unfold the nature and will of the Father. Similarly, the Holy Spirit comes to explain, reveal, interpret, make known, and unfold the nature and will of Jesus (John 16:12–13). As the Teacher, He brings us the truth that is in Jesus, showing Him to be the Revealer of the Father, the Savior, the Forgiver of sins, the risen Lord, the Baptizer in the Holy Spirit, the coming King, and the final Judge. His exegesis, or unfolding, of the truth in Jesus and His reminding them of the words of Jesus guaranteed the accuracy of their teaching and gives us assurance of the inerrancy of the New Testament with respect to both facts and doctrine.

These matters are important, but we must also recognize that the same Teacher Spirit continues His work today, not by bringing new revelation, but by bringing new understanding as He illuminates the truth when we study the written Word. More than simply showing the truth, He sanctifies us by bringing us into the truth, helping us put it into action, making it real and effective in our lives. Thus, not only does Christ dwell within us, but the Holy Spirit helps us carry on the work of Christ in a way that glorifies Him.

A biblical illustration may be found in Acts 9:31, where the church "was strengthened; and encouraged by the Holy Spirit, it grew in numbers, living in the fear of the Lord." The context shows that this growth in numbers and this Christian living was brought about through the Spirit as He anointed the Word and as He quickened, empowered, sanctified, encouraged, and emboldened the believers.

The Christian, therefore, has a responsibility to respond to both the Word and the Spirit in faith and obedience. The Bible was not written to satisfy our curiosity about the past and the future. As 1 John 3:3 says, "Everyone who has this hope in him purifies himself, just as he is pure." Or as Paul puts it, "Since we have these promises, dear friends, let us purify ourselves from everything that contaminates body and spirit, perfecting holiness out of reverence for God" (2 Cor. 7:1). Thus our cooperation is necessary for sanctification to become actual and experiential in our lives. Our holiness must be put into practice, which we can do only with the help of the Holy Spirit.

Since this aspect of sanctification is progressive, the question comes: How far can we progress? or What degree of perfection can we attain in this life? Assemblies of God writers agree that we cannot attain ultimate or final perfection in this life.[26] Even the apostle Paul did not claim to have reached that goal. He says,

> Not that I have already obtained all this, or have already been made perfect, but I press on to take hold of that for which Christ Jesus took hold of me. Brothers, I do not consider myself yet to have taken hold of it. But one thing I do: Forgetting what is behind and straining toward what is ahead, I press on toward the goal to win the prize for which God has called me heavenward in Christ Jesus.

Then he adds, "All of us who are mature should take such a view of things. And if on some point you think differently, that too God will make clear to you. Only let us live up to what we have already attained" (Phil. 3:12–16).

Entire Sanctification

Assemblies of God writers and preachers still occasionally use the term *entire sanctification*, in three different ways. The term is sometimes used of believers who "live up to the light they have." Young Christians or new believers may be far from mature, but if their purpose and desire is to follow Christ and they are doing so the best they know by the help of the Holy Spirit, they are healthy Christians and participate in entire sanctification. E. S. Williams calls it a "life of victory" and emphasizes that through regeneration the power of sin is a dominating force no longer. "By the illumination, the power, the dynamic of the Holy Spirit, Calvary becomes effectual in its operation in us."[27] Thus the believer can live a life of victory over temptations to sin. But as William Menzies, an Assemblies of God professor of church history, points out:

> One gathers readily that this is not to be understood as in any sense a static plateau of perfectionism arrived at through a crisis experience. The emphasis is general: one may be dominated either by the Spirit or by the flesh; the believer can cultivate one form of life or the other, with appropriate results to follow in each case, based on Romans 8. Certainly the believer is not expected to flounder in perpetual struggle and failure, for "the Spirit has come to guide into a holy life."[28]

Pearlman also notes that entire sanctification does not mean absolute perfection, for this quality belongs only to God. He associates it with a relative perfection "which fulfills the end for which it was designed." He further defines it as "the whole-hearted desire and determination to do the will of God"; and "as being complete in the sense of being apt or fit for a certain task or end," an end that may be "attained through growth in mental and moral development" through the Holy Spirit and the Word.[29]

Again, the end or goal is never fully attained in this life. The believer is never free from temptation, and the old nature is still able to make demands. The believer must always be responsive to the Spirit as He continues to mediate the benefits of the Cross, the benefits of the Atonement, that our lives might be "for the praise of his glory" (Eph. 1:12).[30] Yet, as Albert Hoy, a professor emeritus of the Assemblies' Southern California College states,

> No matter how consecrated a Christian may be, it is impossible for him to have perfect knowledge of the application of the Word of God to all the complicated activities of modern life. There is often a good deal of mental confusion in rightly deciding whether God's will conflicts with duty . . . . In the process of sanctification, the believer's response

to revealed truth requires the power of the Holy Spirit in self-denial. As Paul has plainly stated (Rom. 7:16–25), every forward step in holiness is attained only after a struggle between the sensual man . . . and the spiritual man.[31]

Other Assemblies of God writers, however, would argue that this interpretation of Romans 7 is wrong, taking the Greek perfect in Romans 7:14 ("sold as a slave to sin") to mean that the person was and still is a slave to sin and therefore is not a believer.[32] But they would still agree that we have a continuing struggle and a continuing need to crucify the flesh, the sinful nature, in this life. At the same time they would emphasize that through the Holy Spirit we are able not to sin, even though we never come to the place where we are not able to sin.

Assemblies of God writers and preachers may also speak of entire sanctification as the state to which we shall be transformed at Christ's second coming, "in a flash, in the twinkling of an eye, at the last trumpet. For the trumpet will sound, the dead will be raised imperishable, and we will be changed" (1 Cor. 15:52). We shall then be like Christ, "for we shall see him as he is" (1 John 3:2). Then our prayers will be fully answered, and we shall experience the ultimate perfection in our total being that Christ shed His blood to make possible. With new bodies that are immortal and incorruptible, we shall share Christ's glory and thus become completely and entirely sanctified. In the meantime we must maintain "unbroken communion with Christ through the resources of prayer and the Word, seeking divine guidance from the Holy Spirit and striving to 'reach unity in the faith and in the knowledge of the Son of God and become mature, attaining to the whole measure of the fullness of Christ' (Eph. 4:13)."[33]

In every aspect of sanctification there is, of course, perfect cooperation among the members of the Trinity. Paul prayed for the Thessalonian believers: "May God himself, the God of peace, sanctify you through and through. May your whole spirit, soul and body be kept blameless at the coming of our Lord Jesus Christ. The one who calls you is faithful and he will do it" (1 Thess. 5:23–24). At the climax of His prayer for His disciples, Jesus asked the Father, "Sanctify them by the truth; your word is truth" (John 17:17). Jesus had challenged them earlier by saying, "If you hold to my teaching, you are really my disciples. Then you will know the truth, and the truth will set you free" (8:31–32). Continuing, staying, remaining in the word or teaching of Christ is the crux of the whole matter. God has given the Word to set us free from the deception and bondage of sin and Satan. Through the Word He gives us a vision of His will and plan and uses the Word to sanctify, dedicate, and consecrate us to serve Him and do His will.

Jesus went on to say, "As you sent me into the world, I have sent them into the world. For them I sanctify myself, that they too may be truly sanctified" (17:18–19). Jesus demonstrated His sanctification, or dedication and consecration, by obeying the Father and going into the world to do the work for which He was sent. We show our sanctification, dedication, and consecration in the same manner, by putting God's Word and will into practice in our own lives. Progressive sanctification is not something we profess. It is not something theoretical, neither is it something we have to wait until death to become involved in (see Luke 1:74–75; Titus 2:12; 1 John 1:7). We are truly sanctified when we obey God and do whatever work He gives us to do with the same sort of love and self-giving Jesus demonstrated as He obeyed the Father. This kind of sanctification will cause us to do the work that needs to be done, without fanfare and whether or not anyone appreciates it.

Paul uses the same truth as an encouragement for husbands to love their wives, "just as Christ loved the church and gave himself up for her to make her holy, cleansing her by the washing with water through the word, and to present her to himself as a radiant church, without stain or wrinkle or any other blemish, but holy and blameless" (Eph. 5:25–27). Hebrews 10:10 also ties our sanctification with the will of God and the work of Christ: "And by that will, we have been made holy through the sacrifice of the body of Jesus Christ once for all." There again we see that God's will and purpose for us is our sanctification. By Christ's sacrifice, sinful human beings are put into perfect relationship with God. But the purpose of this relationship is to sanctify us, setting us apart for God and His service. As we walk with Jesus in simple faith, we will continue to share in the fruits of His obedience, and we will continue to be free to do God's will. Thus Christ becomes to us and for us, "wisdom from God—that is, our righteousness, holiness and redemption" (1 Cor. 1:30).

The Spirit's Work in Sanctification

The power and help of the Holy Spirit is also just as necessary for our sanctification. Peter addressed the believers as those "who have been chosen according to the foreknowledge of God the Father, by the sanctifying work of the Spirit, for obedience to Jesus Christ and sprinkling by his blood" (1 Peter 1:2). Though the believers were exiles and scattered, they were still a chosen people. They could realize and experience this status by taking the way of consecration and holiness provided by the foreknowledge of God, made possible by the blood of Jesus, made practical through the sanctifying work of the Spirit, and appropriated and expressed through obedience. God wants us to share in His holiness and participate in the divine nature (Heb. 12:10; 2 Peter 1:4). In this connection Peter tells us that Christ has called us to His own glory and virtue, or excellence, which His sinless life offered to God made possible. In fact, the power for life and godliness are made effective through the personal knowledge of Christ, which is also the work of the Holy Spirit. He takes the Word and reveals Christ to us through it. He makes Jesus real. He makes it possible for us to enter into the experience of the apostle Paul, who said, "I consider everything a loss compared to the surpassing greatness of knowing Christ Jesus my Lord,' for whose sake I have lost all things. I consider them rubbish, that I may gain Christ and be found in him, not having a righteousness of my own that comes from the law, but that which is through faith in Christ" (Phil. 3:8–9).

Paul also put this attitude into practice, accepting it as his "priestly duty of proclaiming the gospel of God, so that the Gentiles might become an offering acceptable to God, sanctified by the Holy Spirit" (Rom. 15:16). The Holy Spirit therefore uses the written Word to give us a clear vision of Jesus and inspire us with a deep desire to be like Him.

Zenas Bicket, former academic dean of the Assemblies' Evangel College, draws attention to the Holy Spirit's work in the process of sanctification when he says:

> First, there must be a true reliance on the Spirit to make one holy; misconceptions of the process of sanctification must be renounced. Some Christians conduct themselves as though they believe holiness to be the inevitable result of simply professing Christ long enough . . . . Other Christians apparently believe that sanctification is achieved by an increasing

effort to become godly through one's own strength. But just as growth in a plant is the result of life, not effort, so holiness is the result of an indwelling, living Holy Spirit. Still another misconception about sanctification is that the Christian makes the effort and then asks God to bless it. But the Holy Spirit must do the whole work, or none of it; He will not share the work with man. Without taking Christ's righteousness and the Spirit's application of it, man will find both wind and tide opposed to him.[34]

Bicket goes on to emphasize that the Spirit "serves as the agent to make Christ our sanctification by seeking to bring about a complete and perfect union of Christ and the believer," which He accomplishes through several steps. He makes the believer aware of sin that was either unrecognized or shielded by self-justification. Then the Spirit makes the believer sense his or her own helplessness to achieve holiness and creates a hunger and thirst after righteousness. Then with the help of the Spirit the old man is put off and the new man is put on. With this step a sense of God's acceptance comes that brings peace and comfort. Then there is progress, sometimes by "sudden outbursts of the revitalized life within. . . . Or there may be steady development." The marks of holiness are "imparted through the agency of the Holy Spirit" as the believer "makes new discoveries of things to be surrendered to God or received from Him."[35]

BAPTISM IN THE HOLY SPIRIT

In order to clarify the Pentecostal perspective on sanctification, something further needs to be said about the baptism in the Holy Spirit. Some Oneness, or Jesus Only, Pentecostal groups have gone to an extreme by saying that one is not truly saved until baptized in the Holy Spirit with the evidence of speaking in other tongues. The Assemblies of God and most other Trinitarian Pentecostals recognize the baptism in the Holy Spirit as an experience distinct from regeneration. We do not say that a person who has never spoken in tongues does not have the Holy Spirit working in his or her life. We recognize that regeneration is the work of the Spirit, for the person who is born again is born of the Spirit (John 3:3–8).

We recognize also that it is the Spirit's work not only to give us life but to baptize us into the body of Christ (1 Cor. 12:13). "He plunges us in, no matter who we are, right along with Jews and Gentiles, slaves and free. Then he makes us all drink (be watered, saturated) with the same Spirit."[36] That is, after the Holy Spirit baptizes us into the body of Christ, we are then saturated or filled with the Spirit; the baptism in the Spirit is thus a distinct experience after conversion.

In the six cases in the New Testament that compare John's baptism in water with Jesus' baptism in the Holy Spirit, the word *baptize* is used with the Greek word *en*, which here means "in." But we believe the context in 1 Corinthians 12:13 justifies the translation of *en* as "by," so that the baptism here is "by one Spirit." Anthony D. Palma, formerly dean of the theology division of the Assemblies of God Graduate School (now Seminary) writes:

> The distinction often made by Pentecostal scholars is that the experience Paul speaks of is different from the experience spoken of by John the Baptist and Jesus.
>
> In the two groups of passages under discussion, there are indeed a few similar terms. But it is incorrect to insist that the same combination of words through the New Testament must always be translated in the same way. The Bible is not a handbook on systematic theology. If it were then we could insist that every word or expression or combination of terms must be translated in the same way.
>
> Apart from the similarities, the passages do not have very much in common. As a matter of fact, there are elements in the Pauline passage that are not found in the others. For instance, he mentions the *one* Spirit; he talks about being baptized "into one body." Furthermore, the prepositional phrase "*en* the one Spirit" precedes the verb; in the other passage it follows the verb.[37]

Palma goes on to note that in 1 Corinthians 12:3 and 9, which mention the work of the Spirit, *en* is translated as "by"; furthermore, the rest of the chapter talks about the activity of the Spirit. "By one Spirit" is thus the preferred translation of the phrase in 1 Corinthians 12:13 and is so rendered in the King James Version, the New American Standard Bible, the New International Version, the Revised Standard Version, the Living Bible, Today's English Version, the Twentieth Century New Testament, and the translations by Phillips, Moffatt, Williams, and Beck. Clearly, it is not just Pentecostal hermeneutical bias that makes a distinction between the baptism *by* the Spirit, which incorporates believers into the body of Christ, and the baptism *in* the Holy Spirit, in which Christ is the Baptizer and where the purpose is to empower the believer through the filling of the Spirit (Luke 24:49; Acts 1:8; 2:4).

The president of the Western Canadian Pentecostal College, L. Thomas Holdcroft, points out that some today teach, either by default or design, that the Holy Spirit's total role is to baptize the believer into the body of Christ. Others believe there can be fillings from time to time in the believer's life but do not call them baptisms. Others do distinguish between the baptism by the Spirit into the body of Christ and the baptism by Christ into the Spirit for service but do not accept the evidence of speaking in other tongues as the initial outward evidence for the baptism in the Holy Spirit. Holdcroft suggests further that the rejection of the Pentecostal position and the evidence of other tongues often leads to a downward trend that ends in the neglect of the Spirit's work in the believer's life. Thus, "quite apart from the issue of tongues, it is clearly of manifest spiritual importance to enjoy a meaningful personal baptism with [in] the Spirit."[38]

Pentecostals also recognize that the Old Covenant was abolished at the cross (Eph. 2:15) and that the death of Christ initiated the New Covenant (Heb. 9:15–17). Thus, before Pentecost, Jesus brought those who believed on Him into right relationship with Himself and with God. They were already partakers of His life when He commanded them to wait in Jerusalem for the promise of the Father. Acts 1:8 emphasizes power for service, not regeneration.

We recognize also that speaking in tongues is only the initial evidence of the baptism in the Holy Spirit. It marked the filling of the Spirit on the Day of Pentecost. It was the convincing evidence at the house of Cornelius (*"for* they heard them speaking in tongues," Acts 10:46). Though we make our case primarily from the Book of Acts, we recognize that Luke was a theologian, not just a historian. We recognize also that Paul in the Epistles deals with other people's experiences as well as his own. Even where the Epistles give propositional truth, such as justification by faith, it is related back to a historical event in the experience of Abraham, and when Paul wants to show the importance of grace, he goes back to a historical book and talks about David (Rom. 4). We should note also that when Paul asks the question, "Do all speak in tongues?" (1 Cor. 12:30), the verb is in the present tense, suggesting the meaning, "Do all continue to speak in tongues?"

that is, asking whether all have a continuing ministry to the church of speaking in tongues in the assembly. Paul thus does not rule out tongues as the initial outward evidence. We expect other evidences to follow one's baptism in the Spirit. In the Assemblies of God "Statement of Fundamental Truths," sections 7 and 10, we read:

> With the baptism in the Holy Ghost come such experiences as an overflowing fullness of the Spirit (John 7:37–39; Acts 4:8), a deepened reverence for God (Acts 2:43; Heb. 12:28), an intensified consecration to God and dedication to His work (Acts 2:42), and a more active love for Christ, for His Word and for the lost (Mark 16:20) . . . .
>
> This experience:
>
> a. Enables them to evangelize in the power of the Spirit with accompanying supernatural signs (Mark 16:15–20; Acts 4:29–31; Heb. 2:3–4).
>
> b. Adds a necessary dimension to worshipful relationship with God (1 Cor. 2:10–16; Chaps. 12–14).
>
> c. Enables them to respond to the full working of the Holy Spirit in expression of fruit and gifts and ministries as in New Testament times for the edifying of the body of Christ (Gal. 5:22–26; 1 Cor. 14:12; Eph. 4:11–12; 1 Cor. 12:28; Col. 1:29).[39]

We recognize also that the baptism in the Holy Spirit is not a climactic experience. Pentecost itself was only the beginning of the harvest. It brought believers into a fellowship of worship, teaching, and service. The baptism in the Holy Spirit is thus only a door into a growing relationship with the Spirit as a divine Person and with fellow members of the body of Christ. It leads to a life of service marked by gifts of the Spirit that bring power and wisdom for the spread of the gospel and the growth of the church.

Along with this emphasis on the empowering for service, we do not neglect the sanctifying work of the Spirit, especially with regard to dedication to God and the manifestation of His love. The Holy Spirit, in every aspect of our life with Him, points us to Jesus and pours out the love of God into our hearts and through us to a needy world. Because we are in Christ we are to live in the Spirit and by the Spirit. Every aspect of our lives needs His touch. He desires to make us one with Christ and one with each other as we join in the fellowship of the Spirit.

Whether we receive special manifestations of the Spirit or not, He is always present to guide, direct, and help us. Much of the life in the Spirit is a matter of faithfully carrying on the work of the Lord and the business of life without spectacular interventions. Yet this existence is not drab but is a life of growth in grace and in the fruit of the Spirit. Continuing sanctification thus remains the chief work of the Holy Spirit. However, it should be recognized that since the baptism in the Holy Spirit is not of itself a sanctifying experience, those who are newly baptized in the Spirit need to press on all the more as they cooperate with the Spirit in His sanctifying work.

On the other hand, we believe that the chief object of our Christian life is not to purify ourselves. Growth in grace comes best as we are involved in service. We do not believe that the saint, or dedicated believer should spend every day in nothing but study, prayer, and devotion. Those things are important, but the holy, sanctified life involves much more. We can see an illustration in the holy vessels in the tabernacle. They could not be used for ordinary purposes. No one could take them into their kitchen and cook with them, nor could they take them to their dining table and eat from them. Yet it was not their separation from ordinary use that made them holy. They were not holy until they were taken into the tabernacle and actually used in the service of God. So we are saints, not merely because we are separated from sin and evil, but because we are separated to God, sanctified and anointed for the Master's use.

The ordination, or consecration, of priests in the Old Testament provides another illustration. In the ceremony the blood was first applied to the lobe of the right ear, the thumb of the right hand, and the big toe of the right foot, symbolizing atonement for and cleansing of the whole person. Then they were anointed with oil, which represented the Spirit's work in preparing for service. So we too are cleansed and anointed, as were prophets, priests, and kings (2 Cor. 1:21; 1 John 2:20).

The Holy Spirit gives the power for service, not indiscriminately, but as He wills, through the gifts and ministries of the Spirit (1 Cor. 12:11). But Paul challenges the believers: "Eagerly desire the greater gifts" (v. 31). This command implies that they should strive for whatever gifts are most needed or would be most edifying at the time. It also indicates that we do not receive the gifts of the Spirit automatically, just because we have been baptized in the Spirit. We must be open to the Spirit and respond to Him with active, obedient faith, for He will not force His gifts on us.

First Corinthians 12 also shows that the Corinthian believers, who did not lack any spiritual gift (1:7), needed to exercise them in a better way. They needed to see the value of the gifts and the need for a variety of gifts to build up the body and promote its unity. But they needed more. Paul wrote, "And now I will show you the most excellent way" (12:31)— the way of love.

Love, however, is not one of the charismatic gifts of the Spirit. Rather, it encompasses the fruit of the Spirit and is therefore one of the chief results of the sanctifying work of the Spirit. God's love is a gift to us. Christ has given His love. The Holy Spirit also makes us conscious of the love of Christ (Rom. 5:5). But love is never called a spiritual gift. As a motivating factor in our lives, it is always a fruit of the Spirit.

Paul evidently is not suggesting that love may be substituted for spiritual gifts. The Bible makes it very clear that we need both the fruit and the gifts for Christian life and ministry. What Paul is emphasizing is the contrast between spiritual gifts without love and spiritual gifts with love. He in no way degrades spiritual gifts, nor does he say that love is better than spiritual gifts. But love is necessary to make the gifts effective to the highest degree and to bring the proper reward. Thus, the sanctifying work of the Spirit is needed along with His empowering work.

It should be emphasized also that both are needed today. We clearly need the fruit. But Pentecostals emphasize that we need the gifts as well. I have commented on this matter elsewhere:

> They [the gifts] are part of what God has set (placed, fixed, established) as an integral part of the Church just as He has set the various members or parts of the human body in their place to fulfill their proper function (1 Cor. 12:18, 28). This clearly means that they are intended for the entire Church Age. But they are temporary in the sense that they are limited to the present age. Today they are still needed, but when Christ comes again, the perfect state will be unveiled. We shall be changed into His likeness. No longer shall we be limited to these present decaying bodies. With new bodies, new maturity, and the visible presence of Christ with us, we shall not need the partial gifts. The things that perplex us now will perplex us no more. It will be easy to surrender our present partial and incomplete understanding when we shall see Him as He is (1 John 3:2) . . . . Love, of course, cannot

end, for God is love. The more we have of Him, the more we shall have of love. And since He is infinite, there will always be more throughout eternity. These things that are permanent must therefore be the guide for the exercise of spiritual gifts. Above all, they must be exercised in love.[40]

CONCLUSION

In summary, Pentecostal writers agree that sanctification is related to every part of God's great plan of redemption. Assemblies of God writers see justification and initial sanctification occurring at the same moment, justification giving a new standing before God, sanctification putting one into a new state. Neither justification nor this positional sanctification removes sin, "root and branch," however. Past sins are forgiven, but original sin, in the sense of an inherited tendency to sin, remains. Holiness Pentecostals still hold to a second definite work of grace, which they believe removes original sin entirely and makes it easier to live a holy life. The Assemblies of God and other nonholiness Pentecostals reject this experience and hold to progressive sanctification, which is not complete until our glorification.

Assemblies of God writers could agree with Harold D. Hunter, a holiness Pentecostal, however, when he writes:

Recognition of the believer's dependence on the Holy Spirit for his sanctification does not dissolve the believer's own responsibility. To assert that man is involved in this process, however, is not to share the view that sanctification is a matter of man's own moral improvement. It is extremely difficult to find a suitable way to express the relationship between God and man in sanctification . . . . man's response is important, but so also is the Spirit working in him. The biblical injunctions to righteousness (Rom. 6:13, 19; 8:13; 2 Cor. 7:1; Gal. 5:16, 25) can be understood only to mean that the believer is active in the process . . . . In the Old Testament the Lord sanctifies His people . . . . But also the people must sanctify themselves.[41]

Hunter goes on to point out that this dual responsibility is taught also in the New Testament. He discusses this point in the light of Philippians 2:12, where we are exhorted to keep on working out our own salvation with fear and trembling. This issue is not merely a matter of corporate salvation but involves the individual: the community cannot improve unless each believer individually is making progress. He also points out that the claim to be able to abstain totally from sin in this life "can be predicated only on a faulty definition of sin." He concludes: "Sanctification is a part of the initial salvific experience and it is also a lifelong process of purification."[42] Thus it seems that some holiness and some nonholiness Pentecostals may agree much more today than they did in the early part of this century.

All would agree also that sanctification results in a purity that resists and overcomes temptation (James 4:7; 1 Cor. 10:13; Rom. 6:14; Eph. 6:13–14). It results also in a victorious living that gives glory and praise to God and shows the fruits of righteousness (1 Cor. 10:31; Col. 1:10). It is a life filled with the graces and power of the Spirit, a life lived in fellowship with God and Christ (Gal. 5:22–23; Eph. 5:18; Col. 1:10–11; 1 John 1:7). It is a life of service to God, lived in the power of the Holy Spirit as He baptizes, fills, and refills us. It is a life that receives and becomes a channel for the love of God and Christ. It is also a life of prayer and prayerful study of the Word of God. Finally, as we have already noted from E. S. Williams, sanctification enables us to live above the sin, self-will, and spiritual anarchy of the world and to live for God instead.[43]

BIBLIOGRAPHY

Carlson, G. Raymond. *Our Faith and Fellowship*. Springfield, Mo.: Gospel, 1977.

————. *Salvation: What the Bible Teaches*. Springfield, Mo.: Gospel, 1963.

Fjordbak, Everitt M. *Sanctification*. Dallas: Wisdom House, 1982.

Harris, Ralph W. *Our Faith and Fellowship*. Springfield, Mo.: Gospel, 1963.

Horton, Stanley M. *What the Bible Says About the Holy Spirit*. Springfield, Mo.: Gospel, 1976.

Nelson, P. C. *Bible Doctrines*. Rev. ed. Springfield, Mo.: Gospel, 1948.

Pearlman, Myer. *Knowing the Doctrines of the Bible*. Springfield, Mo.: Gospel, 1937.

Synan, Vinson. *The Holiness-Pentecostal Movement in the United States*. Grand Rapids: Eerdmans, 1971.

Williams, Ernest Swing. *Systematic Theology*. 3 vols. Springfield, Mo.: Gospel, 1953.

Response to Horton

Melvin E. Dieter

Stanley Horton provides an excellent historical summary of the origins of Pentecostalism and the winds of doctrine that were blowing through the American revival movement at the beginning of the twentieth century. The two main roots of Pentecostal theology show up immediately in his account: the second-blessing theology of the Methodist holiness movement and the progressive sanctification teaching of the broad independent Baptist tradition that was strongly influenced by the Moody Bible Institute higher-life position represented by R. A. Torrey. The latter movement emphasized the special work of the Holy Spirit at Pentecost as the basis for receiving power for witness, whereas holiness Pentecostals preached the crisis of sanctification and the accompanying enduement with power.

It might be expected, then, that the Pentecostal theology of sanctification that the Assemblies of God and other baptistic Pentecostal groups espouse would be more eclectic than any of the other positions represented in this volume. At times, indeed, it seems to struggle to find consistent expression. It was formed out of certain reactions against the Pentecostal holiness theology that marked most of the pioneer Pentecostal movement, and it moved in a Calvinistic direction that was more suitable to the native theology of the many former Baptists who had been won to the Pentecostal revival. It is obvious from Horton's essay, however, that the movement has only been partially successful in freeing itself from Pentecostal holiness teaching regarding sanctification and in establishing its own doctrinal understanding.

It is critical to keep sanctification distinct from the new birth as a work of grace in the heart, even though it is begun in the act of regeneration, because our new life in God must be sanctified wholly to His will and purposes. We might allow that there is no reason why the moment of complete cleansing of the heart and perfection of love might not take place immediately subsequent to justification and regeneration. But the real question is, Is that the common pattern of the divine-human encounter? Wesley said that he had not found it to be that way and knew no others who had. In other words, the real issues of sanctification have to do with life after the new birth.

Furthermore, in the light of such Scriptures as 1 John 2:1–5, we must ask all in this series who, because of Reformed theology, find it hard to acknowledge the freedom from sinning that is depicted there as the normal Christian life, how they treat such Scriptures and others that raise expectations of Christian holiness. This kind of Christian life is also described in other passages that indicate that sanctification involves definitive action, taken in a given time and continued as a fact in the present. Of these, Romans 12:1–2 is probably the most vivid in its imagery, most explicit in its language, and most descriptive of the fact that the total yielding of the self to God is something that the born-again Christian must do and that could not be done as part of or prior to the new birth. Such an act, rather than concluding the development of the sanctified life, merely prepares the believer for the life of Christian growth in grace with maturity for its goal.

One notes also how strongly the holiness Pentecostal theology still permeates the Assemblies' position when Horton describes the ways in which the term *entire sanctification* is used in Assemblies circles. Wesleyans would agree with Menzies, for instance, that entire sanctification "is not to be understood as in any sense a static plateau of perfectionism arrived at through a crisis experience." They would also agree that persons who walk in all the light they have are in the highest state of grace they can enjoy and that it is a life of victory over sin and temptation. They would agree with Pearlman that it is a relative perfection "which fulfills the end for which it was designed" (p. 124). And they would strongly support Horton in his affirmation that "through the Holy Spirit we are able not to sin, even though we never come to the place where we are not able to sin" (p. 125)—until that final perfection when we are freed from all the tragic results of the Fall in the new heavens and the new earth, where only righteousness dwells. All of these are familiar definitions for the life that results from the second crisis experience as Wesleyans and even Keswick adherents understand it.

Wesleyans would also follow many of Horton's arguments for the crisis experience of Spirit-baptism beyond the initiation in the Spirit. But it would be difficult for them to allow that one could be filled with the Spirit and not be entirely purified in heart (that is, perfected in love) by the fullness of that presence and power. Paul tells the Thessalonians that it is not for nothing that God has given us His *Holy* Spirit (1 Thess. 4:7–8).

In conclusion, Horton and all Pentecostals continue to remind the whole church powerfully—especially the Wesleyan holiness movement—that both the gifts and the fruits of the Spirit are essential to the edification and witness of the church. In reaction to the challenge of Pentecostal theology, the Wesleyan tradition has often emphasized the ethical nature of sanctification by magnifying the fruits of the Spirit at the neglect of the rich and essential teachings on the gifts of the Spirit. The founding Pentecostal leaders rightly challenged the holiness movement not to be so concerned with the interior life of purity that they lost the dynamic witness in the Spirit, which only the ministry of the gifts in love could provide.

Response to Horton

Anthony A. Hoekema

With most of what Stanley Horton says about sanctification I agree. I concur with his description of sanctification as both "positional" and "progressive"—though I prefer to call the initial aspect of sanctification "definitive." I agree that progressive sanctification is both God's work and our responsibility. I also agree that sanctification involves all three persons of the Trinity, that it is an aspect of our union with Christ, and that we need to be filled and refilled with the Holy Spirit. I appreciate the author's observation that the means of sanctification are the blood of Christ, the Holy Spirit, and the Bible. I concur that it is impossible for us to live without sin in this life. I am also grateful for the author's point that the goal of sanctification—perfection—will not be reached until the life to come.

I do have a little difficulty with Horton's use of the word *cooperate* to describe the relation between our work and God's work in sanctification (pp. 118, 123). To say that we must cooperate with God in our sanctification seems to imply that God and we each do part of the work. But God's working in us is not suspended because we work, and neither is our working suspended because God works. It is better to say that sanctification is a work of God in us that involves our responsible participation.

I also have difficulty with the author's use of the phrase "relative perfection" (p. 124). This expression, it seems to me, is a contradiction in terms. If it is "perfection," it is not "relative," and if it is "relative," it is not "perfection."

My main problem with the chapter, however, is Horton's teaching on "baptism in the Holy Spirit," which is described as an experience distinct from and subsequent to regeneration and conversion (pp. 128–29). This baptism in the Spirit is said to be something that every believer should seek (implied in the chapter, stated specifically in article 7 of the Assemblies of God "Statement of Fundamental Truths": "All believers are entitled to and should . . . earnestly seek the promise of the Father, the baptism in the Holy Ghost . . . ."). When a believer has this experience, he or she is empowered for service through the filling of the Spirit. Speaking in tongues is said to be the initial evidence of this baptism (p. 130). Other evidences of this baptism are a deepened reverence for God; an intensified consecration to God; a more active love for Christ, the Word, and the lost; and growth in the expression of the fruit, gifts, and ministries of the Spirit (p. 131).

At this point I must demur. The teaching here is that only people who have spoken in tongues can be empowered for service through the filling of the Spirit and can enjoy the four additional evidences of baptism in the Spirit just mentioned. In other words, the vast majority of Christians in the world today cannot experience these blessings!

What biblical proof does Horton offer for his view of the doctrine of Holy Spirit baptism? Not a great deal. The second half of 1 Corinthians 12:13 is adduced to prove that the baptism in the Spirit is "a distinct experience after conversion" (pp. 128–29)—though it is admitted that the first half of this text speaks of something different. On page 130 the following texts are referred to, none of which mentions the expression "baptized with the Holy Spirit": Luke 24:49; Acts 1:8; 2:4. On page 129 the author mentions "six cases in the New Testament which compare John's baptism in water with Jesus' baptism in the Holy Spirit" but does not list the texts. And on page 130 Horton alludes to the Day of Pentecost and to the conversion of Cornelius as examples of Holy Spirit baptism.

I reply: there is no biblical basis for the Pentecostal doctrine of baptism in the Holy Spirit as an experience distinct from and subsequent to regeneration. Though the expression "baptism in the Spirit" does not occur in the New Testament, there are seven instances in which the verb *baptize* is used in connection with the Holy Spirit. The expression "to baptize with" or "to be baptized with the Holy Spirit" is found six times in the New Testament: four times in the Gospels and twice in Acts. (Though Pentecostals commonly speak of baptism "in" the Spirit, the King James, Revised Standard, and New International versions all render the Greek word *en* in these texts by "with.")

In the four instances in which the expression "baptize with the Holy Spirit" occurs in the Gospels (Matt. 3:11; Mark 1:8; Luke 3:16; and John 1:33), it describes the future historical event of the outpouring of the Spirit on the Day of Pentecost. In the first of the Acts references, Acts 1:5, the expression, now in the passive voice, also refers to this event: "In a few days you will be baptized with the Holy Spirit." In these five instances, therefore, "baptism with the Holy Spirit" does not mean an experience that believers must go through after conversion but refers to a historic event that occurred at Pentecost—an event that, like the resurrection of Christ, is not repeatable.

What does the expression mean in Acts 11:16, the second Acts reference? Peter is in Jerusalem, telling the Christians in Judea what had happened at the house of Cornelius in Caesarea a few days before. What happened in Caesarea was indeed a "baptism with the Spirit," but it was not an experience distinct from and subsequent to conversion; it was simultaneous with conversion. The meaning of the Spirit's baptism of Cornelius is described in verse 18: "So then, God has granted even the Gentiles repentance unto life." It meant the bestowal of the Spirit for salvation on people who previously were not Christian believers.

The one other New Testament passage that mentions Spirit-baptism is 1 Corinthians 12:13. Here the word *en* is rendered "by" in most versions: "For we were all baptized by one Spirit into one body . . . and we were all given the one Spirit to drink." The first half of this verse tells us that *all* Christians have been Spirit-baptized. Spirit-baptism here is the act of God whereby we are made one with Christ. You do not need to seek such a baptism as a post-conversion experience, Paul is telling us here; if you are in Christ, you have already been Spirit-baptized!

Horton, however, while granting that the first half of this text describes something that happens to all Christians, maintains that the second half of the verse describes Spirit-baptism in the usual Pentecostal sense. He argues that, whereas the other texts that speak of Spirit-baptism say that Christ baptizes

142 | Five Views on Sanctification

us *in* the Spirit, the first half of the Corinthians text states that we are baptized *by* the Spirit and thus describes something different (pp. 129–30).

The second clause of the Corinthians text, however, is clearly parallel to the first clause, since both clauses stress the oneness of all believers. Besides, how can one base an argument on the distinction between a baptism by the Spirit and a baptism by Christ? If something is done by Christ, is it not done through the Spirit? And if something is done by the Spirit, is it not also done by Christ?

Response to Horton

J. Robertson McQuilkin

Many will be indebted to Stanley Horton for the succinct and accurate history of the Pentecostal movement and for the clear theological distinctions identified among the various branches. For example, it was helpful to find the distinction drawn between the three crisis experiences advocated by the Pentecostal groups that were rooted in Wesleyan holiness origins and the two crises advocated by those whose origins were baptistic (such as the Assemblies of God). This distinction has much to do with one's doctrine of sanctification, though such implications were not outlined for us. The historical section would have been even more useful had the charismatic renewal movement beginning in the 1960s been included.

Furthermore, it would have been helpful for comparative studies had the Reformed, Wesleyan, and Pentecostal chapters dealt with the implications of the doctrine of eternal security for the process of sanctification. There are other lesser matters, such as the distinction drawn between baptism *by* the Spirit (into the body of Christ at the time of the initial salvation encounter) and baptism *in* the Spirit ("filling" in a subsequent necessary encounter). The doctrine is far too important to rest on a highly disputed lexical argument such as Horton gives.

The great surprise for me was to discover, in the first two-thirds of the exposition on sanctification, no significant teaching in the Assemblies of God branch of the Pentecostal movement (as distinct from other branches) that would not be applauded on a Keswick platform. The divergence became apparent only in the last pages of the presentation. Only when Horton moves—seemingly almost as a postscript—into the teaching on speaking in tongues as the necessary sign of a theologically necessary second work of grace did the wide divergence become apparent. But since he makes the surprising (to an outsider) statement that baptism in the Spirit (filling) is not of itself a sanctifying experience (p. 132), I am caused to wonder if the experience is essential to the sanctifying process and if indeed there may be less divergence than one might suppose. This line of thinking is further reinforced by the fact that sanctification, or the pursuit of holiness, is considered by many leaders in the modern charismatic renewal movement to be neither a distinctive of the movement nor a major emphasis. For them the charismatic experience is more for worship, enhancement of one's relationship with God, personal freedom to find fulfillment, and, for some, power for service. Would not both the historic Pentecostal and the contemporary charismatic renewal groups assist themselves and others by addressing the issue of the relationship between the baptism and sanctification more thoroughly and publicly?

Space considerations do not permit an adequate consideration of the two related questions of whether a second crisis experience is necessary for sanctification and whether speaking in tongues is presented in Scripture as the necessary evidence of such a "baptism" or "filling." For the record, however, let me register my concerns that this position lacks an adequate basis in Scripture, hermeneutics, and church history.

Nowhere is a second crisis experience advocated in Scripture; yet, if true, it would be second in importance only to the teaching of salvation. Scripture consistently points sinning, failing Christians back to their original experience of God's grace. Some in the Pentecostal and charismatic movements have said that this teaching was not advocated because the people to whom the New Testament was addressed already had such an experience. This answer raises many other questions. For whom was the Bible written, and how many other crucial doctrines were omitted because they had already been experienced? Furthermore, salvation had certainly been known by the recipients of New Testament letters, yet it is consistently taught, and commands to seek an experience of it are common. Then why not the necessary second experience as well? Furthermore, if the Corinthian Christians, for example, did not need a sanctifying experience, who does? How are we to interpret the complete omission of any such teaching from the New Testament letters, which were written primarily for the very purpose of enabling Christians to live the Christian way? Since the experience is not taught in Scripture, much of the doctrinal discussion is based on what took place as recorded in the Book of Acts. Without analyzing the specifics, as a general principle I hold that doctrine based on history without the corroboration of apostolic teaching is insecure. History uninterpreted by Scripture may not be made normative, since Scripture does not treat historical data that way and, if such a hermeneutic principle is admitted, the potential abuses are virtually limitless.

Apart from the lack of biblical evidence for baptism in the Spirit as a necessary second (or third) experience and for speaking in tongues as a sign rather than a gift, joining the two experiences by elevating the tongues experience to be the indispensable sign of the baptism presents an even greater—and critical—problem. This joining of the two experiences not only lacks biblical evidence, it lacks solid historical precedent as well. Although both the teaching of a second work of grace and the experience of glossolalia have appeared periodically throughout church history, the two were never joined until January 1, 1901, in the incident Horton alludes to (p. 105). Tongues as a necessary sign (as distinct from a gift given to some) is nowhere taught in Scripture. The idea that such a manifestation is the indispensable evidence of a theologically necessary second experience was new "revelation" made to a group of first-year Bible school students while the teacher was absent from the school during its first—and only—year of existence. For those who do not accept postbiblical revelation as establishing authoritative norms for the church, the foundation for this crucial doctrine may well continue to be viewed as inadequate.

Having outlined briefly—and unsatisfactorily—my problems with the teaching, I must return to my earlier conclusion that, glossolalia aside, when the discussion is limited strictly to the way a newborn Christian or a failing Christian may grow toward likeness to Jesus Christ, the position of Assemblies of God spokesman Stanley Horton and much of the contemporary charismatic movement is not that far distant from the Keswick approach.

Response to Horton

John F. Walvoord

Stanley Horton documents well the progress in doctrine that is seen in the Pentecostal movement and also records the refinement and stabilization in Pentecostal truth in contemporary Assemblies of God. His discussion of the many scriptural evidences for true spirituality and sanctification is commendable.

Non-Pentecostals note that early Pentecostal beliefs were based mostly on experience rather than solid Scripture exegesis. Speaking in tongues was erroneously taken as evidence of spirituality and of spiritual power, whereas 1 Corinthians 12 (vv. 8–10, 28–30) indicates that tongues is the least of the spiritual gifts. The concept of a second work of grace, which to some extent has been perpetuated in the contemporary holiness movement, is also viewed by non-Pentecostals as unjustified and not scriptural in its terminology. Many also object to the teaching that believers should crucify their sin nature, which is not supported by Scripture and actually is impossible. The crucifixion of our old life (not our old nature) took place when Christ died in our place. Galatians 2:20, properly translated in the New International Version, states, "I have been crucified with Christ." This truth should be appropriated by faith. Furthermore, since justification and positional sanctification occur at regeneration, and all three, as acts of God, are irreversible, we cannot accept the teaching that salvation is lost when any sin occurs after the second work of grace.

Current teaching in the Assemblies of God has corrected most of these errors in interpretation, but further clarification would be helpful. Much would be accomplished by distinguishing the baptism of the Spirit from the filling of the Spirit, though this confusion is not limited to the Pentecostal movement. The Bible speaks of only one baptism of the Spirit. Although believers may be filled with the Spirit repeatedly, there is no record of anyone being baptized by the Spirit more than once. Furthermore, every genuine Christian is, at the time of regeneration, baptized by the Spirit, as the Assemblies of God themselves teach and as is indicated in 1 Corinthians 12:13. The filling of the Spirit occurs many times (cf. Acts 2:4; 4:8, 31; 7:55), though its first instance in the Book of Acts is simultaneous with the baptism of the Spirit. Speaking in tongues is not an evidence of spirituality or spiritual power, a fact that should be evident when one recalls that the Corinthian church, which by Paul's definition was carnal (1 Cor. 3:1 KJV; "worldly" NIV), not spiritual, nevertheless majored in speaking in tongues and needed the correction that Paul gave (1 Cor. 12–14).

When it is recognized that the Pentecostal movement includes widely divergent views on sanctification, its most accurate contemporary source is the Assemblies of God. As pointed out in Horton's discussion, a believer in Christ at the initial moment of salvation is regenerated, baptized by the Spirit, justified, and given positional sanctification. The Assemblies make clear that this original sanctification is not complete; that is, it is followed by progressive sanctification in subsequent experience. They also teach correctly that ultimate sanctification, or complete separation from the sin nature and all acts of sin, occurs when we stand complete in heaven. Horton summarizes this teaching in the following paragraph, with which most non-Pentecostals would agree.

> The early Assemblies of God writers agree also that sanctification is twofold. In one aspect it is positional and instantaneous, and in another, practical and progressive. Nelson, Pearlman, and Williams all draw attention to Paul's addressing the Corinthian believers as saints and as already sanctified in Christ (1 Cor. 1:2; 6:11). Yet, at the same time, they were far from perfect; many were not walking worthy of their high calling, and some were even involved in open sin (p. 113).

Though the Pentecostal movement in its early days promoted theological concepts that non-Pentecostals do not accept, the blessing of God was on the movement because of its sincere looking to God for holiness and spiritual power. In its current refined definition in the Assemblies of God, the approach taken to the doctrine of sanctification is quite similar to that of the Wesleyan movement and even to those of other theological points of view.

Chapter 4

THE
KESWICK
PERSPECTIVE

J. Robertson McQuilkin

THE KESWICK PERSPECTIVE

J. Robertson McQuilkin

Average is not necessarily normal. For example, the average temperature of patients in a hospital may be 100 degrees, but such a temperature is not normal. The average score for a group of friends on the golf course may be 85 for the day, but par may be only 72. So it is with the Christian life. The average experience of church members is far different from New Testament norms for the Christian life.

The normal Christian is characterized by loving responses to ingratitude and indifference, even hostility, and is filled with joy in the midst of unhappy circumstances and with peace when everything goes wrong. The normal Christian overcomes in the battle with temptation, consistently obeys the laws of God, and grows in self-control, contentment, humility, and courage. Thought processes are so under the control of the Holy Spirit and instructed by Scripture that the normal Christian authentically reflects the attitudes and behavior of Jesus Christ. God has first place in life, and the welfare of others takes precedence over personal desires. The normal Christian has power not only for godly living but for effective service in the church. Above all, he or she has the joy of constant companionship with the Lord.

But what is the average Christian experience? Church members typically think and behave very much like morally upright non-Christians. They are decent enough, but there is nothing supernatural about them. Their behavior is quite explainable in terms of heredity, early environment, and present circumstances. They yield to temptation more often than not, lusting when their body demands it, coveting what they do not have, and taking credit for their accomplishments. The touchstone for their choices is self-interest, and though they have a love for God and others, it does not control their life. There is little change for the better; in fact, most church members do not expect much improvement and are little concerned by that prospect. Scripture is not exciting, prayer is perfunctory, and service in the church demonstrates little touch of the supernatural. Above all, their life seems to have an empty core, for it does not center around a constant, personal companionship with the Lord.

SOLVING THE PROBLEM

In considering any spiritual problem, most would agree that there are both divine and human initiatives. God's part is to provide salvation, and human responsibility is to receive it. If salvation includes all that God does in redeeming a lost sinner, from initial contact through final transformation into the perfect likeness of Christ, then surely the provision of ability to live a normal Christian life is part of God's saving work. As in other elements of salvation, individuals are responsible by faith to appropriate God's provision.

But as we develop the relation between God's part and the human part and especially as we work out the solution in life, we tend to emphasize one side and neglect the other. Much of the controversy over sanctification, or how to live successfully a normal Christian life, stems from stress on God's part to the neglect of human responsibility or from stress on human responsibility to the neglect of divine initiative. The so-called Keswick approach, however, seeks to provide a mediating and biblically balanced solution to the problem of subnormal Christian experience.

THE KESWICK APPROACH

The History and Message of Keswick

Keswick (pronounced without the *w*) is the name of a resort town in England's lake district where annual conventions "for the promotion of practical holiness" have been held since

1875. Over the years, several other conference centers have been established for the purpose of spreading the same message of hope—for example, America's Keswick and the now-defunct Canadian Keswick. But of more widespread influence, perhaps, have been annual conventions held in various places around the world, modeled after the original Keswick pattern.

The original initiative came from Americans, but from the first Keswick Convention onward, the leadership was British. Without exception, the leaders were people who had become increasingly frustrated with their own low-level (albeit average) Christian experience and who longed for a life lived in the power of the Holy Spirit. They found such a life at Keswick and joined with other "normal Christians" to spread the good news that such an experience was possible for all. The leadership came from various denominations, with many noted churchmen from the Anglican, Baptist, Presbyterian and other communions leading the Keswick Conventions in the decades around the turn of the century.

Keswick is not a doctrinal system, much less an organization or denomination, which perhaps explains why participation in it has been so broad. Though leading churchmen and noted scholars led the movement, no Keswick leader has written a treatise on its teaching. Since there is no official theological statement, some outside the movement have misunderstood its teaching, and a broad variety of doctrinal positions have been held and taught by those associated with the name *Keswick*. Nevertheless, it is proper to speak of a common Keswick message or approach. We are indebted to Steven Barabas for providing a definitive treatment of the history and message of the Keswick Conventions.[1] Although Barabas himself was not a Keswick leader, his scholarly and warmly positive analysis won the endorsement of Keswick leadership.

Barabas concludes that the best summary of the Keswick message is expressed in the "call" to the original convention—a "Convention for the Promotion of Practical Holiness."[2] He gives more extended definitions as well:

> In the very first issue of *The Christian's Pathway to Power* the editor stated what he conceived to be the practical possibilities of faith. "We believe the Word of God teaches that the *normal* Christian life is one of uniform sustained victory over known sin; and that no temptation is permitted to happen to us without a way of escape being provided by God, so that

we may be able to bear it." Keswick has never departed from this faith. From the beginning until the present it has taught that a life of faith and victory, of peace and rest, are the rightful heritage of every child of God, and that he may step into it . . . , "not by long prayers and laborious effort, but by a deliberate and decisive act of faith." It teaches that "the normal experience of the child of God should be one of victory instead of constant defeat, one of liberty instead of grinding bondage, one of 'perfect peace' instead of restless worry. It shows that in Christ there is provided for every believer victory, liberty, and rest, and that this may be obtained not by a life-long struggle after an impossible ideal but by the surrender of the individual to God, and the indwelling of the Holy Spirit."[3]

At one of the meetings of the 1890 Convention, H. W. Webb-Peploe put the difference between the ordinary teaching and this in a crisp sentence. "Before I expected failure, and was astonished at deliverance; now I expect deliverance, and am astonished at failure."[4]

Though these statements have a common theological ground and may be viewed as a summary of the message, Keswick theology overall is basically mainstream Protestant theology; thus, it has been possible for the leadership to be drawn from virtually all major streams of theological thought. Therefore the various emphases of Keswick, which can best be understood from the method of the conference itself, are crucial for understanding its message.

The Method of Keswick

A traditional Keswick Convention pursues a specific topic each day. The first day emphasizes sin. God's standard of holiness and human failure are held before the people with the express intention of promoting a deep conviction of sin and spiritual need.

On the second day God's provision for victorious Christian living is presented. The finished work of Christ provides more than justification—it provides identification. In fact, union with Christ is seen as the heart of Pauline theology.

> The place in the New Testament where the truth of the believer's identification with Christ in His death and resurrection is most clearly set forth is the sixth chapter of Romans. It would not be possible, I think, to exaggerate the

importance of this chapter for the doctrine of sanctification. It
has rightly been called the Magna Charta of the soul and the
Emancipation Proclamation of the Christian.[5]

God's provision for successful Christian living is found not
only in the finished work and living presence of Christ but also
in the inner work of the Holy Spirit. Of the members of the
Trinity, it is He who sanctifies the believer. He works to
counteract the downward pull of sin. He does not eradicate the
susceptibility to sin, nor does He displace human responsibility
to believe and choose. Rather, the Spirit exercises a counter-
force, enabling the surrendered and trusting believer to resist
successfully the spiritually downward pull of his or her natural
disposition. Keswick does not teach the perfectibility of human
beings prior to the eternal state, but it does teach the possibility
of consistent success in resisting the temptation to violate
deliberately the known will of God.

The third day is absolutely crucial. Consecration is the
theme, and people are challenged, in the light of their own
failure and inability and in the light of God's full provision, to
surrender unconditionally to God. The Keswick maxim, "No
crisis before Wednesday," derives from the conviction that
individuals must clearly see their own bankruptcy and God's
abundant provision before they can adequately respond to the
challenge of unconditional surrender.

"Life in the Spirit" is the theme of the fourth day. This
topic is also extremely important, for Keswick teaches most
distinctively that living a life filled with the Spirit is the
birthright of every Christian.[6] Being "full" is held to mean
"controlled by." Those who have an obedient heart experience
the condition of being filled with the Spirit.[7] A distinction is
sometimes drawn between the normal condition of being
"full," or under the control of the Spirit, and the experience of
being "filled," which is viewed as a special enduement for a
particular occasion. The Holy Spirit is God's provision both for
holy living and for effective service.

Originally conventions had these four consecutive emphases: sin, God's provision, consecration, and being filled
with the Spirit. Soon a fifth theme was added: service. The idea
of this final emphasis was to turn the newly prepared saints
outward toward their responsibility to serve God and other
people in the power of the Spirit. But almost from the
beginning a special emphasis in service emerged, an emphasis

that soon became a hallmark of the Keswick Convention, namely, missions, or the cause of world evangelization. Volunteers for missionary service soon numbered in the thousands, and the mother convention, at least, financially supported those who responded to God's call at the convention and received reports from them in years to come.

Marginal Ambiguities

Because Keswick is a broad fellowship encompassing those of varying theological convictions, it should not be surprising that differences would arise among the leaders, even on doctrines relating to the Christian life. But in comparison with the major platform emphases outlined above, these differences have been minor. In these areas of ambiguity one should not seek to establish an official Keswick position, for there is none.

Able Not to Sin

Keswick has periodically been accused of teaching perfectionism, the view that it is possible to live without sinning. B. B. Warfield, for example, in "The Victorious Christian Life," the final chapter of his definitive work *Studies in Perfectionism*, asserted that Keswick held such a position.[8] Keswick leaders have consistently, officially, and emphatically denied these allegations.[9] But the signals are not always clear. Some Keswick speakers have spoken of a spiritual condition in which one is able not to sin, which is normally considered a "perfectionist" position.

The problem seems to lie in the definition of sin, as is so often the case in differences among theologians on the subject of human perfectibility. Is sin defined as the deliberate violation of the known will of God? Then the ability not to sin in that sense is available to every Christian, not as the extraordinary capacity of some supersaint, but as the normal expectation— indeed, the indispensable evidence—of genuine Christianity. Keswick clearly teaches that Christians, by the power of the indwelling Spirit, have the ability to choose consistently not to violate deliberately the known will of God.

But does sin also mean any falling short of the glory of God? Is it wrong to fall short in disposition and attitude of the glorious character of Christ? Do I sin when I fail to love as God loves, to be as self-controlled, contented, humble, and courageous as Jesus was? If Jesus' life is the standard of Christian living, who can attain it, even for a moment? If sin is defined to include this falling short unwittingly, Keswick does not teach that a person ever in this life has the ability not to sin. Yet, since so much of the emphasis of "victory" centers in the very area of disposition, spokesmen have often given the impression that consistent victory is possible, not only over temptation to conscious, deliberate acts of sin, but also over falling short in unconscious attitudes as well. But the "official" teaching has consistently been that every believer in this life is left with the natural proclivity to sin and will do so without the countervailing influence of the Holy Spirit.

The Old Nature

Another area of marginal ambiguity concerns the vexing problem of the relationship between natural human inclinations and the new life in Christ. Some who have spoken at Keswick Conventions have held the view that the Christian life is a battleground between one's old nature and one's new nature. The "old man" and "new man" of biblical analogy are taken to indicate an old nature, which one has by birth, and a new nature, which is imparted at the new birth. But this interpretation is not the mainline Keswick teaching. There is general agreement that the old nature, called in Scripture "the flesh," means a natural disposition to sin.[10] The "natural man" behaves in this way, as do many Christians. Such Christians are said to be under bondage, when they should be free through their union with Christ in His death and resurrection. They should henceforth claim that liberty and live accordingly!

The "old nature" is generally considered to be incapable of improvement,[11] though not all hold this position. The antidote to living life in conformity with one's natural disposition is the counteracting power of the Holy Spirit.[12] So there is a battle. Besides the "rest of faith," there is also the "wrestle of faith." The conflict is not between old and new natures, however, but between the old nature and the indwelling Holy Spirit.[13]

Keswick teaching, then, includes these two areas of marginal ambiguity: what does it mean to say that "a Spirit-filled Christian is able not to sin"? And what happens to one's old natural inclinations in his or her new life? Answers from within Keswick are neither uniform nor clear. Given the lack of a detailed system of Keswick theology, one may articulate a so-called Keswick perspective on sanctification as long as it is consistent with the basic emphases of the movement. The following sections represent such an attempt.

SANCTIFICATION

To sanctify is, literally, to set apart, and in the biblical context it means set apart to God. Originally this setting apart was both moral and ritual. An object such as a bowl could be set apart from common use for exclusive use in the temple ritual. It was then considered *holy* (from the same root as *sanctify*). But of deeper and more enduring significance was, on the one hand, a person's separation from sin and, on the other hand, his or her consecration to God. One who is set apart from sin (sanctified) is rightly called a *saint* (from the same root as *sanctify* and *holy*). This moral and theological sense of sanctification is the one we are considering in this book.

To be sanctified is of utmost importance, because otherwise no one will see God (Heb. 12:14). That is, until the sin problem is cared for, no one is qualified to associate with a holy God, one who is Himself completely without sin and who, moreover, cannot countenance sin in any form.

God is not only holy, however; He is supremely a God of love, and therefore His ultimate desire for human beings is for them to be restored to full, loving fellowship with Himself. But there is a barrier: sin. For complete unity of heart, two persons must be in harmony of spirit. They must have the same purposes, outlook, and way of life. If one is sinful and the other holy, what oneness can there be? Their total mind-set is in conflict. So in order to accomplish the ultimate purpose of our existence, namely, to live in loving oneness with God, the sin barrier must be removed. The removal process is called sanctification, and it comes in three stages, all of which are God's own work of grace.

The first step is positional sanctification, in which the sinner is set apart from his or her sin for the purpose of becoming God's own possession. One is set apart from sin in three ways.

First, a person is forgiven, so that the result of sin, eternal punishment, is done away with.

Second, a person is justified, so that his or her guilt is removed, the guilty record is expunged. God views the person no longer as a weak, stubborn, and failing sinner but now as an individual who is as clean and pure as His holy Son, Jesus. These two aspects of positional sanctification are judicial, that is, a transaction between the Father and Son that declares the sinner forgiven and made right with God.

Third, the forgiven, justified person is regenerated, or set free from the controlling authority of a sinful disposition. Some make this step a part of experiential sanctification, since it is a condition experienced more than a legal standing granted, as in the case of forgiveness and justification. I include it under positional sanctification, since it is part of the initial salvation transaction and results in a position that is the condition of every true believer. The change is so radical as to be comparable to the change that a person experiences at birth (John 3) or death (Rom. 6). Though there is continuity with the same human personality, as in the case of birth or death, in regeneration also there is passage into a totally different dimension of human life, with totally different characteristics of personal being. Sin is the prevailing characteristic of persons who live apart from God. They do not have the desire or power to choose consistently the right or to change their condition. Upon union with God the process is reversed, and right begins to prevail. A new life-force has been introduced that has power to prevail against a sinful disposition. Christians may not behave in this way, but such is their true condition and potential.

In these three ways, every believer has been sanctified through the atoning death of Christ (Heb. 10:10), has been made holy (Eph. 4:24), and is thus legitimately called a saint (1 Cor. 1:2; 6:11). Not all believers are saintly, as we shall see, but all true believers are saints, officially released from the condemnation due their sins, the guilty record, and the tyranny of a sinful disposition. This first element in sanctification has been called "positional sanctification" because it is the condition of every true child of God.

The second element of sanctification has been called "experiential sanctification," the outworking of one's official position in daily life. Holiness means more than a legal standing—it means salvation from sinful attitudes and actions. Sons are disciplined so that they may experience God's kind of holiness (Heb. 12:10). We are called on to complete, or perfect, the measure of holiness we have (2 Cor. 7:1). This process of sanctification is available to all who are, by God's grace, in the position of having been set apart from sin to God's ownership.

Finally, there is the complete and permanent sanctification, which occurs when the believer is totally transformed into the likeness of Jesus—when "we shall see him as he is" (1 John 3:2). This final condition, commonly called "glorification," is a state of complete sanctification; one is no longer tainted with sin or even susceptible to it.

Though there are these three meanings, or stages, in God's project of making unholy people holy, the doctrine of sanctification ordinarily concentrates on the second meaning—how may the believer experience freedom from sinful thoughts and actions? Why is it that the average Christian is not very saintly, does not reflect the character of Christ very clearly, lives much like any morally upright but unbelieving neighbor, and also relies on basically the same resources?

THE ROOT CAUSE OF SUBNORMAL CHRISTIAN EXPERIENCE: UNBELIEF

Scripture recognizes a basic difference among Christians. It distinguishes between carnal ("of the flesh") Christians, who behave like unconverted people, and spiritual Christians, whose life is dominated by the Spirit of God (1 Cor. 3:1–3). All Christians are indwelt by the Holy Spirit (Rom. 8:9), but some Christians are "filled with the Spirit." The Bible speaks both of immature (or retarded) Christians and of mature Christians (Heb. 5:11–6:3). More than exhibiting simply a difference in degree of growth, Christians' lives manifest qualitative differences: some Christians have a life pattern of defeat, whereas others have a life pattern of spiritual success.

A student once asked me, "How long can you be 'carnal'?" An interesting question! Did he mean, "How long can you live in sin without losing your salvation?" Or did he mean, "How long can you live in sin before you prove that you never were really in the family of God?" Or was he hoping that one could choose the low road and follow it all the way safely home? The question perplexes sincere believers, fascinates theologians, and divides Christendom. But Scripture does not favor us with a consideration of that question. Though the issue of eternal security is important, I am emboldened by the biblical approach to the problem of the sinning Christian to suggest that for pastoral (or evangelistic) purposes, in seeking to rescue the helpless person mired in the bog of subnormal Christian experience, it may be legitimate to by-pass the question, at least for the time being.

The Bible consistently deals with people where they are and only rarely answers the theoretical problems that plague us. For example, to fearful saints who desperately want to please God, Scripture gives an abundance of reassurance. No power can ever separate them from God (John 10:28–29; Rom. 8:31–39), and they will surely complete their course successfully by His grace (Phil. 1:6). But to those who continually and deliberately reject the known will of God, Scripture gives, not reassurance, but only fearful warnings.

> By their fruit you will recognize them. Do people pick grapes from thornbushes, or figs from thistles? Likewise every good tree bears good fruit, but a bad tree bears bad fruit. A good tree cannot bear bad fruit, and a bad tree cannot bear good fruit. Every tree that does not bear good fruit is cut down and thrown into the fire. Thus, by their fruit you will recognize them. Not everyone who says to me, "Lord, Lord," will enter the kingdom of heaven, but only he who does the will of my Father who is in heaven. Many will say to me on that day, "Lord, Lord, did we not prophesy in your name, and in your name drive out demons and perform many miracles?" Then I will tell them plainly, "I never knew you. Away from me you evildoers!" (Matt. 7:16–23).
>
> No one who lives in him keeps on sinning. No one who continues to sin has either seen him or known him. . . . He who does what is sinful is of the devil . . . . This is how we know who the children of God are and who the children of the devil are: Anyone who does not do what is right is not a child of God; neither is anyone who does not love his brother . . . . We know that we have passed from death to life, because we love our brothers. Anyone who does not love remains in death. (1 John 3:6, 8, 10, 14).

These passages and many others (e.g., Matt. 23; 25:31–46; John 15:2, 6; Heb. 3:6–19; 6:1–8; 10:26–31) show clearly the position that Scripture takes in addressing the sinner: repentance is the only option.

But how does one reconcile the two lines of teaching? Are church members living in sin saved, or are they lost? Have they been saved? Will they prove to have been saved? Have they lost their salvation? I have opinions—even convictions—about the theological answers to some of those questions, but since the Holy Spirit did not feel it necessary to answer them directly in Scripture, I feel under no compulsion to do so in the context of addressing professing Christians who are living in sin. Rather than attempting to play God and answer the question they raise, I can with confidence answer the basic question that ought to be asked: what must I do to be saved? Whatever standing people may have before God (which is unknown to me), if they are not now in a right relationship with God, they need to be. If they continue to reject the known will of God and are comfortable in that condition, I can assure them on the authority of God's Word that they have no biblical basis for any assurance of salvation. Their only option is repentance. Just as a lost person can do right (Acts 10:4, 35) but cannot consistently choose to do right (Rom. 8:7–8), so a saved person can do wrong (James 3:2; 1 John 1:8) but cannot consistently choose to do wrong (1 John 3).

Along with these truths, however, it is clear from Scripture that there are sinning Christians (1 Cor. 8:12; 15:34; 1 Tim. 5:20; 1 John 5:16), that many do live like people of the world, and that they have settled for a subnormal Christian experience. Somehow, the New Testament picture of a supernatural quality of life lived in the power of the Spirit seems to elude them. What are the reasons?

Ignorance

Paul remonstrates, "Don't you know?" (Rom. 6:16). His readers ought to know what happened when they came to Christ, and they ought to know how to live godly lives today— but maybe they do not. So Paul explains. In fact, the abundance of biblical teaching on the subject of sanctification implies that it is possible to be ignorant, that a person needs to learn what is right and wrong and how to do right.

But there is little direct teaching about the problem of ignorance, especially as a reason for one's failure to live like a normal Christian. Perhaps the lack is because there is a moral responsibility for ignorance. A newborn believer may be excused for ignorance and spiritually infantile behavior (Heb. 5:11–6:3), but to continue in that condition is not only unnecessary but also wrong (2 Peter 1:5–9, 12–13, 15; 3:1–2). In other words, to some extent people are responsible for their ignorance about their own sub-Christian condition, about God's provision for successful Christian living, and about their own responsibility to appropriate that provision. If they were responding to the light they had, God would be providing all the information they need to keep progressing in a normal Christian life.

Having said this, however, I recognize that many Christians have never been exposed to teaching concerning the possibility and necessity of living triumphantly. They need to be enlightened. At the point of enlightenment, the root cause of failure becomes clear. If the root cause is primarily ignorance, there will be an immediate response to the new information, accepting it and living by it. If, on the other hand, the true reason all along has been disobedience or unbelief, masquerading under the guise of ignorance, there will be resistance to any exhortation to repent or to trust God for a radically different quality of life. Because a common cause of failed expectations in the Christian life is ignorance of the possibilities and resources, God's people need constant instruction. The more common and more basic reason for failure, however, is unbelief.

Unbelief

By *unbelief* I refer to a lack of the only response acceptable to God. Biblical faith is two-sided, including the more passive aspect of reliance and trust and the more active aspect of obedience. In the Old Testament, *faith* might be more accurately rendered *faithful* in most instances, for the objective aspect of an obedient response to God was intended. The more common word was *fear*, or reverent awe—the unconditional amen of the soul to God, the expression of the same basic requirement for any acceptable relationship between creature and Creator.

In the New Testament, the subjective aspect of reliance predominated in the writings of John and Paul, but the original concept of obedience was never lost. It was lost to some people, but Paul warned against this misperception, and James explored fully the relationship between obedience and trust as aspects of saving faith. Though they are two aspects of a single response, sometimes one is more prominent by its absence (or presence) than the other. It is, therefore, often helpful, in searching for the root cause of subnormal Christian attitudes and conduct, to distinguish between disobedience and lack of trust.

Disobedience

Active rebellion. This cause for failure in the Christian life is easiest to identify. God is still available, He has not changed, and He is capable of winning the conflict. But "your iniquities have separated between you and your God" (Isa. 59:2 KJV). No one who is deliberately rejecting the known will of God in one area of life can expect to receive His enabling to live supernaturally in other areas, a truth that most Christians who are actively rebellious know.

Passive drift. This second way of disobedience is far more common and not as easily identified. Through failure to pursue actively God's highest standards, through neglect of Bible meditation, prayer, or active church involvement, or through the accumulation of small, hardly conscious disobediences into a callous pattern of spiritual insensitivity, a person may leave his or her "first love" (Rev. 2:4) and become lukewarm and actually obnoxious to God (3:15–16). Passive drift will distance a person from God just as surely as active rebellion, though it may take longer and prove more difficult to identify. Because the relationship is not easily recognized, especially by the person experiencing it, this condition is more dangerous than that of conscious rebellion. The original covenant relation with God has been violated, and the person can no longer experience the normal, Spirit-empowered life God promises. I believe that this passive drift into a condition of disobedience is the most common reason for failure in the Christian life.

Lack of Trust

Some earnest, fearful souls may be guilty of unbelief in a second way. They seem to long for holiness of life, to be unconditionally yielded to God's will, to strive and struggle, but yet they fall short. Such failure may partly be due to unbiblical expectations, which we shall consider later, but often the root problem is lack of trust in God that He will do what He promised.

Sometimes people demonstrate this lack of trust by relying on their own religious activity or moral effort to live a life pleasing to God (Gal. 3:3). In fact, this self-reliance is the common failure of most sincere church members. They made a start "in the Spirit," as Paul says, but now are foolishly attempting to live the Christian life in their own strength. But just as it is futile to attempt initial salvation through self-effort, so it is impossible to attain godliness through self-effort. If it was necessary to make a start by the power of the Spirit, "by the Spirit let us keep on making our pilgrim journey" (Gal. 5:25, my paraphrase). "As you received Christ Jesus as Lord, continue to live in him" (Col. 2:6). The first step toward normalcy for many Christians is to abandon self-effort as the path to success, recognizing that God alone is adequate to the task.

We have identified disobedience and lack of trust as the reasons most Christians subsist in a subnormal condition of defeat and spiritual poverty. These reasons reflect the common malady of unbelief, for which the cure of faith is necessary.

CURE FOR SPIRITUAL FAILURE: FAITH

First, let us reaffirm that there is a cure. There is indeed deliverance from the wretched condition of bondage to sin and failure: it comes through Jesus Christ our Lord (Rom. 7:24–25). It is possible to live in the Spirit and not fulfill the desires of our sinful disposition, to be more than conquerors in Christ, indeed, to participate in "all the fullness of God" (Eph. 3:19).

> Now unto him that is able to keep you from falling, and to present you faultless before the presence of his glory with exceeding joy, to the only wise God our Saviour, be glory and majesty, dominion and power, both now and ever. Amen. (Jude 24–25 KJV).

When Scripture faces the problem of failing Christians and offers a better way, it consistently points back to what happened when a person first experienced saving grace. "Even so reckon ye also yourselves to be dead unto sin, but alive unto God in Christ Jesus" (Rom. 6:11 ASV). In fact the central biblical passage on the subject, Romans 6, repeatedly points back to the initial transaction, the original sanctification in which the sinner was saved from sin. Recognize and rely on what has already happened to you, says Paul.

The problem of Christians who behave just like non-Christians is dealt with in 1 Corinthians 3. What is the solution? Paul points his readers back to the time of their "planting," to the original laying of the foundation: "Know ye not that ye are the temple of God, and that the Spirit of God dwelleth in you?" (v. 16 KJV). Paul excoriates the sinning Christians of Corinth, but he does not exhort them to seek some as yet untasted experience. Rather, he calls into question their salvation: "Examine yourselves to see whether you are in the faith; test yourselves. Do you not realize that Christ Jesus is in you—unless, of course, you fail the test?" (2 Cor. 13:5).

Peter exults in the fact that God has given us, with Christ, all the resources needed for life and godliness. After describing the incredibly beautiful life that the Christian has, he admits that not all Christians experience such a life. What are they to do? "But if anyone does not have them [these glorious characteristics of a fruit-filled life], he is nearsighted and blind, and has forgotten that he has been cleansed from his past sins" (2 Peter 1:9).

I know of no exception to the consistent teaching of New Testament authors that the solution for defeated, failing, sinning Christians is to return to what took place at salvation. They were brought from death to life, they were joined to Christ, they were possessed of the Spirit.

Scripture treats failure in this way because success in continuing the Christian life, like success in beginning it, does not depend upon the mastery of some complex doctrinal system or upon the achievement of some esoteric additional experience but upon a relationship with a Person. And that relationship is so simple that a child may understand and experience it. (Perhaps only a child may do so!) Simple faith is the secret, whether for initial salvation or for salvation today, whether for positional sanctification or for experiential sanctification. The covenant, or contract, relationship of faith is the answer to the sin question—both for the unredeemed sinner and for the redeemed sinner.

Although correct doctrine and life-changing experience are vitally important, the key to the problem of subnormal Christian experience is found in a personal relationship. People, therefore, who are confused by the doctrinal controversy swirling about the subject as well as those who are unsure about their past experiences or frustrated about their inability to reproduce the experience of another need only take stock of their present relationship. Is Jesus Christ Lord of their life? Then He has assumed the responsibility for making the failing saint successful. But if that initial faith-contract has been violated, there is no need to seek for some new and different experience. The original covenant must be reaffirmed. Then, just as repenting, believing sinners received life by God's grace, so now the yielded, trusting saint will receive abundance of life by God's grace.

Faith is needed because God is needed. People cannot save themselves and cannot sanctify themselves either. God is needed to deliver from sin, and God is needed if one is to live a successful Christian life. But His wisdom and power do not come automatically. God will not impose His blessings on unwilling people. So if individuals want to receive anything from God, they must trust Him for it (James 1:6–7). Self-confident people can achieve whatever their resources can produce, but these resources cannot produce reconciliation with God or Godlike living. The God-confident person, on the other hand, has available the resources of God. The object of our faith is thus of supreme importance.

Some people go astray by relying on personal experience or feeling. To be sure, a loving response to God and the resulting genuine experience of Him are essential, but a past experience or present emotion must not substitute as the *object* of faith. Other people have faith in faith—the important thing, they hold, is not what you believe but whether you believe. These gods are false. God Himself must be the object of our faith if we are to receive His blessing.

Faith is thus the key to appropriating God's provision for successful Christian living. We cannot live the Christian life until we have that provision; by faith we are justified and receive the life of the Spirit.

After this, as we continue to trust God the Holy Spirit, the means of grace become operative in our lives. Even though the Holy Spirit gave Scripture, we must approach it in belief; otherwise it becomes a means of destruction and not a blessing. Again, we do not know how to pray as we ought, but when we rely on the Spirit and pray through His enabling, this means of grace becomes effective. And so it is with the church and the other means of grace. Faith throws the switch, releasing the current of divine power. Without faith there is no light, no power.

What Faith Is

Often a distinction is made between heart (emotional) faith and head (rational) faith. It is said that a person may mentally believe the facts about God and yet, if there is no heart belief, still be eighteen inches away from salvation. But this distinction is not biblical. It is just as well, for how does one distinguish theologically, let alone psychologically or anatomically, between the reasoning and emoting activities of the mind? The Bible does make a distinction, however, between heart faith and mouth profession (e.g., Matt. 15:7–9), between what we may call true faith and false faith.

False Faith

False faith can be faith in the wrong object. If I rely on past experiences, on my own resources, or on a misappropriated promise, I do not have saving, or sanctifying, faith. Again, some may deceive themselves into believing that they are trusting God, when actually they are presuming on His goodness. For example, if someone's motive is for personal glory rather than for God's glory, such "faith" is in reality presumptuous (John 5:44), and presumption is a form of false faith.

Another variety of false faith is incomplete or partial faith. Saving and sanctifying faith involves a person's whole being, including intellect, affection, and will. That is, true faith involves understanding, love, and decision. If one of these elements is missing, faith is inadequate. Many Christians live defeated lives because, though they believe the facts and feel warmly about the Lord Jesus and sorrowful about their own failure, they do not make the choices God demands.

Definition of Faith

Some people feel that faith is a miraculous gift of the Holy Spirit that flies in the face of evidence. Others take the opposite view that faith is induced by intellectually impelling evidence such as the Bible, philosophical proof, or experience. Charles Hodge, whom some have called "the prince of theologians," said that faith is the persuasion of truth founded on testimony.[14] He used *persuasion*, not *proof*. Again, he used the word *testimony*. Historical evidence differs from mathematical proof or scientifically observed events. Persuasion is based on evidence, to be sure, but it is the evidence of testimony—in the case of Scripture, the testimony of the prophets and the apostles. There are many reasons for considering this testimony thoroughly trustworthy, such as the character of those who gave it, the unity of the testimony, its content, and so on. The evidence alone, however, does not compel acceptance. The work of the Holy Spirit is needed, and thus faith is a miraculous gift that confirms the evidence and even carries one beyond the evidence if necessary. It does not contradict evidence, nor is it "sight" based on irrefutable scientific proof.

Faith is at once the gift of God (Eph. 2:8) and our own responsibility. How God's sovereign, autonomous authority and our responsibility to believe relate to one another is not clarified in Scripture. Scripture makes it clear, however, that we must respond in obedient faith in order to receive God's promises of salvation. In summary, faith is a choice to commit all of oneself unconditionally to the person of God, who is revealed in the Bible and witnessed to by the Holy Spirit (1 Cor. 2:14; Rom. 10:17).

Degrees of Faith

Are there degrees of faith? Must it be absolute to be effective? Scripture seems to answer both yes and no. When the disciples asked for an increase in faith, Christ responded that if they had even the smallest amount, it would be quite adequate (Luke 17:5–6). In this sense, any faith at all is adequate, since it is not the faith itself that saves but the object of one's faith. One may have strong faith in thin ice and drown but have weak faith in thick ice and be safe.

On the other hand, Paul speaks of the measure of faith, indicating that there are different degrees of faith (Rom. 12:3–8). The father of the demon-possessed son cried out, "Lord, I believe; help thou mine unbelief" (Mark 9:24 kjv). The degree of faith necessary to effect a release of God's power is apparently related to the three aspects of faith noted above. One's intellectual understanding of the facts may be quite inadequate. Again, one may not have an emotion of confident assurance, or heart peace, about the matter. And yet, if he or she chooses to act in obedience to God and launches out in response to what is known to be God's will, this choosing is saving faith or sanctifying faith. Such a person may feel quite unsure and may be fearful and unable to predict the outcome of the step of obedience. But the key question is, "What is the response of the will?"

Evidences of Faith and Unbelief

A person who is living by faith may have—indeed ought to have—an inner tranquility, Christlike behavior, a doctrinally correct confession of faith, and unwavering conviction and assurance. None of these, however, is the key evidence of sufficient faith. A person can have inner peace with confidence in the wrong object—as do some devotees of false gods, as well as those Christians who have confidence in some misappropriated Bible promise. Again, one's emotional state may vary with changes in health or circumstances.

A Christlike character is the result of true faith. On the other hand, not all character comes from biblical faith. It is quite possible for a person in ideal circumstances to develop a commendable degree of personal integrity and good behavior without God's regenerating power. So far as correct doctrine is concerned, even the devils know the truth.

The most important evidence of faith, as we have seen, is unqualified commitment to doing the will of God. Obedience may not evidence full or mature faith, but it certainly gives evidence of some faith. Abraham proved his faith through obedience (James 2:21–24), and Israel proved its unbelief through disobedience (Heb. 3:18–19). The choice to obey is absolutely necessary for birth into God's family or growth as God's child because God does not force a person. Faith frees the Holy Spirit to work. Unbelief, or disobedience, stops that work.

Note that it is quite possible for the will to speak contrary to the emotions, as Christ demonstrated in the Garden of Gethsemane when He initially cried out in anguish for deliverance but in the end chose the will of the Father. Ordinarily, the other two elements in faith—emotional response and understanding—will follow the choice to obey (John 7:17).

As we have seen, it may be possible to be an unsurrendered Christian, although there is no legitimate biblical ground for assurance of salvation for the one who is deliberately rejecting the known will of God. "If you live according to the sinful nature, you will die" (Rom. 8:13). At the least, without this basic confidence of a saving relationship with God, growth in the Christian life is impossible. If there is a longstanding rejection of the known will of God, a person is certainly not living by faith; moreover, the Bible clearly teaches that God is saving those who are believing. Thus, the essential element of faith for one who is disobedient is obedience. The unyielded person must surrender.

Scripture gives many evidences of an unsurrendered heart: unreconciled personal relations, unforgiving spirit, a complaining attitude, unloving criticism, persisting in a wrong even after realizing one is sinning, grieving more over what hurts oneself than what hurts God, making decisions on the basis of personal benefit rather than promotion of God's purposes, and seeking the praise of other people. Even if one displays no conscious rebellion, behaviors such as these indicate that the individual must choose to surrender unconditionally to the will of God.

For Christians who are experiencing a subnormal life, reentry into normal, supernatural Christian living is through the gate of surrender. They may concentrate their energies on gaining a more accurate understanding or on experiencing some emotional sense of release or well-being, but such efforts will all prove fruitless until they make the choice to yield.

Depending on the intensity of conflict, the length of time out of fellowship, and one's personality, this decision may be a major emotional crisis. But even without any emotion, in the sense of a turning point or a decisive event, this decision is rightly called a crisis. For such a person, a normal, successful Christian experience is not the product of a gradual process of spiritual development, let alone automatic progress. A decisive turning point is needed.

Is such a crisis event necessary in the life of every believer? As we have seen, Scripture points the failing Christian back to his or her original covenant relationship with God. Ideally, then, a person who enters that saving relationship can and should maintain it; there is no theological necessity for a second spiritual crisis. But in practical experience most believers do violate their covenant responsibilities, either through open rebellion or through spiritual drift, and therefore need to make a decision to turn from what they have become to what they can and should be in Christ.

In summary, then, God Himself is the key to successful Christian living, and both He and His resources are available only to the person of faith. By faith alone we enter and maintain a personal relationship that releases an unending flow of grace. This biblical faith is both choice and attitude. The choice is to obey; and obedience begins with repentance, continues in a yielded spirit, and proves itself in aggressive participation in using the means of grace and in eager affirmative action to be all that God intends. The attitude is childlike trust, relying with loving confidence on Him alone.

RESULTS OF A FAITH RELATIONSHIP WITH GOD

Faith results in salvation by the grace of God, but how do we define this salvation? Some hold that "full salvation" means a morally perfect life. As we have seen, the only way to describe any mortal as morally perfect is to define sin as the

172 I Five Views on Sanctification

deliberate violation of the known will of God and perfection as
a condition in which one consistently chooses to act obediently.
Let us examine these definitions.

First of all, is the distinction between deliberate and
unintentional sin biblical? Though direct teaching on this
subject is limited, it is certainly present and serves to solve
some basic dilemmas about the doctrines of sin and sanctification. The Old Testament clearly draws a sharp distinction
between deliberate (or presumptuous) sin, on the one hand,
and unintentional (or unwitting) sin, on the other (e.g., Exod.
21:12–14; Num. 15:27–31). A very great distinction is made
between the two in the sin itself, the guilt incurred, and the
punishment imposed.

This distinction between deliberate and unintentional sin
helps solve the problem of the teaching about sin in 1 John, for
example, where the apostle tells us in the same short letter that
(1) those who say they have no sin are lying (1:8–10) and
(2) those who sin are not Christians at all (3:6, 8–10)! The
apparent contradiction is at least partially alleviated when we
note that the verb tense (in 3:6, 8–10) may easily be understood
as referring to a continuing activity of sin, which by definition is
at least conscious, if not certainly deliberate. This continuing
sinful activity, says John, is the sure sign of an unconverted
state. At the same time, when a person claims to have no sin
whatsoever, he includes, by definition, all varieties of sin,
including unintentional, even involuntary and dispositional
sin. No one can claim freedom from all sin, says John, so no
one is sinlessly perfect on biblical grounds, for at least he or she
is constantly guilty of falling short of God's perfection, even
when unconscious of the shortfall. On the other hand, to
continue on deliberately in the practice of sin is to evidence
alienation from God. So the distinction between presumptuous
sin and unwitting sin is biblically valid.

Though the distinction between deliberate and unintentional sin may be doctrinally sound and a helpful key to
unlocking some of the mysteries of our salvation, in everyday
life the borderline between these two cannot always be easily or
precisely identified. For example, when one becomes angry, is
this attitude deliberate and conscious or is it involuntary?
Perhaps it was involuntary to begin with, but if one continues
in a state of anger, it surely becomes voluntary. But at what
precise point does sin begin and perfection become forfeit (for
one who believes in perfection)? No one wants to lose such a

preferred condition, so it is much easier simply to baptize the response and call it "righteous indignation." It may have been, of course, but if people consider themselves to be in a state of perfection, the temptation is to redefine many subnormal responses as valid. The greatest hazard in distinguishing between presumptuous sin and unwitting sin is the infinite human capacity to rationalize. Furthermore, should we classify habitual sins like drunkenness or gluttony as voluntary or involuntary?

Having recognized the difficulties of distinguishing between sins that are conscious and voluntary and those that are unconscious and involuntary, especially where they intersect, we must admit that for most behavior the distinction is clear and readily identified: people deliberately choose to do what they know is wrong or, on the other hand, they are genuinely unaware of their failure to measure up to God's perfection. But the problem here is much more basic: I believe that neither the definition of sin (as limited to deliberate choices) nor that of perfection (as the absence of volitional sin) is biblical.

As we have pointed out, sin, according to the Bible, is any falling short of the glorious perfection of God Himself (e.g., Rom. 3:23). Such failure is viewed in Scripture not as evidence of nonmoral human finitude but as sin. According to that definition, no one is perfect, even momentarily. So sinless perfection is not the result of one's initial encounter with God nor of any subsequent encounter, and to hold out such an expectation can be profoundly frustrating for those who have not achieved it and extraordinarily dangerous for any who think they have. The Bible does speak of Christian perfection (e.g., Matt. 5:48; Phil. 3:15; James 1:4), but the Greek word is often used of *maturity*, a term that fits the biblical teaching on sanctification much better than does the idea of being flawless; and it is this term that has been preferred by most contemporary translations.

Though not all will agree on these definitions, perhaps in the interest of working together to solve the practical problem of subnormal Christian experience, others could accept as a working hypothesis a view of *sin* as both deliberate violation of God's known will and falling short of God's moral perfection. With such a definition, what does a covenant relationship of faith produce?

A New Person

As we have seen, individuals who are united with Christ by faith are forgiven and justified. But they also have become new persons. By the regenerating power of the Holy Spirit, they are no longer subject to the controlling tyranny of the sinful disposition. Although subject to its influence, they are no longer legally under its control. Thus believers have the ability consistently to choose the right. They still fall short of God's perfect disposition in failing to love as He loves, to be as self-controlled, contented, humble, and selfless as Jesus was. But when the thought or activity rises to the level of the conscious choice, they can choose God's way. Even then, however, they do not do so in their own strength, not even in their own "new person" strength.

A New Relationship

Those persons who enter into this covenant relationship with God enter a new relationship in which God not only adopts them as His own children but actually comes to live with them in a special sense as their constant companion. This relationship is the key to successful Christian living.

The moment one turns to God in saving faith, the Father, the Son, and the Holy Spirit come to live with that one in a unique, new sense (John 14:16–17, 20, 23; Rom. 8:9; Gal. 2:20; Eph. 3:16–19; Col. 1:26–29). This presence is the exceeding great power working in us (Eph. 3:20) that strengthens us—not an abstract power but His Spirit within (v. 16), Christ living in our hearts (v. 17), God Himself filling us with all His fullness (v. 19). The secret to a victorious life, then, is not vainly struggling and resolving in my own strength but "Christ in you, the hope of glory" (Col. 1:27). Any hope we have of demonstrating His glorious character through our lives is based on His living personally within us and providing us with all the resources of the God of the universe.

But how, specifically, does Christ enable us to overcome, to grow, to succeed? How does He enable us to have a pattern of success in place of the old pattern of failure? Does He displace our personalities with His? The beauty and glory of God's victory in our humanity is that He does not by-pass or replace us. Rather, he renews the new person after the likeness of God Himself (Col. 3:10). As we shall see, this renewing work is primarily accomplished through the various means of grace that God provides, in the use of which we cooperate with Him. But because God in us is not an impersonal resident force or influence in our lives but a person, the new life is one of delightful personal companionship. Like a good friend, His presence does wonderful things for us. He comforts us when we are discouraged, and sensitizes our moral judgment through giving us understanding of His Book. His very presence galvanizes our will when we are weak; His counsel clarifies issues when we are confused. He works within us to change our thought patterns and outside us to control our circumstances for our long-term good.

Scripture speaks of each member of the Trinity living in us, but because the agent for effecting God's purposes in this world is the Holy Spirit, most of the teaching in the New Testament on normal Christian living focuses on the work of the Holy Spirit. The person who is in covenant relationship with God is said to have been baptized by the Spirit into the body of Christ, to have been born of the Spirit, to be indwelt by the Spirit, to walk in the Spirit, to bear the fruit of the Spirit, and to have been sealed by the Spirit. Of all these analogies, the most common is the idea of being filled with the Spirit. What does this picture language mean literally?

A tank may be empty, half-full, or full, and some Bible teachers refer to the filling of the Holy Spirit almost in such material terms. But we speak of a person, not a force, much less a liquid. Others use physical/figurative ideas similar to being full-blooded genetically or full of alcohol, meaning, for example, that people may have a lot of alcohol in their system and may be so affected by it that they have little control over themselves. This notion is better than the material concepts of fullness and has the advantage of an apparent biblical analogy: "Don't be drunk with wine, but be filled with the Spirit" (Eph. 5:18, author's paraphrase). There are many parallels between the effects of drunkenness and God-intoxication, no doubt, but we are left in the realm of the figurative and still do not know what the expression means literally. It cannot be physical, because the Holy Spirit does not have a physical dimension, though in some sense He exists in the physical bodies of believers.

Some speak of being filled with the Spirit as a spiritual experience or event and might ask, "Have you been filled with the Spirit?" Certainly the disciples' filling on the Day of

Pentecost (Acts 2) and after a prayer meeting a few weeks later (4:31) and Paul's filling with the Spirit in Acts 9:17 and again in 13:9 were all momentous experiences and specific events. But by virtue of being time oriented, the answer to the question "Have you been filled with the Spirit?" can tell us something only about the past.

The more important question is about the present—"Are you filled with the Spirit?" In this sense the expression seems to indicate a state or condition. This use of the expression must also be valid, because we are commanded to be filled continually with the Spirit (Eph. 5:18). One problem is that many take the state to refer primarily to a subjective feeling, similar, perhaps, to our expression, "filled with joy." If the condition is limited to a subjective one, it could be misconstrued or prove unstable. Nevertheless, Scripture does promise us a life of awareness of God's presence. Thus, one who is filled with the Spirit may have a continuous sense of the divine presence, a gift that must be at the very pinnacle of God's good gifts. But we are not very much closer to identifying the literal meaning of this figurative expression.

Another biblical use of the expression seems to refer to a personal characteristic. When we say that a man is full of pride, sinful, or even "full of Muriel," we mean that he is characterized by pride or sin or infatuation with some person. Used in this sense, the expression "filled with the Spirit" would mean that the person was characterized by Godlikeness, by God's being the predominant person or the pervasive influence in one's life. This must have been the meaning when people in Scripture were said to be Spirit-filled (e.g., Acts 6:3). Others could watch them and tell that their lives were characterized above all else by their association with God and by the results of that association.

There is one other possible meaning of the expression. When a person was said to have a devil (or demon), Scripture meant more than that the person was devilish, or characterized by devil-like thinking or behavior. It meant that Satan and his forces were the dominant influence in that person's life, at least at that point in time. Since the Holy Spirit, like the unholy spirits, is a person, this use of the term "filled with the Spirit" would seem to be very appropriate. The figurative expression would then literally mean that the Holy Spirit dominated, had full control, possessed, exercised imperious claim to the whole being, though the domination would be gracious, by invitation only, and would not, like demon-possession, displace or override one's personal choice. In the central biblical passage on the Holy Spirit, Romans 8, this concept of control is clearly taught (e.g., v. 9). This meaning of the term is at least the starting point, for without this relationship of unconditional yielding to the will of God, one does not receive the Holy Spirit to begin with nor benefit by His continuing presence. This definition of the expression "Spirit-filled" is the one advocated by Keswick teachers, by Campus Crusade for Christ, and by many others.

Someone who has in mind the idea of the Holy Spirit as the dominant characteristic of his or her life might hesitate to claim to be such a person. It might be more fitting to join Paul in claiming to be "the chief of sinners." Others should make such a judgment. Perhaps only others are competent to judge how godly a person is. But if a person has in mind the idea of control by the Spirit, a relationship of trusting obedience, that one certainly is competent to judge and perhaps alone can know for sure.

Much of the confusion over the way Spirit filling is understood stems from the fact that Scripture uses the expression, just as our English language uses the term *full*, in a variety of ways. How do we put them all together? The nearest I can come to it is this: "Filled with the Spirit" is a figurative, poetic expression that refers primarily to the relationship between two persons in which one is in charge, a relationship that began as a specific event that was intended to initiate a continuing condition. The relationship normally results in a glorious sense of the divine presence and certainly results in a transformed life. Such a person may legitimately be said to be filled with the Spirit.

To complicate matters even further, there seems to be another sense in which the expression is used. People whom the Bible designates as Spirit-filled are, on specific occasions, said to receive a filling (e.g., Acts 4:8, 31; 13:9). Here again, the emphasis on relationship is helpful. Under the figure of *filling* we are talking not about the infusing of some spiritual power but about a personal relationship. We may speak of a standard relationship that continues and a special plus in that relationship for a special occasion. To change the analogy, an automobile running under full power may nevertheless use a passing gear for an emergency. The sail of a vessel is normally full of wind, enough to get it to its destination, perhaps, but then there are times when a welcome breeze comes up and the sails billow in even greater fullness. So the normal life of the Christian may indeed be Spirit-filled, but there are times when a special power is needed for a special problem or opportunity. Spirit-filled believers can trust God for a fresh "filling," a passing-gear thrust to carry them through triumphantly.

To dissect a specimen is to kill it. I trust the same is not true of theological analysis. If this discussion has seemed too analytical, however, let us return to the simple, beautiful assurance that the most wonderful Person in all the universe offers us more than doctrinal truth, more than exciting experiences; He offers us Himself in an intimate relationship that can be described adequately only as *full*. And when we respond to Him in uncomplicated—and unreserved—faith, the blessed Holy Spirit gives us, with Himself, truth that we may know all He intends us to know, fruit that we may be all He designed us to be, and gifts that we may do all He purposed for us to do. This new relationship with God initiates a process and results in a new potential.

A New Potential

Simply stated, the new potential is for victory and growth. As we have seen, the new person in Christ has the ability to choose the right and to do so consistently. Such a person need never—and should never—deliberately violate the known will of God. This experience is victory, and this potential comes immediately and fully with the beginning of the new life and, when forfeited by the violation of contract, may be renewed by the reaffirmation of the original faith-covenant. Since this kind of victory is initiated by a decision at a specific point in time, many have so concentrated on this crisis experience as to minimize or ignore the all-important biblical teaching of growth. On the other hand, others emphasize the process of growth to the neglect or exclusion of the necessary initial decision. But Scripture is clear on both the crisis and the process. We have considered the faith-decision in some detail, so let us turn now to the process of growth.

The normal Christian life is one of spiritual growth toward greater and greater likeness to Jesus Christ. This truth is central in the New Testament discussion of Christian living. Those who teach that nothing changes in the persons themselves and those who teach that a particular experience can so transform people that they are perfect and no longer in need of change must answer, not a few isolated proof texts, but the whole fabric of New Testament teaching, as the following texts illustrate.

> Do not conform any longer to the pattern of this world, but be transformed by the renewing of your mind. (Rom. 12:2)

> And we . . . are being transformed into his likeness with ever-increasing glory, which comes from the Lord, who is the Spirit. (2 Cor. 3:18)

> We will in all things grow up into him who is the Head, that is, Christ. From him the whole body, joined and held together by every supporting ligament, grows and builds itself up in love, as each part does its work. (Eph. 4:15–16)

> Not that I have already obtained all this, or have already been made perfect, but I press on to take hold of that for which Christ Jesus took hold of me. Brothers, I do not consider myself yet to have taken hold of it. But one thing I do: Forgetting what is behind and straining toward what is ahead, I press on toward the goal to win the prize. (Phil. 3:12–14)

> [You] have put on the new self, which is being renewed in knowledge in the image of its Creator. (Col. 3:10)

> We instructed you how to live in order to please God, as in fact you are living. Now we ask you and urge you in the Lord Jesus to do this more and more. . . . Yet we urge you, brothers, to do so more and more. (1 Thess. 4:1, 10)

> His divine power has given us everything we need for life and godliness through our knowledge of him who called us by his own glory and goodness. Through these he has given us his very great and precious promises, so that through them you may participate in the divine nature and escape the corruption in the world caused by evil desires. For this very reason, make every effort to add to your faith goodness; and to goodness, knowledge; and to knowledge, self-control; and to self-control, perseverance; and to perseverance, godliness; and to godliness, brotherly kindness; and to brotherly kindness, love. For if you possess these qualities in increasing measure, they will keep you from being ineffective and unproductive in your knowledge of our Lord Jesus Christ. (2 Peter 1:3–8)

From this sampling of biblical teaching on the subject, who can deny that God intends the normal Christian life to be a life of

180 I Five Views on Sanctification

change, advancing in knowledge and in likeness to Jesus Christ?

Nature of Growth

- *Inner mind.* God is primarily in the business of remodeling our thought processes—our values, attitudes, ways of viewing things. This inner mind is the primary arena for growth. A normal Christian loves more and more like God loves; grows in self-control, contentment, humility, and courage; grows in understanding of God's ways; and is increasingly other-oriented and less self-oriented in the choices of life.

- *Outer behavior.* The inner transformation is visible in outward conduct. One's character changes, and even those personality traits that reflect sinful thought patterns are changed. Note that this growth into more Christlike behavior is in areas of unconscious sin or sins of omission, falling short of Godlike qualities. In deliberate sin there is no pattern of gradual growth. People do not reduce their bank robberies annually as they "grow in grace." They do not lie less frequently or cheat in fewer matters. In the Old Testament there was no redemption for presumptuous sins (e.g., Exod. 21:14; Num. 15:30–31), and in the New Testament that type of deliberately chosen sin occurs consistently in lists that identify those who are unredeemed and under judgment (e.g., 1 Cor. 6:9–10; Gal. 5:19–21; Rev. 21:8).

In matters where a person makes a deliberate choice, the normal Christian will choose God's way. But much of our behavior falls short of Christlikeness involuntarily and even unconsciously. It is in this area that the normal Christian grows steadily to reflect more and more accurately the likeness of Christ.

Means of Growth

God does influence our minds directly, but His primary method of bringing about growth is through what are commonly called "means of grace," or conduits of divine energy. In these means we are not passive but must participate actively. Even though God indeed works in us both the willing and the doing of His good pleasure, we are to work out our own salvation with fear and trembling (Phil. 2:12–13).

Prayer. Through prayer our companionship with God reaches its highest intensity. Not only do we grow more like Him through this companionship, but we find that prayer is the great means of victory at the moment of temptation.

Scripture. The Bible is God's means of revealing His character and thus His will for our thoughts and actions. Therefore, the more we know His Word, the higher potential we have for conforming to His will. It is the milk and bread and meat of the soul. Furthermore, Jesus demonstrated in His hour of temptation that Scripture is a great weapon in spiritual warfare. As we study it diligently to understand it and as we meditate on it constantly to apply it to life, we will be prepared to use it effectively to overcome temptation.

Church. The congregation of God's family is indispensable for spiritual growth. United worship and observance of the ordinances, teaching, fellowship, discipline, service, and witness within the responsible structure of the church are God's ordained means for the growth of each member.

Suffering. Suffering may be God's great shortcut to spiritual growth. Our response to suffering determines its benefit to us, of course, for the same adversity may be destructive or life building. The response of faith, that is, confidence that God has permitted the trial for His glory and our own good, transforms a potentially evil circumstance into a means of making us more like the Suffering Servant Himself.

These four "tools of the Spirit" are indispensable to Christian growth. But though they are equally available to all, not all Christians seem to mature at the same pace.

Rate of Growth

Affirmative action. Some Christians use the means of grace more diligently than others. Although in a passive sense all believers may be equally "yielded" to the will of God, the Christian life is nevertheless a war, and some are more aggressive and seem to have more of a will to fight. Though faith must rest, relying on God to do what we cannot do, it also must wrestle, struggling in warfare. Satan is the great adversary and destroyer, constantly seeking to immobilize, if he cannot destroy, God's people. Furthermore, Christians live in a world that is opposed to all they yearn to be. Some seem more aware of these adversaries and more persistent in opposing them.

In a sense, failure to do battle aggressively could be considered a spiritual flaw needing correction. At the same time this difference among Christians may simply be another sign of different levels of maturity. One should, in these matters, deal stringently with oneself and generously in judgment of the other person—both of which responses are the opposite of our natural inclinations!

More apparent than real. In the first place, I am not responsible to judge my brother (Rom. 14:3–12); furthermore, I cannot do so very accurately, even for myself, let alone for others (1 Cor. 4:4). Another reason for caution in making such judgments is that the differences may be more apparent than real. What is the standard of comparison?

One must have God's perspective in order to make a proper evaluation, and who among us has that? Therefore, we are fools if we compare ourselves among ourselves (2 Cor. 10:12), for we can never have God's full perspective. If we must make a comparison, we should compare ourselves with our model, the Lord Jesus. On the other hand, it is proper to compare ourselves either with what we once were or with what we would be, apart from the grace of God. Comparisons along these lines give God the credit and bring us closer to His perspective.

To compare ourselves with others is foolish for several reasons. In the first place, each begins his or her growth from a different level of unlikeness to God. For this reason a non-Christian gentleman with a good early environment may be a much nicer person to be around than some veteran Christian who is actually Spirit-filled. The question is, however, what that veteran Christian would be if God had not been at work and what the non-Christian gentleman could have been had God been in control. In the second place, each normal Christian is at a different stage of growth, though all are in a covenant relationship of full acceptance of the authority of the Spirit in their lives. To compare one to another is to have the wrong basis of comparison. In the third place, the data for making an accurate judgment are available only to God. We are therefore wise to leave these judgments to Him, especially when we do not have a responsibility for the spiritual development of the other person.

CONCLUSION

What glorious good news! No matter what may or may not have occurred in the past and no matter how inadequate my understanding, if my relationship to God is one of unconditional surrender and confident expectation that He will keep His word, I can experience a life of consistent victory over temptation and growth toward His own likeness, I can see His purpose for my ministry supernaturally fulfilled, and above all, I can daily experience loving companionship with my Savior.

Though Keswick does not have an officially articulated theology of sanctification, the doctrinal statement I have presented here is fully compatible with the Keswick message. I have attempted to avoid the constant temptation to develop some facet of divine truth to an extreme and have tried to stay at the balanced center of biblical tension. To the extent I have succeeded, this approach may provide a mediating position among the different perspectives on sanctification. Certainly we all seek to bring honor to our God by putting His glorious character on display in mortal flesh.

BIBLIOGRAPHY

[1] Barabas, Steven. *So Great Salvation*. London: Marshall, Morgan & Scott; Grand Rapids: Eerdmans, 1952. The definitive study of the Keswick movement (historically) and the Keswick message (theologically). A thirteen-page comprehensive bibliography on Keswick is included.

McQuilkin, Robert C. *The Life of Victory*. Chicago: Moody, 1953. A typical devotional exposition of Keswick teaching, it is in the format of personal testimony by one who participated in bringing the movement to the United States in the early part of the century.

Two authors who attack the movement and are universally held by Keswick speakers to have misunderstood the teaching:

Packer, J. I. *Keep in Step With the Spirit*. Old Tappan, N.J.: Revell, 1984.
Warfield, B. B. *Studies in Perfectionism*. New York: Oxford, 1931.

Response to McQuilkin

Melvin E. Dieter

J. Robertson McQuilkin's article demonstrates two facts about the views of the doctrine of sanctification presented in this volume: (1) these Evangelical traditions, all of which appeal strongly to scriptural authority, describe the biblical vision of Christian holiness in remarkably similar terms; one is struck more by their correspondence than by their difference; and (2) of all the positions represented, the Keswick higher life and the Wesleyan holiness views are more similar in the expression of that vision than any two others. The Keswick doctrine takes most seriously certain key elements of the Evangelical-Arminian theology that underlies the Wesleyan view. Keswick takes the Wesleyan vision of the possibility and even necessity of the invasion of the Christian life by the fullness of God and incorporates it into a view of the holy life, at the same time looking to basic features of Reformed theology to shape its definitions.

History gives some insight into the often turbulent relationship between these two movements. One of the high points of the continuous interchange between American and British revivalism was the influx of American revivalists into England after the American Civil War. During that period the influence of the American holiness evangelists was second only to the influence of Dwight L. Moody, the premier evangelist of the day. Their message generated a renewed emphasis on Wesley's doctrine of Christian holiness where it might have been most expected—within its native soil, British Methodism. But more important, through the influence of Charles G. Finney, Asa Mahan, and other Oberlin evangelists who accommodated "second blessing" teaching to the Reformed tradition, the message gained entrance to the broad Evangelical Calvinist circles of England and the Continent. The theology of that higher-life movement, itself an Arminianized Calvinism, opened English and European Evangelicalism to interest in holiness and higher-life teaching, despite the strong aversion of traditional Calvinism to anything smacking of perfectionism.

Out of that mix, the Keswick movement was born through the ministry of Robert Pearsall Smith, William Boardman, and others in the 1870s. A higher-life coalition supported Smith's remarkable ministry among British Evangelicals of all stripes, in spite of his strong affiliations with Methodist (perfectionist) "second blessing" teaching. The early breakup of the coalition was undoubtedly occasioned by his fall from grace at the height of the movement's success in 1875. The precipitous abandonment of Smith by British Evangelicals, already on edge over the strong Wesleyan element in his message, set the tone for the future. The ongoing Keswick movement, which picked itself up from the ruin of Smith's fall, was Calvinist oriented, as it set up the patterns of distinction that sought to put all the distance possible between its understanding of the Spirit's work in the deeper-life experience and that of the American holiness movement out of which it was born. The conflict, therefore, that has marked Keswick and holiness relationships has significant historical as well as theological roots.

Throughout McQuilkin's excellent exposition of a classical Keswick position, the influences of the Wesleyan holiness position constantly appear. Regeneration is recognized as the beginning of a process-crisis-process pattern of growth in holiness. This life of daily victory over sin is entered by the total offering of oneself to God in entire consecration; it is the actual participation in the holiness of God through faith in the redemptive work of Jesus Christ by the indwelling Spirit. It is a life, not of any kind of sinless perfection, but of being enabled by the grace of God not to sin. The emphasis is not on looking back to the crisis moment of total commitment but on looking ahead and asking, "What more, Lord?" This position is essentially the Wesleyan message that Smith and others preached in non-Wesleyan terms to Evangelicals rooted in the Reformation tradition.

The result is that, in spite of the strong parallels between the Keswick and Wesleyan positions, the distinctions with which they have struggled historically arise from whether the concepts are set in a Reformed or a Wesleyan context. Since the Wesleyan view gives larger place to human responsibility, it considers sanctification as more a matter of rectifying the attitude, the will, and the affections in the perfection of the divine-human relationship than a matter of any conception of sinlessness as matching perfectly a code of moral rectitude. As a result, when it comes to defining the life of perfect love and what places a person into a position of culpability before God, it is perfectly possible to define sin in Wesleyan terms of "willful transgression against the known will of God." It is then possible to say that we have known God's grace in an experience of utter surrender in which the warped wills that we inherited from the Fall are freed to obedience rather than disobedience and enabled to love God with wholeness. Having such a defective will is the essence of what it means to be in the flesh; to be cleansed from all remnants that would enslave the will to sin is the essence of holiness and Christian perfection.

Freedom from sin is not freedom from temptation and the fallenness of our humanity but freedom from any necessity to respond willingly to the many temptations to which that fallenness exposes us. Because Keswick chooses to explicate these truths in light of a theology that includes much broader definitions of the nature of the divine-human relationship and a different definition of our human situation, there will always be this difference in the understanding of how Christian holiness is wrought in the believer's heart and how its dynamics may be defined. These differences that distinguish the Wesleyan and Keswick teachings are at the heart of the differences between the Wesleyan view and the others in this volume as well; the others, however, are often more stark in their contrasts.

A final point of concern with the Keswick view is its failure in the minds of some to provide a theology broad enough for the ethical and social sides of the life of fullness and wholeness. The teaching has tended to give most of its attention to inner piety as the final goal of the holy life. In practice, however, the movement has often moved beyond that theology. For example, the movement's strong missions thrust is widely recognized; it flows naturally from lives fully committed to God's will but finds little explication or reinforcement in the theology of the movement.

Response to McQuilkin

Anthony A. Hoekema

There is much in J. Robertson McQuilkin's chapter with which I agree. I appreciate the emphasis on victory—the New Testament does indeed describe the Christian life as a life of victory (Rom. 8:37; 1 John 5:4). I appreciate also McQuilkin's insistence on union with Christ as the heart of Paul's theology and on the importance of being filled with the Spirit. I agree that a life of holiness is the purpose of our salvation. I concur with the author's affirmation that the believer still has a natural proclivity to sin and that it is not possible for a Christian to live without sin in this life.

I also agree with McQuilkin when he says that some, possibly many, Christians need to surrender their wills in total commitment to the Lord some time after their conversion. The Corinthians who were living carnally (1 Cor. 3:1–3 KJV) certainly had this need, as did the church in Ephesus (Rev. 2:4). I disagree, however, that a specific post-conversion crisis experience of this sort needs to be programmed into the lives of most Christians (p. 171).

I have major problems with the chapter in two areas. The first is the question of the definition of sin. On page 153 McQuilkin quotes, as a true representation of the Keswick message, the following statement: "We believe the Word of God teaches that the *normal* Christian life is one of uniform sustained victory over known sin." On page 173, however, "sin according to the Bible" is defined as "any falling short of the

glorious moral perfection of God Himself (e.g., Rom. 3:23)." On
the basis of this second definition of sin, the author goes on to
say, "No one is perfect, even momentarily." I appreciate the
disavowal of the possibility of attaining sinless perfection. But
now I have questions about the possibility of "uniform
sustained victory over known sin."

First, if "sin according to the Bible" is what was defined on
page 173, is this definition not known? Does not God require us
in His law to love Him with all our hearts, souls, and minds,
and to love our neighbors as ourselves (Matt. 22:37–39)? Can
any one of us keep this broadest requirement perfectly?
McQuilkin admits that to "fall short of the glory of God" (Rom.
3:23) in this sense is sin. But is not such sin against a *known* law
of God?

Second, the author works with two definitions of sin. One
is "according to the Bible." The other is "deliberate violation of
God's known will." Is Keswick then operating with something
less than the biblical definition of sin?

Third, even the expression "known sin" has its problems.
How terribly easy it is not to recognize sin as sin. Often what
we call "sinful anger" in others we deem "righteous indignation" in ourselves. Our sins, as someone has said, are like notes
pinned to our backs; others see them, but we do not. Did not
David say, "Who can discern his errors" (Ps. 19:12)? Did not
Paul affirm, "My conscience is clear, but that does not make me
innocent" (1 Cor. 4:4)? How, then, can we be sure that, when
we avoid what we think are known sins, we are really doing
God's will?

Finally, how about the matter of motivation? Do we ever
do anything from perfectly pure motives? Do we perform our
"good works" *solely* out of love for God and the neighbor? Does
nothing of self enter in? Isaiah complains, "All our righteous
acts are like filthy rags" (Isa. 64:6). Was not Herman Bavinck
right when he said, "In every deliberation and deed of the
believer . . . the good and the evil lie, as it were, mingled
through each other"?[1] How, then, can believers claim to have
"uniform sustained victory over known sin"?

The second major problem concerns McQuilkin's distinction between two types of Christians. The distinction is

---

[1] Herman Bavinck, *Our Reasonable Faith*, trans. Henry Zylstra (Grand
Rapids: Eerdmans, 1956), p. 495.

expressed in various ways: between "carnal" and "spiritual" Christians, between those who "have a life pattern of defeat" and those who "have a life pattern of spiritual success," between "subnormal" and "normal" Christians, or between "unsurrendered" and "surrendered" Christians.

I grant that Christians live on various levels of maturity, that some live closer to God than others, and that some are more consistent in their Christian life than others. But is it right to divide believers into two distinct categories?

First, there is no biblical basis for the distinction between "carnal" and "spiritual" Christians. The New Testament does distinguish between people who have been born again and those who have not (John 3:3, 5), between those who believe in Christ and those who do not (v. 36), between those who "live according to the flesh" and those who "live according to the Spirit" (Rom. 8:5 RSV), and between the "unspiritual man" and the "spiritual man" (1 Cor. 2:14–15 RSV). It never speaks of a third class of people called "carnal Christians."

The reference in 1 Corinthians 3:1–3 is not to such a third class of people but to immature Christians, to "mere infants in Christ" (v. 1). Though they are still infants, they are "in Christ." Their carnality is a behavior problem, which they must outgrow. Since they are in Christ, they are indeed "new creatures" (2 Cor. 5:17 KJV), "sanctified" (1 Cor. 1:2; 6:11), and spiritually rich (3:21–23).

The distinctions in question would seem to open the way for two erroneous and spiritually harmful attitudes: depression and discouragement on the part of the "lower class" of believers; pride or possible complacency on the part of the "upper class" (see 1 Cor. 10.12).

Further, the distinctions are too extremely stated. Is it really true that "most Christians subsist in a subnormal condition of defeat and spiritual poverty" (p. 165)? Is it true that the "average Christian" yields to temptation "more often than not" (p. 152)? On the other hand, the description of the life of the "normal Christian" on page 151 seems too good to be true. Is it true that such a believer "authentically reflects the attitudes and behavior of Jesus Christ" and "consistently obeys the laws of God"?

I believe it is more true to Scripture to say that we who are in Christ are at various points on the pathway of sanctification. We experience neither total defeat nor total victory over sin. We are in Christ, but we need to grow up into Him more and more.

We are indwelt by the Spirit, but we need to be more consistently filled with the Spirit. We have yielded ourselves to Christ as Lord, but we need to surrender more fully. We try to resist known sin, but we do not always succeed, and we are not always sure what is sinful and what is not. We continue to struggle against the "lusts of the flesh" in the strength of the Spirit, but we sometimes give in.

We live a life of victory, but it is a qualified victory. We are not yet what we shall be. We are not yet totally like Christ (1 John 3:2). We live in the tension between the "already" and the "not yet." We are *genuinely* new persons but not yet *totally* new.

Response to McQuilkin

Stanley M. Horton

Many Pentecostal writers have expressed a debt to the classic Keswick position. I have heard many sermons from our pulpits encouraging a life of victory over known sin. Sometimes this has led people to ask one another (in an encouraging way), "Do you have the victory?"

We have a similar emphasis on the finished work of Christ and on union with Him. We recognize the work of the Holy Spirit in the progressive sanctification of the believer, and we expect His help in resisting temptation. We would agree that this demands complete consecration, unconditional surrender to the will and purpose of God as revealed in His Word.

We differ in our definition of being filled with the Spirit and being full of the Spirit. We recognize that the fullness of the Spirit is available to those who ask (Luke 11:13), and we identify the initial filling with the baptism in the Holy Spirit (with its initial outward evidence of speaking in other tongues). Most Pentecostals would agree, however, that new special fillings are available to meet special needs, as when Peter faced the Sanhedrin (Acts 4:8) and when Paul faced Elymas the sorcerer (Acts 13:9). We also recognize that the baptism in the Holy Spirit is not a climax. It occurs when we enter into a life relationship with the Spirit and He comes to abide. He is present with us continually, whether we are aware of His presence in any way or not. Yet, he does not take away our free will. It is still up to us whether we yield to His control or not.

It is important also to recognize that "the spirits of the prophets are subject to the control of the prophets" (1 Cor. 14:32). When the Spirit prompts us to minister in one of the gifts, it is still our responsibility to minister in love and courtesy, fitting into the flow of the Spirit and not interrupting the ministry of others. It is my experience that we do not lose anything by holding steady until there is opportunity to minister a gift of the Spirit in a way that will edify. In fact, if we wait and the gift is really for this occasion, the Spirit will deepen and intensify the manifestation of the gift when it is ministered.

The Keswick emphasis on service and missions has been picked up by the entire Pentecostal movement. Our whole emphasis is that the primary purpose of the baptism in the Spirit is power for service. That this has been effective is seen in the fact that Assemblies of God membership overseas is now about fifteen times its membership in the United States.

Like the Keswick leaders, we deny the possibility of "sinless perfection" in this life. We also teach that the Christian, instead of expecting to sin, should expect not to sin, as far as acts of sin are concerned. We, however, recognize that we are still in a battle and must continue to be on guard, for the tendency to sin is still with us. We agree that we must daily claim the help of the Holy Spirit and put to death the deeds of the old nature. But, as in the Keswick movement, the relation between the old nature and the new life in Christ is not always clearly defined by our preachers.

In that we recognize all believers as saints, our definition of and distinction between positional and experiential sanctification is similar to those in Keswick circles. We recognize also that some Christians are carnal, and we recognize that all have carnal moments, but we would say that Christians who continue to sin are in danger of losing their salvation. Like the Keswick position, we put considerable emphasis on the warnings of Scripture, warnings that would have no meaning if it were not possible for professing Christians to be lost. In other words, we are more openly Arminian than Dr. McQuilkin seems to be.

We would agree that faith involves both knowledge and obedience and that active pursuit of holy living through prayer and the Word is necessary. Faith must also be in God.

Among Pentecostals there is no agreement about whether a crisis experience is essential. However, most would agree with

McQuilkin that in practice a crisis event (surrender and consecration) is often necessary in order to experience victorious Christian living.

We differ from the Keswick position, however, with respect to being filled with the Spirit. They seem to take the Spirit-filled life as primarily a matter of maturity. We see the baptism in the Spirit as an empowering experience that does not automatically produce maturity. Maturing is a gradual process that comes through growth as we continue walking in the Spirit and applying the truth of God's Word in our lives. But God does not wait to use us, nor does the Spirit withhold His gifts until we are mature. However, we would accept as scriptural what Dr. McQuilkin says about the nature of spiritual growth.

Actually, Pentecostals do not deny that many Christians do live on a high level of Christian victory without having experienced the Pentecostal baptism. But we contend that the Holy Spirit helps them, recognizing that the truth of the Pentecostal experience has been neglected over the centuries. The Scriptural pattern is first new life by the Spirit, then the empowering experience of the baptism in the Holy Spirit, then a life of spiritual growth that makes progress in both sanctification and service.

Response to McQuilkin

John F. Walvoord

Those holding to the Augustinian-dispensational perspective on sanctification will find little with which they need to take issue in J. Robertson McQuilkin's presentation of the Keswick perspective. As is true of the Pentecostal, Wesleyan, and Reformed positions, so also within Keswick circles there is a wide variety of approaches to the doctrine of sanctification. Yet, although each writer in this symposium on sanctification has come from his own perspective, there is concurrence in the recognition of justification as a decisive act by God, with initial sanctification occurring at the same time. Each writer has disclaimed that there is any experience by which anyone can reach sinless perfection and freedom from both deliberate and unconscious sins. Each writer points to ultimate sanctification in heaven, and at the same time each one emphasizes the responsibility to grow in sanctification in the Christian's experience on earth.

In the opinion of some, the problem with Keswick teaching is that it seems to imply that by an act of the will the Christian can reach a plateau of spiritual perfection. Yet, practically all Keswick teachers will freely admit that such a person can sin following his initial decision. The corrective that is presented by McQuilkin is the same as that of the Augustinian-dispensational perspective and some of the other points of view, namely, that experiential sanctification depends on a daily life of obedience to the exhortations of Scripture and of constant dependence upon the Holy Spirit to provide the necessary power—the transforming power that can only come from God Himself. While in every perspective there may be those who will go to extremes that contradict the mainstream of their perspective, when conservative and sober judgment is applied, it is remarkable how similar the various views on sanctification are.

The treatment by McQuilkin is to be especially commended for its warm and sympathetic tone, reflecting as it does the work of the Holy Spirit in the writer himself. One senses a winsomeness and an attractiveness to the Christian life that is what God intends and the Scripture prescribes. While the life of relatively complete victory in Christ may not be normal, it is certainly the high standard to which each believer should press with full recognition of all that God has provided in Christ, in the Scriptures, and in the indwelling Holy Spirit to produce the progressive sanctification that is real and honoring to God.

From the Augustinian-dispensational point of view, clarity would be introduced in all perspectives if the baptism of the Spirit, like justification, would be recognized as a once-for-all act of the Spirit at the time of conversion. Moreover, it would be helpful if the filling of the Spirit would be emphasized as God's means of transforming the Christian life and if the means by which one may be filled with the Spirit would be carefully delineated. The ultimate goal in sanctification of the church is "to present her to himself as a radiant church, without stain or wrinkle or any other blemish, but holy and blameless" (Eph. 5:27).

Chapter 5

THE AUGUSTINIAN-DISPENSATIONAL PERSPECTIVE

John F. Walvoord

THE AUGUSTINIAN-DISPENSATIONAL PERSPECTIVE

John F. Walvoord

THE MORAL CHARACTER OF A PERSON BEFORE AND AFTER SALVATION

Ever since the time of the early church fathers, theologians have struggled to delineate the moral character of individuals before and after their salvation. There is general agreement that a person is sinful before salvation, but what has been debated is the extent of the transformation after the new birth. Some emphasize the tremendous change that takes place with the new birth, quoting, for example, 2 Corinthians 5:17, "Therefore, if anyone is in Christ, he is a new creation; the old has gone, the new has come!" Some picture the transformation as gradual, culminating in perfection in heaven. Others offer the possibility of totally eradicating sin—at least as willful sin. Others describe people after salvation as having two natures: the old nature, or sin nature, which they had before salvation, and a new nature like the divine nature of God, which includes eternal life.

Theological discussion in the English language struggles with the word *nature*, for "there are few words more dangerously ambiguous than 'nature.'"[1] The problem arises because in the Bible at least one Hebrew word and three Greek words are translated "nature." Even the same Hebrew or Greek word is used in different senses. This lack of clear definition of the word *nature* has led to much of the theological debate regarding the transformation that occurs at regeneration. Strangely, many writers begin discussing the subject without any consideration of the varieties of meaning in the English word or the relevant words in the original languages. Many theologians avoid the word *nature* and try to find another word that would indicate some type of indwelling sin.

The early church fathers taught that Christians have two distinct natures, with Augustine, in particular, discussing the matter at some length. T. A. Hegre suggests that "if Ambrose (340–397) introduced the idea of a *sinful* nature, it was Augustine (354–430) who developed the idea of the believer's *two* natures and introduced it as a respectable doctrine of Christianity."[2] After questioning whether Augustine got this teaching from Scripture, Hegre errs in trying to account for Augustine's position on the basis of his experience with Manicheanism.[3] Augustine, however, characteristically did not refer to two natures but to the flesh, which is a scriptural idea.

Throughout the history of the church, Christians continued to discuss the concept of the two natures. The Protestant Reformers seemed to follow Augustine. Nineteenth-century Calvinists such as Charles Hodge also adopted the concept of an old and a new nature in the believer. Twentieth-century Calvinists such as Anthony A. Hoekema follow essentially the same concept of the two natures in Christians. Hoekema states the following in the introduction to his helpful study on the subject:

> Most of us would indignantly resent the suggestion that we bear any resemblance to the notorious Dr. Jekyll–Mr. Hyde of Stevenson's famous novel—the man who, though a respected and competent physician by day, committed fiendish crimes by night. However much we may dislike admitting this fact, however, there is a sense in which every converted person is a kind of Jekyll-Hyde combination. For the Scriptures clearly affirm that there is a continual struggle within every converted man between his old nature and his new. Though he may grow in grace and the knowledge of our Lord and Savior Jesus Christ, there is no armistice in this war, there is no cessation of hostilities—until we die.[4]

In the discussion that follows, Hoekema traces the doctrine through scholasticism, Calvin, and Luther. He reviews important Scriptures such as Galatians 5:16–24 and Romans 7:14–25 and then closes with the theological implications of the struggle.[5]

C. I. Scofield and many twentieth-century Evangelicals, particularly dispensationalists, have adopted the two-nature theory as a biblical concept. The central problem for all these views was and continues to be the extent and power of sin in Christians after their conversion and the means of sanctification, or a holy life, in view of the sin factor that remains.

The problem of the meaning of the word *nature* plagues the theological discussion. One of the important Greek words for nature is *phusis*, used of a person's sinful nature before salvation. Ephesians 2:3 states "All of us also lived among them at one time, gratifying the cravings of our sinful nature [the flesh, Gk. *sarx*] and following its desires and thoughts. Like the rest, we were by nature [Gk. *phusis*] objects of wrath." On the basis of this passage of Scripture, there is little question that people by nature are sinful before conversion. The word *phusis* is also used of "the divine nature" (2 Peter 1:4), which makes it difficult to use this word for a person's new nature after conversion. The question remains open, then, of what the best term is for referring to people's continued sinfulness as well as to their new desires for holiness after conversion.

THE AUGUSTINIAN CONCEPT OF SIN

Because of his sense of the profound sinfulness of human beings, Augustine gave a great deal of attention to a person's sinful character, even after his or her conversion. However, he seldom referred to either aspect of an individual's new character after conversion as a nature, preferring to use the word *flesh* (Gk. *sarx*).

In his *Confessions*, Augustine compared his own struggles with sin to those described by Paul in Romans 7:14–25. Augustine wrote:

> In vain did I "delight in Thy law after the inner man," when "another law in my members warred against the law of my mind, and brought me into captivity to the law of sin which is in my members." For the law of sin is the violence of custom, whereby the mind is drawn and held, even against its will; deserving to be so held in that it so willingly falls into it. "O, wretched man that I am! who shall deliver me from the body of this death" but Thy grace only, through Jesus Christ our Lord?[6]

At this point in Augustine's *Confessions* it is not clear whether he was talking about his experience before salvation or his experience subsequent to salvation. In his later writings, however, Augustine definitely took the position that this passage in Romans refers to the struggle that takes place within a Christian.[7]

Charles Hodge supports this understanding of the situation. In reference to Romans 7:14–25, Hodge comments at length that Augustine and others held that this passage refers to a Christian, not to one who is still unsaved and, thus, still under the law. According to Hodge,

> It appears that during the first three centuries, the Fathers were generally agreed in considering the passage as descriptive of the experience of one yet under the law. Even Augustine at first concurred in the correctness of this view. But as a deeper insight into his own heart and a more thorough investigation of the Scriptures led to the modification of his opinion on so many other points, they produced a change on this subject also. This general alteration of his doctrinal views cannot be attributed to his controversy with Pelagius, because it took place long before that controversy commenced. It is to be ascribed to his religious experience, and his study of the Word of God. The writers of the middle ages, in general, agreed with the later views of Augustine on this, as on other subjects. At the time of the Reformation, the original diversity of opinion on this point, as in all others connected with it, soon became manifested. Erasmus, Socinus, and others, revived the opinion of the Greek fathers; while Luther, Calvin, Melancthon, Beza, etc., adhered to the opposite interpretation.[8]

Hodge defends at some length the view that this passage applies to Christians and notes that, generally speaking, Calvinists have taken this position but Arminians have not. For Hodge, this difference "is indeed the natural result of the different views of scriptural doctrine of the natural state of man."[9]

Recognizing the conflict between sin and righteousness in a Christian, Augustine, in writing *Palatinus*, stated,

> "Watch, therefore, and pray that you enter not into temptation." Such prayer is indeed in itself an admonition to you that you need the help of the Lord, that you ought not to rest upon yourself your hope of living well. For now you pray, not that you may obtain the riches and honours of this

present world, or any unsubstantial human possession, but that you may not enter into temptation, a thing which would not be asked in prayer if man could accomplish it for himself by his own will.[10]

In his *City of God*, Augustine commented on the flesh:

> In enunciating this proposition of ours, then, that because some live according to the flesh and others according to the spirit, there has arisen two diverse and conflicting cities, we might equally well have said, "because some live according to man, others according to God." For Paul says very plainly to the Corinthians, "For whereas there is among you enmity and strife, are ye not carnal, and walk according to man?" So that, to walk according to man and to be carnal are the same; for by *flesh*, that is, by a part of man, man is meant.[11]

In his discussion of continence, Augustine quoted Galatians 5:16–17, "For neither were those other than members of the Church unto whom he thus spake, 'Walk in the spirit, and fulfill not the lusts of the flesh. For the flesh lusteth against the spirit, and the spirit against the flesh; for these are opposed the one to the other; that ye do not what ye would.' "[12] Noting that the word translated here as "flesh" is rendered "sinful nature" in the New International Version, we can clearly see that Augustine found in the Christian both the continuance of sin in some form and a resulting conflict of the flesh with the new nature and with the Holy Spirit.

If a Christian has indwelling sin, described in Scripture as "flesh"—something that was not eradicated by the new birth—the question remains whether this factor should be referred to as "the sin nature." In order to understand the problem, we must go back to Hodge's concept of nature as a substance, a concept that is derived from his concept of the two natures in Christ—the hypostatic union of the divine and the human.

THE CONCEPT OF NATURES IN
THE PERSON OF CHRIST

In commenting on the hypostatic union in Christ, Hodge clearly presents his position, namely, that a nature is a substance.

> There is a union. The initial elements united are the divine and human nature. By *nature*, in this connection, is meant substance. In Greek, the corresponding words are [*phusis*]

and [*ousia*]; in Latin, *natura* and *substantia*. The idea of
substance is a necessary one. . . . The first important point
concerning the person of Christ is that the elements united or
combined in His person are two distinct substances, humanity and divinity; that He has in His constitution the same
essence or substance which constitutes us men, and the
same substance which makes God infinite, eternal, and
immutable in all His perfections.[13]

Hodge's point is that this position is orthodox theology.

B. B. Warfield has much the same to say about this doctrine
of the two natures in Christ. He states:

One of the most portentous symptoms of the decay of vital
sympathy with historical Christianity which is observable in
present-day academic circles is the widespread tendency in
recent Christological discussion to revolt from the doctrine of
the Two Natures in the Person of Christ. The significance of
this revolt becomes at once apparent, when we reflect that a
doctrine of the Two Natures is only another way of stating
the doctrine of the Incarnation; and the doctrine of the
Incarnation is the hinge on which the Christian system turns.
No Two Natures, no Incarnation; no Incarnation, no Christianity in any distinctive sense. Nevertheless, voices are
raised all about us declaring that the conception of Two
Natures in Christ is no longer admissible; and that very
often with full appreciation of the significance of the declaration.[14]

It may be concluded that in Christ the human nature must
include all that is genuinely human apart from sin and that the
divine nature must include all that is divine. This concept of
nature as a substantive entity is usually assumed by those who
deny that a Christian still has a sin nature and in turn has led to
the struggle to find a substitute word or to deny as much as
possible the presence of sin in the person of a Christian. While
the view of the substantive character of *nature* in the person of
Christ is generally accepted as orthodox, most theologians who
hold that believers have both a sin nature and a divine, or new,
nature use the word *nature* in this context in a lesser sense. No
one holds that the divine nature in a Christian ever existed as a
separate person, as was true in the case of Christ, although the
sin nature characterizes a person before salvation. The problem
remains of how to define *nature* as used in connection with a
believer.

THE AUGUSTINIAN-DISPENSATIONAL DEFINITION OF THE SIN NATURE

Charles Ryrie discusses this concept of nature in the believer:

> The moment one accepts Jesus Christ as his personal Savior he becomes a new creation (2 Cor. 5:17). The life of God within him begets a new nature which remains with him along with the old as long as he lives. Understanding the presence, position and relationship of the old and new within the life of a believer is essential to experiencing a wholesome and balanced spiritual life. Sometimes the sin nature is referred to as the flesh. Actually, the word *flesh* has several meanings. (1) Sometimes it simply means the material body of a person (1 Cor. 15:39). (2) Often it indicates people as a whole (Rom. 3:20). (3) But frequently it is used in Scripture to indicate the sin nature (Rom. 7:18). What does it mean when used in this way? To answer this question it is necessary to find a satisfactory definition of the word *nature.* Too often when people think of the sin nature and the new nature they picture two distinct people who live inside their bodies. One is a grisly, horrifying, degenerate man while the other is a handsome, young, victorious-looking man. Representations like this are not necessary to be discarded entirely though they often lead to the idea that it is not really I who do these things but the "little man" inside me. In other words, they often lead to a false disjuncture in the individual personality.[15]

Ryrie goes on to define *nature* as "capacity."

> It is far better to define nature in terms of a capacity. Thus the old nature of the flesh is that capacity which all men have to serve and please self. Or one might say that it is the capacity to leave God out of one's life. It would not be inclusive enough to define the sin nature in terms of a capacity to do evil, because it is more than that. There are many things which are not necessarily in themselves evil but which stem from the old nature.[16]

Paul, however, in Romans 7:14–25 seems to indicate that the flesh, or sin nature, is more than capacity. Many additional concepts seem to be indicated, such as the depravity of the old nature, or its natural tendency (or predisposition) to sin. In harmony with Scripture, all these concepts can be properly incorporated into the concept of the old nature.

Calvinists generally recognize that an unbeliever has a sin nature. Lewis Sperry Chafer, for example, states:

"In seeking to analyze more specifically what the sin nature is, it should be remembered that it is a perversion of God's original creation and in that sense is an abnormal thing. Every faculty of man is injured by the Fall, and the disability to do good and the strange predisposition to evil arise from that inner confusion."[17]

While dispensationalists commonly hold that believers continue to have a sin nature, Chafer clearly limits the concept of the word *nature*:

"Were it not for a secondary meaning of the word *nature*, it would not be a proper designation as it is now being used. A nature, primarily, is a thing created by God, such as the unfallen human nature which reflected the image and likeness of God. In its secondary meaning, the term *nature* designates the perversion, with its unholy dispositions, which the Fall engendered."[18]

From the writings of Calvinists such as Hodge and twentieth-century dispensationalists such as Ryrie and Chafer, it may be concluded that the Augustinian-dispensational perspective considers the sin nature an entity with less substantive character than the two natures of the incarnate Christ. While Ryrie prefers the word *capacity*, Chafer uses the word *nature* in the sense that includes the inclination of even a Christian, who has a new nature, to continue in sin.

Though C. I. Scofield has numerous notes on the concept of sin, his discussion of the sin nature itself is comparatively brief. In connection with his exposition of Romans 7:14, he states, "In this passage (vv. 15–25) of profound spiritual and psychological insight, the apostle personifies the struggle of the two natures within the believer—the old or Adamic nature, and the divine nature received through the new birth (1 Peter 1:23; 2 Peter 1:4; cp. Gal. 2:20; Col. 1:27)."[19]

Though a dozen other definitions could be debated, the concept of a sin nature can probably be best summarized as a complex of human attributes that demonstrate a desire and predisposition to sin. At the same time, in one who has experienced Christian salvation, there is a new nature, which may be defined as a complex of attributes having a predisposition and inclination to righteousness. These definitions fairly summarize the Augustinian-dispensational concept of the two natures in a person. The word *nature* is used by contemporary dispensationalists but in a lesser sense than when it is used of the two natures in Christ. The tendency to limit the character of sin in a believer is seen in Ryrie's use of the word *capacity* and in other dispensationalists' use of a phrase such as "indwelling sin" or any other expressions that avoid using the word *nature.* When the word *nature* is not used, however, it is often difficult to find a good substitute for it.

Some contemporary dispensationalists, however, have gone much further in redefining the concept of the sin nature in a Christian. David C. Needham, for instance, so emphasizes the idea of a Christian as a new creation that he almost eliminates the concept of sin in a believer. He states, "I believe that it is completely illogical to hold that Romans 7:14–25 is describing the typical experience of a believer who is looking at life through the truth of Romans 6 and 8."[20] In his discussion he avoids any reference to the two natures in Christ, as do most others who deny there is a sin nature in a believer. The use of *nature* in theology for the human and divine attributes of Christ undermines the possible contention that the two natures in the believer imply that human personality is divided and schizophrenic. Christ certainly was one person with two natures. Needham's definition of what is remaining as sinful for those in Christ views the new nature as the "inner man" and the factor of sin in a believer as the "more shallow self."[21] Overall, his discussion magnifies the concept of a person as a new creature in Christ and minimizes the presence of sin in any form. Needham, while writing in a dispensational context, is not a typical dispensationalist. He seems to be unaware of the historic position of Augustine and Calvinists, which is far more realistic and definitive concerning indwelling sin in a person than his portrayal is. He also ignores the light cast on the problem by the fact of the two natures in Christ. His contention that the concept of the sin nature is "illogical" is not sustained by his argument.

OTHER TERMS RELATED TO THE SIN NATURE

As we have seen, Augustine's concept of the flesh seems synonymous with the concept of the sin nature. In earlier discussion we noted that not all instances of the word *flesh* (Gk. *sarx*) refer to the sin nature. In Romans 7:18, however, it is used as a synonym for the sin nature, or that which remains in a person after he or she becomes a Christian.

Other terms that need definition are the concepts *old man* and *new man*. Many contemporary dispensationalists follow Scofield in defining the old man as "all that man was in Adam, both morally and judicially, i.e. the man of old, the corrupt human nature, the inborn tendency to evil in all men."[22] By contrast, Scofield holds that "the regenerate 'new self' is distinguished from the old self (Rom. 6:6, note), and is a new self as having become a partaker of the divine nature and life (Col. 3:3–4; 2 Pet. 1:4), and in no sense the old self made over, or improved (2 Cor. 5:17; Gal. 6:15; Eph. 2:10; Col. 3:10). The new self is Christ 'formed' in the Christian (Gal. 2:20; 4:19; Col. 1:27; 1 Jn. 4:12)."[23]

There are some grounds to question this identification of the old man with the sin nature and the new man with the new nature. Colossians 3:9–10, for instance, states "Do not lie to each other, since you have taken off your old self [the old man] with its practices and have put on the new self [the new man], which is being renewed in knowledge in the image of its Creator." It is obviously impossible to put off the old man or the old self, just as it is impossible by human effort to put on the new man or the new self, if these refer to the old and new natures. The old self mentioned in Romans 6:6 and Colossians 3:9–10 seems to be related to the former life rather than to the former nature. Likewise, the new self as indicated in Ephesians 4:24 seems to refer to the new manner of life stemming from the new nature and manifested in a Christian's experience. The exhortation here to "put on the new self" means that the new nature should be allowed to manifest itself. This putting on can also be taken as something already accomplished (as in Col. 3:9–10). Similarly, the old man, or old self, is pictured in Romans 6:6 as having been crucified at the time Christ was crucified. Hence, Paul states, "I have been crucified with Christ and I no longer live, but Christ lives in me" (Gal. 2:20). Not only is the death of Christ sufficient to take away the guilt of sin for the believer, but also His death and resurrection provide power for deliverance from the old habits and old life that characterized a person before salvation.

SUMMARY OF A PERSON'S SPIRITUAL STATE AFTER SALVATION

In light of the foregoing discussion, we may conclude that, once a person is saved, the spiritual state of that person includes a new nature and an old nature. That is, the believer still has an old nature—a complex of attributes with an inclination and disposition to sin; and the new nature, received (along with eternal life) at the time of the new birth, also has a complex of attributes, but these attributes incline and dispose the Christian to a new manner of life, one that is holy in the sight of God. From the Augustinian-dispensational perspective, the basic problem of sanctification is how individuals with these two diverse aspects in their total character can achieve at least a relative measure of sanctification and righteousness in their life.

Redeemed individuals cannot lead a holy life apart from divine help. The old nature has a tendency to sin and the new nature a tendency to act in righteousness; hence, these two natures are in the struggle that is described in Romans 7:14–25. Moreover, just as the old nature cannot produce a righteous life, so also the new nature cannot in itself produce one either. Accordingly, the Augustinian-dispensational perspective holds that a holy life is possible only by the grace of God and the enablement that God has provided for every Christian. The ultimate sanctification of believers in heaven is assured, but Christians do not automatically experience sanctification on earth simply because they have been made new creatures in Christ. On the divine side, it requires provision for the Christian's spiritual need; on the human side, it requires appropriation.

THE REGENERATION OF A PERSON

An essential element of the dramatic change of a person in salvation is the work of the Holy Spirit in regeneration, the renewal that takes place at the moment of salvation. The word *regeneration* (Gk. *palingenesia*) is used only twice in the New Testament (Matt. 19:28; Titus 3:5 KJV, NASB). Only in Titus 3:5, however, does it describe the new life that a believer receives from God at the time of salvation: "He saved us, not because of righteous things we had done, but because of his mercy. He saved us through the washing of rebirth [Gk. *palingenesia*] and renewal by the Holy Spirit." The concept of regeneration, however, is prominent in Protestant theology, for over the centuries the church has debated its meaning in relation to that of such terms as *conversion, sanctification,* and *justification.* In contemporary Reformed theology, *regeneration* relates to the impartation of eternal life. Charles Hodge states,

> By consent almost universal the word *regeneration* is now used to designate, not the whole work of sanctification, nor the first stages of that work, comprehended in conversion, must less justification or any mere external change of state, but the instantaneous change from spiritual death to spiritual life.[24]

In this sense a redeemed person is a new creation in Christ, for he or she has received eternal life.

In Scripture, regeneration embodies the meaning of three figures.[25] First, regeneration is a new birth, or being "born again" (John 3:7). As natural birth is the product of human parentage, so the divine birth relates a believer in Christ to the eternal life that is in God.

A second figure used in the Bible compares the new birth with spiritual resurrection (John 5:25; Eph. 2:5–6; Col. 2:12; 3:1–2). Christians are described as "those who have been brought from death to life" (Rom. 6:13).

A third figure is used in the term "new creation": "Therefore, if anyone is in Christ, he is a new creation; the old has gone, the new has come!" (2 Cor. 5:17) On the basis of being a new creation and having its new perspective, the Christian is exhorted to manifest good works and a transformed life (Eph. 2:10; 4:24).

Following Augustine, Reformed theology views regeneration as distinctively a work of God that is accomplished, not by means, but immediately by the Holy Spirit at the same time one places faith in Christ. Although producing experience, regeneration in itself is not an experience and is inseparable from salvation.

Insofar as regeneration involves the bestowal of eternal life it is also inseparable from the new nature given to the regenerated person. All spiritual experience that follows temporally the act of regeneration characterizes the new creation that it has brought about. In Reformed theology the act of regeneration is irreversible and results in the eternal security of a believer in Christ. Once saved, regenerated persons no longer question their salvation but are prepared to confront the problem of experiential sanctification. From Scripture, regeneration in itself clearly does not bring perfection of character or freedom from a sin nature.

THE BAPTISM OF THE HOLY SPIRIT

Though there is general agreement in Reformed theology on the doctrine of regeneration, the meaning of the baptism of the Holy Spirit has frequently been debated.[26] For dispensationalists, sanctification rests upon the foundation of Reformed theology, but in the doctrine of the baptism of the Holy Spirit there is a departure from, or at least a further refinement of, previous Reformed theology. In general the doctrine of the baptism of the Spirit has been ignored in Reformed theology, as illustrated in Abraham Kuyper's *Work of the Holy Spirit*. This volume of more than six hundred pages contains no discussion of the baptism of the Spirit.[27]

Confusion in understanding the baptism of the Holy Spirit has accompanied confusion over the nature of the church in the present age. Although the baptism of the Spirit is not mentioned in the Old Testament, many have taught that the saints of all the ages belong to the church. Dispensationalists, however, hold that the church consists only of saints of the present age. Some scholars have also mistakenly identified the baptism of the Spirit with either regeneration, the indwelling of the Spirit, the filling of the Spirit, or the manifestation of various gifts of the Spirit. The truth becomes clear, however, by careful attention to the use of the term in the New Testament.

In the four Gospels, the baptism of the Spirit is always mentioned as a future work of God (Matt. 3:11; Mark 1:8; Luke 3:16; John 1:33). Even in Acts 1:5, shortly before the ascension of Christ, the baptism of the Spirit is still regarded as a future event. In later Scriptures, however, it is viewed (as far as believers are concerned) as something that has already occurred (Acts 11:16; 1 Cor. 12:13; cf. Gal. 3:27; Eph. 4:5; Col. 2:12).

Much of the confusion on the doctrine is avoided by proper exegesis of 1 Corinthians 12:13, the definitive text: "For we were all baptized by one Spirit into one body—whether Jews or Greeks, slave or free—and we were all given the one Spirit to drink." According to this verse, the baptism of the Spirit is the placing of the believer "into one body," that is, the church. The human body is used as a figure of all believers, who are repeatedly referred to as "in Christ." This relation fulfills the prophecy of Christ in John 14:20, "On that day you will realize that I am in my Father, and you are in me, and I am in you." The concept of believers as forming a living body whose head is Christ (1 Cor. 11:3; Eph. 1:22–23; 5:23–24; Col. 1:18) is a spiritual and theological truth that is peculiar to the present age.

The definitive character of the baptism of the Spirit as embodied in New Testament revelation leads to the dispensational concept that the church is a term relating to the present age only. Though the word *church* [Gk. *ekklesia*) is found frequently in the Old Testament Septuagint, it there refers only to a local assembly that is geographically related rather than to a body of believers without respect to location. Accordingly, while the word *saint* is properly used of those who are redeemed in every age, dispensationalists hold that the word *church* has specific reference to believers in the present age.

While the doctrine of the baptism of the Spirit has largely been neglected in Reformed circles, it has attracted a good deal of attention in current Pentecostal teaching as well as in dispensational theology. James D. G. Dunn's *Baptism in the Holy Spirit* illustrates the renewed attention to the baptism of the Holy Spirit. This study critiques Pentecostalism and its understanding of the New Testament doctrine of spiritual gifts. Although Dunn's concept of the baptism of the Spirit is not always accurately defined, he does see it as "a figurative way of describing the act of God which puts a man 'in Christ.' "[28] While Dunn stops short in some respects of embracing the full-orbed doctrine of the baptism of the Spirit as held by dispensationalists, he comes remarkably close. The book is noteworthy for the attention given by a non-Pentecostal to the doctrine of the baptism of the Spirit.

The concept of the church as being in Christ introduces a significant element in the dispensational understanding of sanctification, a concept that is often referred to as "positional sanctification." In his discussion entitled "Seven Figures of the Church," Lewis Sperry Chafer comments at length on the believer's position "in Christ." Chafer develops the concept of the church as a new creation and refers to several New Testament passages (2 Cor. 5:17–18; Gal. 3:27–28; 6:15; Eph. 2:10, 15; 4:21–24; Col. 3:9–10).[29]

Because every believer is equal in having a position in Christ, a relationship that has never changed, it is the basis for the common use in the New Testament of the word *saint*. The great majority of allusions to sanctification in the New Testament are in the use of the word *saint*, which is used indiscriminately for all genuine Christians. Although *saint* applies to the redeemed of all the ages, in the present age it means in particular one who is baptized by the Holy Spirit into the body of Christ, and this baptism is never mentioned as an accomplished fact before Pentecost or as a future work after the second coming of Christ.

The baptism of the Holy Spirit, which occurred first on the Day of Pentecost (contrast Acts 1:5 with 11:16), identifies the believer with Christ in His death, burial, and resurrection (Rom. 6:1–4; Col. 2:12). This identification is not simply one of divine reckoning but is also related to our union with Christ in eternal life as embodied in the concept of regeneration.

The baptism of the Holy Spirit should not be confused with the filling of the Spirit, as is commonly done, just because both occurred at the same time on the Day of Pentecost, nor should it be confused with the indwelling of the Holy Spirit, which also occurred on the Day of Pentecost. The act of baptism of the Spirit is a once-for-all work of God at the moment of salvation, placing the believer into living union with all fellow believers and with Christ. This new union is an essential ingredient in God's program of sanctification, providing at once a new position in Christ, which is a complete and finished work, and (at the same time) a unity with Christ as the Head and with the church as the body of Christ. From this union spring spiritual fellowship, the capacity to bear fruit, the supply of spiritual power, and the direction that Christ, who is the head of the church, gives to the members of His body. This truth, accordingly, is foundational and essential to the doctrine of salvation as well as to the doctrine of sanctification. Failure to comprehend the distinctive character of the baptism of the Spirit is a major cause of confusion in understanding the work of the Holy Spirit in and for the believer and the work of God in the progressive sanctification and maturity of the members of Christ's body.

THE INDWELLING OF THE HOLY SPIRIT

Though the work of the Holy Spirit may be traced throughout the entire Scriptures and is intrinsic in every work of God from eternity past to eternity future, a distinct new provision of the Spirit's presence has been realized since the Day of Pentecost. The Old Testament records occasional special ministries of the Holy Spirit in enabling individuals to perform some task for God. We assume that the Spirit of God worked in the prophets and in the writers of Scripture as well as in the sanctification of those who were saved. The universal indwelling of the Holy Spirit, however, was not realized until the Day of Pentecost, as indicated in the prophecies of Christ that the indwelling was yet future.[30]

In the four Gospels, just as there was prophecy concerning the future baptism of the Spirit, so Christ prophesied a new, distinct ministry of the Holy Spirit:

> On the last and greatest day of the Feast, Jesus stood and said in a loud voice, "If a man is thirsty, let him come to me and drink. Whoever believes in me, as the Scripture has said, streams of living water will flow from within him." By this he meant the Spirit, whom those who believed in him were later to receive. Up to that time the Spirit had not been given, since Jesus had not yet been glorified. (John 7:37–39)

This passage clearly distinguishes the past ministry of the Spirit from that which is future.

The night before His crucifixion Christ announced again this new ministry of the Spirit: "And I will ask the Father, and he will give you another Counselor to be with you forever—the Spirit of truth. The world cannot accept him, because it neither sees him nor knows him. But you know him, for he lives with you and will be in you" (John 14:16–17). Before His ascension into heaven, Christ also instructed the disciples concerning the future work of the Spirit, speaking of the Spirit's future baptism (Acts 1:4–5) and infilling (v. 8). Subsequent to Pentecost the Holy Spirit's indwelling is mentioned repeatedly (Acts 11:17; Rom. 5:5; 8:9, 11; 1 Cor. 2:12; 6:19–20; 12:13; 2 Cor. 5:5; Gal. 3:2; 4:6; 1 John 3:24; 4:13). It should be obvious from these many references that the indwelling presence of the Holy Spirit is one of the outstanding evidences of the salvation of the individual and also the means by which God can effect sanctification in the experiential and progressive sense.

It is impossible to overestimate the importance of the Spirit's residence in a new convert. His very presence is a proof of divine ownership, of security and grace, and of God's intention to produce through the new convert the fruit of salvation. The Holy Spirit is God's seal of ownership (2 Cor. 1:22; 5:5; Eph. 1:14). The fact that the Holy Spirit indwells believers makes their body His temple (1 Cor. 6:19). The presence of the Holy Spirit is also God's seal of security for believers in respect to salvation, certifying God's purpose to present them perfect in heaven. The indwelling of the Holy

Spirit, like the baptism of the Spirit and the regeneration of the Spirit, is accomplished once for all at the moment of salvation and provides the basis for God's future work of grace, namely, sanctification and ultimate glorification. With the presence of the Holy Spirit come spiritual gifts and the possibility of their exercise in the power and blessing of God.

THE FILLING OF THE HOLY SPIRIT

Though all Christians are regenerated by the Spirit, baptized by the Spirit, indwelt by the Spirit, and sealed by the Spirit, not all Christians are filled with the Spirit. This important variable explains the wide difference in spiritual experience and spiritual power that exists among various Christians. The filling of the Spirit is the source of all important ministries of the Spirit in believers subsequent to their salvation. The filling of the Spirit is not to be confused with experiences that precede salvation (such as the conviction of the Spirit), nor is it to be confused with the works that occur once and for all at the time of salvation. The filling of the Spirit is a work of God that occurs repeatedly in the life of believers, and as such it is obviously the source of sanctification as well as all spiritual fruitfulness.[31]

The quality of spirituality in a Christian is variously demonstrated throughout life. A new believer may be immature and quite ignorant of God and His truth but even so can have a measure of spirituality and can experience the filling of the Spirit, as illustrated by the conversion of Cornelius (Acts 10) and the conversion of John's disciples (Acts 19). As Christians mature, however, their spirituality may deepen and broaden and take on new characteristics. Accordingly, spirituality, while related to maturity, is the quality of spiritual life in a believer at any given moment. With growth and maturity, spirituality may clearly become more significant and effective. The combined qualities of spirituality, or filling of the Spirit, and spiritual maturity, which is achieved gradually, are the two major factors that determine the quality of a Christian's spiritual life.

Though various definitions of the filling of the Spirit have been given, the term refers basically to the unhindered ministry of the Holy Spirit in the life of a Christian. Such ministry brings for the time being a control of a believer's life by the Holy Spirit and the infusion of spiritual power, enabling a Christian to do far more than he or she could do naturally. Such spiritual control of a Christian, however, is not permanent and is dependent upon the constant renewed filling of the Spirit.

In the Old Testament, the filling of the Spirit seems to be primarily related to useful service for God and sometimes is connected with skills of various kinds. In the New Testament, the filling of the Spirit is more related to spirituality and to a spiritual state in activity that is associated with God's will for the individual Christian. In all, there are fifteen New Testament references to the filling of the Spirit. The Greek verb most commonly used is *plēthō* (Luke 1:15, 41, 67; Acts 2:4; 4:8, 31; 9:17; 13:9). The verb *plēroō* is used in Acts 13:52 and Ephesians 5:18, the latter being one of the most important New Testament references on this subject. Both verbs are built on the stem *ple.* Five instances of the adjective *plērēs* are also found in connection with the Spirit's filling (Luke 4:1; Acts 6:3, 5; 7:55; 11:24).

In all of these instances, excluding the exceptional case of the infant (John the Baptist, Luke 1:15), the believer who is filled with the Spirit does not get more of the Spirit quantitatively, but rather the Spirit is able to minister in an unhindered way in the believer and in a sense has all of the believer. Accordingly, the issue is not one of getting more of the presence of God but rather of realizing the power and ministry of God's presence in the believer's life.

Early references in the Gospels to the filling of the Spirit as it was experienced by Christ (Luke 4:1), by John the Baptist (1:15), and by John's parents, Elizabeth and Zechariah (vv. 41, 67), are anticipations of similar experiences of Christians in the Book of Acts. A milestone in the filling of the Spirit is observed on the Day of Pentecost, when all the Christians were filled with the Spirit (Acts 2:4). Subsequent experiences of filling are recorded in the case of Peter before the Sanhedrin (4:8) and that of the early Christians after praying together (4:31). Later instances include the filling of the Spirit in the lives of Stephen (6:3, 5; 7:55), Paul (9:17), Barnabas (11:24), and the disciples at Antioch in Pisidia (13:52). In every instance, the filling of the Spirit signifies the empowering presence of the Spirit of God, enabling the individual to accomplish the will of God.

One of the most important texts in the New Testament is Ephesians 5:18, where Paul declares, "Do not get drunk on wine, which leads to debauchery. Instead, be filled with the Spirit." The work of the Holy Spirit is both illustrated by and contrasted with the effect produced by wine. Just as wine with its alcoholic content permeates the entire body of an individual and changes one's capacity to act, so the Spirit fills an individual and enables that one to fulfill the will of God. As is implied in the command to be filled with the Spirit, a person can be a Christian without being filled with the Spirit. The same individual may be filled at one time and not at another. This operation contrasts with the permanent works of the Holy Spirit that are wrought at salvation (such as regeneration, baptism, and indwelling).

In the Greek of Ephesians 5:18, the verb rendered "be filled" is in the present tense, which suggests the meaning of "keep on being filled." The Spirit's filling, therefore, is related to experience, which extends over a period of time, in contrast to the baptism of the Spirit, with which it is often confused. The Greek verb rendered "baptized" in 1 Corinthians 12:13 is in the aorist tense, which indicates a single definitive act occurring once for all. With respect to the filling of the Spirit, however, an individual may seek to have an experience of being controlled and empowered by Him on a repeated and moment-by-moment basis. If the Holy Spirit's filling of the believer is a central aspect of a believer's spiritual life, it then raises the question of what a Christian can do to receive this filling.

The New Testament is clear that the filling of the Spirit results when Christians meet the necessary conditions. Early in His ministry, Christ stated that no one can serve two masters (Matt. 6:24). The issue facing Christians after their conversion is whether they will submit completely to the will of God. This issue is raised repeatedly in Romans as Paul deals with the outworking of salvation in terms of the doctrine of sanctification. He challenges his readers to yield themselves to God, as, for example, in Romans 6:11–14.

> In the same way, count yourselves dead to sin but alive to God in Christ Jesus. Therefore do not let sin reign in your mortal body so that you obey its evil desires. Do not offer the parts of your body to sin, as instruments of wickedness, but rather offer yourselves to God, as those who have been brought from death to life; and offer the parts of your body to him as instruments of righteousness. For sin shall not be your master, because you are not under law, but under grace.

In this passage, Paul contrasts offering one's body to repeated acts of sin with offering oneself to God as a definite

218 | Five Views on Sanctification

act. (Paul uses the present tense in the commands "do not let sin reign" and "do not [continue to] offer the parts of your body to sin" but uses the aorist tense in the command "offer yourselves to God.") This offering to God is the initial act of recognizing the lordship of Jesus Christ and the right of the Holy Spirit to control and direct the life of a believer. This same truth is emphasized in Romans 12:1–2, where the exhortation summarizes the implications of all the previous theological material in the Book of Romans. Here Paul writes, "Therefore, I urge you, brothers, in view of God's mercy, to offer your bodies as living sacrifices, holy and pleasing to God—which is your spiritual worship. Do not conform any longer to the pattern of this world, but be transformed by the renewing of your mind. Then you will be able to test and approve what God's will is— his good, pleasing and perfect will." Furthermore, the initial act of yieldedness should continue, an imperative that is suggested in 1 Thessalonians 5:19 ("Do not put out the Spirit's fire."). In other words, do not resist or say no to the Spirit.

The experience of continued filling of the Spirit involves the believer in a relationship to God in a number of particular areas. First of all, a believer must understand and be yielded to the will of God as it is revealed in the Scriptures. As Christians gain experience and maturity and fuller revelation of His will, they must continually obey the commands of Scripture and yield to the Holy Spirit as conditions for continued filling. Note that guidance for the Christian life must be distinguished from Scriptural revelation. Scriptural revelation provides the general principles and moral standards of conduct, whereas guidance is the application of the general teaching to the individual's personal life.

Another most important area to which Christians must yield is the providential work of God in their life, which often includes undesired experiences of sorrow, disappointment, and frustration. Submitting to God's providential dealing fosters additional maturity and insight into truth about God and His ways.

The supreme illustration of the filling of the Spirit is provided in Christ Himself, as stated in the familiar passage of Philippians 2:5–11. In His own yieldedness to the will and plan of God, Christ submitted to the limitations of being a man on earth, to the trials and temptations that this brought into His experience, and to His ultimate humiliation in dying on the cross for the sins of the world. This passage describes Christ as willing to be what God chose, willing to go where God chose, and willing to do what God chose. This high standard of conformity and yieldedness to the will of God is the example and standard for the individual Christian. The filling of the Spirit, as Christ demonstrated most perfectly, is possible only as the Holy Spirit empowers and controls one's life.

Speaking realistically, however, we know that Christians fall into sin. This experience does not reverse one's salvation, nor does it cause one to lose the Holy Spirit, but it must be corrected. This requirement is referred to in Ephesians 4:30, where Paul taught, "And do not [continue to] grieve the Holy Spirit of God, with whom you were sealed for the day of redemption." Here the indwelling presence of the Holy Spirit is referred to as God's seal, the evidence of His ownership and the safety and security of the believer in Christ. Since the Holy Spirit does indwell the believer, any sin that he or she commits grieves Him.

Grieving the Holy Spirit begins as an initial act of rebellion, or of resisting the Spirit. Resisting the Spirit not only grieves Him but also hinders His ministry to the individual and makes it impossible for His full-orbed work to be manifested in one's life. This resistance affects one's fellowship with God, fruitfulness, and discernment of spiritual truth. However, just as God provides salvation for the lost sinner, so He provides restoration for the sinning saint. In 1 John 1:9, the apostle, aware of our spiritual experience and needs, offers this solution: "If we confess our sins, he is faithful and just and will forgive us our sins and purify us from all unrighteousness." By confessing their sin, Christians acknowledge that what they have done is contrary to God's will. In that confession, they seek forgiveness, which is already provided in their salvation, and seek the restoration that only God can provide in grace. Just as salvation is conditioned on faith (believing in Christ), so restoration is dependent on confession of sin. Believers are assured that God will forgive and purify and is perfectly just in doing so because of the full atonement provided in Christ. Confession is the human side, but on the divine side the apostle John goes on in 1 John 2:1–2 to speak of the advocacy of Christ as the believer's High Priest in heaven: "My dear children, I write this to you so that you will not sin. But if anybody does sin, we have one who speaks to the Father in our defense—Jesus Christ, the Righteous One. He is the atoning sacrifice for our sins, and not only for ours but also for the sins of the whole world."

Although forgiveness is by grace, believers are warned against continuing in sin, for God will discipline His children who are straying from Him. In this connection, Paul instructed the Corinthian church in 1 Corinthians 11:31–32, "But if we judged ourselves, we would not come under judgment. When we are judged by the Lord, we are being disciplined so that we will not be condemned with the world." As Hebrews 12:5–6 indicates, the discipline of God is not to be taken lightly. Peter exhorts Christians not to suffer as sinners (1 Peter 4:14–15). To be filled with the Spirit involves yieldedness and then, whenever there is departure from the will of God, confession of sin.

Probably the most difficult aspect of the spiritual life is to obey fully the exhortation found in Galatians 5:16 ("So I say, live by the Spirit, and you will not gratify the desires of the sinful nature."). The word "live" is literally "walk" (see KJV and NASB). Walking by the Spirit involves continued dependence. When people walk physically, they depend upon the strength of their limbs to support their body. Christians going through life must likewise walk spiritually in constant dependence upon the Holy Spirit. Variations in conscious dependence upon Him correspond to the variations in people's experience of being filled with the Spirit. The exhortation teaches clearly that the spiritual life must be lived moment by moment in relationship to the Holy Spirit as the Christian's source of strength and direction for life. The program of God for the Christian's sanctification must be viewed in the context of the doctrine of the Holy Spirit both in salvation and in the everyday life of the Christian, with full recognition, on the one hand, of the believer's new nature secured in salvation and, on the other hand, of the believer's sin nature carried over from the former life.

THE RESULTING EXPERIENCE OF PROGRESSIVE SANCTIFICATION

Although a believer in Christ still has the potential for grievous sin and personally cannot attain anything corresponding to God's standard of sanctification, yet because of the indwelling presence of the Holy Spirit and His power and direction, a Christian can progressively grow in sanctification. Although the old nature is present, by the power of the Spirit the new nature can be enabled to manifest the fruit of the Spirit, namely, "love, joy, peace, patience, kindness, goodness, faithfulness, gentleness and self-control" (Gal. 5:22–23). This fruit of the Spirit, which was manifested supremely in Christ, is possible for a believer, not in one's own strength or because of one's new nature, but as a result of the Spirit of God using the human body as His instrument for manifesting these evidences of God's grace. In this sense a believer can be Christlike, even in this life. This fruit of the Spirit is also related to the vital union of a believer in Christ, as illustrated in Christ's discourse on the vine and the branches (John 15). Believers, because of their relationship to Christ as well as to the Holy Spirit, are able to bear fruit, but as the dependence of the branch upon the vine illustrates, they are at the same time dependent upon the Holy Spirit for the manifestation of any evidences of sanctification in their lives.

The progressive sanctification of believers also results in their service for God. The Scriptures are clear that every aspect of believers' ministry on God's behalf is a result of the work of the Spirit and a part of their increasing sanctification. As mentioned above, Christians, by applying God's Word, can be guided as to God's particular will for their lives. Guidance becomes one of the more important evidences, not only of salvation, but also of spirituality. Progressive sanctification also brings with it increasing assurance that one is a child of God. As Paul mentions in Romans 8:16, "The Spirit himself testifies with our spirit that we are God's children." While Scripture teaches that Christians are secure in their salvation as a work of God, their experience and assurance of salvation are often related to their walk with the Lord and the ministry of the Spirit to them.

The Holy Spirit ministers also in true worship, in which Christians can lift their heart in adoration and praise to God, who is the source of all their grace and blessing. In connection with the filling of the Spirit, Ephesians 5:19–20 speaks of worship in the form of "psalms, hymns and spiritual songs."

The prayer life of the believer is likewise related to the ministry of the Holy Spirit. Because we are often ignorant of our true spiritual needs, the Spirit of God, according to Romans 8:26, has to help us in our prayer to God and offers intercession on our behalf. His ministry to us as believers reveals our true spiritual needs and directs us in seeking the guidance and will of God for our life.

The Spirit of God in His progressive sanctification also makes possible a Christian's service for the Lord as a source to others of the "streams of living water" that Christ predicted in John 7:38–39. The inexhaustible source of this water is the Holy Spirit Himself. From the Spirit of God working in the believer in unhindered ministry, a mighty work for God can be accomplished.

THE RELATION OF SOVEREIGN GRACE TO HUMAN RESPONSIBILITY

The issue of the interrelation of sovereign grace and human responsibility is intrinsic to the whole consideration of divine sanctification. Characteristically, Arminian theology emphasizes human responsibility and Calvinistic theology emphasizes divine sovereignty. All agree, however, that grace is essential for an unbeliever to become a Christian. Differences arise in explaining how this grace operates at the moment of salvation. Careful students of the subject agree that there are essentially inscrutable elements in the process of a fallen person's believing in Christ and finding salvation, but some aspects do require definition.

Calvinists confidently assume, from abundant Scriptures, that those who are saved have been elected to salvation before the foundation of the world. It was God's sovereign purpose that elect individuals, at some point in their life, should come to the moment of complete salvation in Christ. The question is how someone who is dead spiritually and incapable of faith comes to the place of believing and being saved.

Christ in the Upper Room stated that when the Spirit of God came, He would deal with this problem, for "he will convict the world of guilt in regard to sin and righteousness and judgment: in regard to sin, because men do not believe in me; in regard to righteousness, because I am going to the Father, where you can see me no longer; and in regard to judgment, because the prince of this world now stands condemned" (John 16:8–11). Properly interpreted, this passage deals with the experience of individuals prior to conversion and indicates a process by which the Holy Spirit graciously reveals to fallen persons the nature of salvation and their need of it. A person can experience conviction, however, without then coming to Christ as Savior. In theological terms, the convicting work of the Spirit is preparatory rather than efficacious in salvation. The Scriptures indicate that at the moment of salvation an unsaved person believes in Christ. The Gospel of

John repeatedly refers to the necessity of faith in Christ for salvation. According to John 20:31, the main purpose of John's writing was "that you may believe that Jesus is the Christ, the Son of God, and that by believing you may have life in his name." But how can a fallen person who is dead in sin believe?

The answer given by Arminians and Calvinists alike is that grace is administered, although how this is accomplished is not entirely clear from Scripture. God's grace at salvation is both supernatural and also effective. Calvinists, accordingly, refer to it as efficacious, or irresistible, and Arminians refer to it as sufficient.

The controversy between Arminians and Calvinists culminated in the Synod of Dort (1618–19), at which Arminianism was condemned and Calvinism asserted in the strongest possible terms. In the process, confusion arose between grace administered to enable a person to believe and regeneration, which is the bestowal of eternal life on the believers, for the synod seems to have identified the two as the same. More moderate Calvinists, however, while agreeing that the work of God in grace and regeneration occurs at the same time, see a cause-and-effect relationship that makes grace the enabling power given to a person to believe and regeneration as a result of believing. The Synod of Dort seems to teach that regeneration precedes faith, and in this case the sovereignty of God prevails and a person, for all practical purposes, is a robot who does not actively participate in his or her own salvation.

This emphasis on the sovereignty of God and on salvation as something that is wholly God's work is sometimes carried over into the doctrine of sanctification. Some Calvinists historically have taken the position that world-wide preaching of the gospel was unnecessary (if God elected people to salvation, He would see to it that they were saved), and some likewise have viewed sanctification as a sovereign work of God in which human beings participates only incidentally. While most Calvinists allow a place for human responsibility, the tendency to emphasize the sovereignty of God at the expense of human interaction has, to some extent, continued to permeate the Calvinistic approach to sanctification.

Some of the typical differences between the Augustinian-dispensational approach to sanctification and that of contemporary Reformed theology are reflected in B. B. Warfield's critique of Lewis Sperry Chafer's book *He That is Spiritual*. In his thoughtful review, which appeared shortly after the book was originally published, Warfield finds that Chafer, to a large degree,

> makes use of all the jargon of the Higher Life teachers. In him, too, we hear of two kinds of Christians, whom he designates respectively "carnal man" and "spiritual man," on the basis of a misreading of I Cor. ii. 9 ff (pp. 8, 109, 146); and we are told that the passage from one to the other is at our option, whenever we care to "claim" the higher degree "by faith" (p. 146).[32]

Warfield objects to Chafer's point of view because he considers it a blending of Arminian and Calvinistic theology. According to Warfield,

> These two religious systems are quite incompatible. The one is the product of the Protestant Reformation and knows no determining power in the religious life but the grace of God; the other comes straight from the laboratory of John Wesley, and in all its forms—modifications and mitigations alike—remains incurably Arminian, subjecting all gracious workings of God to human determining. The two can unite as little as fire and water.[33]

In general, dispensationalists, while usually Calvinistic, object to making conversion and sanctification wholly the sovereign acts of God apart from human participation. Though agreeing that both conversion and sanctification flow from the grace of God and that it is impossible for people to accomplish either one by themselves, dispensationalists hold that the many exhortations of Scripture become meaningless if there is not some human responsibility associated with these aspects of salvation. To eliminate the element of human responsibility is to carry the sovereignty of God beyond what the Bible indicates. The truth is that God has sovereignly given human beings a will that, in the case of Christians, has been supernaturally and graciously enabled to make choices. These choices are critical for a person's experience of sanctification in this present life. The contemporary Augustinian-dispensational perspective on sanctification embraces not Arminianism but a more moderate type of Calvinism than that which the Synod of Dort approved. Chafer's view of sanctification and the spiritual life, instead of being ambiguous and contradictory, actually brings together the sovereignty of God and human responsibility, which is assumed in Scripture in every exhortation.

In comprehending the work of God in conversion, we must

balance God's sovereign act and man's human response in obedience. In sanctification also, the Scriptures affirm that God is the sanctifier and that He accomplishes in individuals what they could not accomplish by themselves. At the same time, however, the Scriptures are just as clear that people are responsible for responding to the truth of God and to the work of the Holy Spirit, which permits God to work out His program of sanctification. In the New Testament revelation of the grace of God as manifested in Christ, a person is never put under the conditional blessings outlined in the Mosaic covenant, where blessing was conditioned on obedience.

In the New Testament, however, one's experience of sanctification is clearly conditioned on one's response to the sanctification that the Holy Spirit intends to provide. Accordingly, the New Testament is full of exhortations that encourage believers to respond to God's revealed will and by faith and appropriation to avail themselves of the power of the indwelling Holy Spirit, the power of the Word of God, and all the other elements of the contemporary experience of grace. Though sanctification is the work of God in the heart of an individual, it is accomplished only in harmony with the human response. Most scholars agree, however, that in spite of imperfect response to the grace of God and a resulting imperfect sanctification in this life, believers' standing in the presence of God in heaven will be perfect, not by human attainment, but by the divine grace of God and the sovereign purpose of God to make them like Christ. While sanctification in our present life is sovereignly determined by God to be conditioned on human response, ultimate sanctification is assured, regardless of human imperfections.

ULTIMATE PERFECTION IN HEAVEN

Though Christians can have relative perfection in this life and can often manifest godliness in a significant way, the degree of their perfection is limited until they stand in God's presence in heaven. This truth is clearly taught in Scripture, though relatively few passages deal with it directly. Ephesians 5:25–27 is one such passage. It deals with the whole work of Christ for His church—including His death on the cross, His present work of sanctification, and His future perfecting of the church. He will "present her [the church] to himself as a radiant church, without stain or wrinkle or any other blemish, but holy and blameless." In heaven the believer will be as perfect as Christ is. The apostle John also speaks of this condition when he states, "But we know that when he appears, we shall be like him, for we shall see him as he is" (1 John 3:2). Though believers' present position in Christ is perfect, their spiritual state maintains some imperfection until they stand in the presence of God in heaven. At that point, their sin nature will be no more, and sin will depart forever from their spiritual experience.

In Scripture, from beginning to end, sanctification is the work of God for human beings rather than their work for Him. It is grounded in the death of Christ, which makes it possible. It is continued in the present ministry of the Holy Spirit in the life of the Christian and is ultimately perfected as the Christian stands in God's presence—forever free from sin, with its guilt and stain. The believer is destined to reflect forever the holiness of God, as an example of what the grace of God can do. The Christian doctrine of sanctification is separated forever from human attainment and is thus totally removed from all legalistic systems of non-Christian religions. In the end, sanctification is all to the glory of God and an evidence of His infinite perfections.

BIBLIOGRAPHY

Chafer, Lewis S. *Systematic Theology.* 8 vols. Dallas: Dallas Theological Seminary, 1947–48.
Dunn, James D. G. *Baptism in the Holy Spirit.* Naperville, Ill.: Allenson, 1970.
Hegre, T. A. *The Cross and Sanctification.* Minneapolis: Bethany Fellowship, 1960.
Kuyper, Abraham. *The Work of the Holy Spirit.* Trans. Henri de Vries. New York: Funk & Wagnalls, 1900.
Needham, David C. *Birthright.* Portland: Multnomah, 1979.
Ryrie, Charles C. *Balancing the Christian Life.* Chicago: Moody, 1969.
Walvoord, John F. *The Holy Spirit.* Findley, Ohio: Dunham, 1958.
Warfield, Benjamin B. *The Person and Work of Christ.* Ed. Samuel C. Craig. Philadelphia: Presbyterian and Reformed, 1950.

Response to Walvoord

Melvin E. Dieter

John Walvoord's extended discussion of the meaning of *nature* as it is used to describe the state of men and women after their new birth in Jesus Christ is very helpful. It moves the discussion away from the concept of the old nature as some substantial, quantifiable element of sin in the life of the believer to the more holistic biblical understanding of remaining sin as a capacity to sin, or the inclination or propensity to sin. Similarly, the essence of the new nature may be described as the inclination to obedience and righteousness. This understanding moves the issue toward the Wesleyan contention that the essential problem in the sanctification of the Christian life is not one of fixed polarities that are set in constant confrontation and war. Rather, the basic concerns are those of the proper adjudication of relationships between persons—between God and individuals, and individuals with each other.

If one further allows that sin may be defined better as a failure of love rather than as concupiscence, as in the classical Augustinian definition, then the remedy is a divine work of grace. This operation releases the new nature granted the believer through justification and regeneration from the bent to sinning, which best describes the nature of humankind after the Fall. Individuals may be free to love and obey the divine will. Because the heart of the biblical truth of sanctification is faith working by love, Wesley felt confident in narrowing his definition of sin to that of the voluntary transgression of known law. In this area, men and women need the freedom to be able not to sin, to be spiritual persons. A willing heart is what God promises in Christian perfection, not the knowledge of maturity or perfection of action. In all these latter areas of imperfection, the blood of Jesus Christ cleanses from all sin as we walk in the light by His grace and power.

Walvoord's dispensationalist views of the life of Christian holiness are also very close to the Wesleyan position on the work of the Spirit, including the baptism and infilling of the Spirit. Although many Wesleyans and Pentecostals would disagree on his understanding of the baptism of the Spirit as being restricted to the initial baptism into the body of Christ and would use the language of Spirit-baptism to describe the crisis of entire sanctification and the filling of the Spirit, they would readily agree with Walvoord's excellent statement that "the believer who is filled with the Spirit does not get more of the Spirit quantitatively, but rather the Spirit is able to minister in an unhindered way in the believer and in a sense has all of the believer" (p. 216).

Walvoord comes even closer to the Wesleyan understanding of the work of the Spirit in the entirely cleansed and Spirit-filled life when he describes the necessity for the Spirit's infilling for the accomplishment of God's will. He falters, however, when he notes that the infilling may not be as permanent or steady as the work of the Spirit in regeneration and indwelling. Such a contrast is not necessary in the Wesleyan understanding, because the permanence of all these works of grace depends on a willing heart and an unbroken relationship with God in Christ and rests on faith and the power of the Spirit, just as our initiation into the Christian life did. The strictures on the permanence of this subsequent work of the Spirit lie in the presuppositions of a Reformed understanding of election and perseverance that is readily applied to the first works but not to the ongoing relationships of life in the Spirit in the freedom from sin, even though Walvoord eloquently describes this freedom in his challenge to Christians to let sin be their master no longer, because they are no longer under law but under grace.

Walvoord's general description of the entrance into the Spirit-filled life is one that most Wesleyans would accept. When the infilling of the Spirit takes place, something happens that clears the way for a more stable and rich experience of God and for more powerful service to God than could have been realized otherwise. His section "The Resulting Experience of Progressive Sanctification" Wesleyans would probably entitle "Growth in Grace," "Going on to Maturity," or "The Experience of Practical Sanctification." When the heart is cleansed and flooded with the presence and love of God, it is ready to grow in grace and to know God more intimately each succeeding day as life is lived in the ongoing reality of that moment of total commitment.

Finally, Walvoord rightly understands the tension in Scripture between divine sovereignty and human response in salvation and sanctification, although it would seem that the presuppositions of evangelical Arminianism, as closely related as they were in Wesley to the heart of the Reformed tradition, would make for a smoother explication of Walvoord's strongly biblically supported concerns for Christian holiness. Benjamin Warfield was probably right when he noted the significant shift toward Wesleyanism that Calvinists made who began to take seriously the biblical injunctions to lead a Spirit-filled life. It is very difficult to apply consistently the nature of the divine-human relationship in the initial works of grace in one theological pattern and then to represent the operation of God's grace in a different theological pattern when describing the experience of "the higher Christian life."

Response to Walvoord

Anthony A. Hoekema

The points made in John Walvoord's chapter with which I agree include the following: that the Holy Spirit plays an indispensable role in sanctification, that sanctification involves both sovereign grace and human responsibility, that sanctification must be progressive, and that the baptism of the Holy Spirit means the placing of people into the body of Christ—a divine blessing that is to be distinguished from the filling of the Holy Spirit (see my *Holy Spirit Baptism* [Grand Rapids: Eerdmans, 1972]). I also agree with Walvoord that the regenerated person has eternal security, that the believer cannot attain sinless perfection in this present life, and that such perfection will be reached only in the life to come.

Walvoord's main point, as I see it, is that Christians have two distinct natures: a "sin nature" and a "new nature." The sin nature is described as "a complex of human attributes that demonstrate a desire and predisposition to sin," and the new nature as "a complex of attributes having a predisposition and inclination to righteousness" (p. 206).

I have some difficulty with the expression "sin nature." I prefer the term "sinful nature," which is used in the best-known Reformed creed, the Heidelberg Catechism, and in the NIV. Questions of terminology aside, however, I agree that Christians do have a sinful nature, as defined here, which struggles against the new nature that is received in regeneration. I agree that, according to Galatians 5:16–17, believers must still fight against sinful impulses coming from "the flesh" (the literal translation of the Greek word *sarx*) and that the word *flesh* as used in this text (and in many other New Testament passages) means the tendency within human beings to disobey God in every area of life. I also agree that Christians have a new nature, as defined above.

My basic problem with Walvoord's presentation is that, in my judgment, he fails to do full justice to the fact that a decisive break with sin was brought about by Christ for believers (Rom. 6:6)—so that sin, though still present in the believer, no longer has dominion (v. 14)—and to the amazing truth that the believer is now indeed a new creature, old things having passed away (2 Cor. 5:17). When the author says (p. 209) that "the basic problem of sanctification from the Augustinian-dispensational perspective is how individuals with these two diverse aspects in their total character [the old nature and the new] can achieve at least a relative measure of sanctification and righteousness in their life," he gives the impression that the Christian is something like a spiritual seesaw with two contradictory types of inner tendencies. With both tugging at one's heart, a believer can go either way.

This picture of inner conflict may be true as far it goes, but where does the newness of the Christian enter in? Does not the believer now live a life of victory in the Spirit's strength (Rom. 8:4; 2 Cor. 5:15; Gal. 5:16–24; 1 John 5:4)? Granted, this victory is not sinless perfection, but is it not nevertheless a real victory? Are we not indeed new persons in Christ? Do we not now "walk in newness of life" (Rom. 6:4 RSV)? When Christians look at themselves, should not the emphasis fall on the new rather than on the old? (See my book *The Christian Looks at Himself*, 2d ed. [Grand Rapids: Eerdmans, 1977].)

Walvoord interprets the "old man," or "old self," as meaning "the former life" of the believer, and the "new self" as meaning "the new manner of life stemming from the new nature" (p. 208). I do not believe that this view does justice to Paul's teaching. "Old self" I understand to mean the total person enslaved by sin—this total person we Christians no longer are (Rom. 6:6; Col. 3:9). "New self" means the total person ruled by the Holy Spirit. This new self the believer has put on, but it is being continually renewed (Col. 3:10). Believers, therefore, should see themselves as new persons who are being progressively renewed—*genuinely* new but not yet *totally* new. (The biblical basis for this view of the old and the new self can be found in my chapter, pp. 78–82.)

Another basic point of difference I have is the interpretation of Romans 7:14–25. Walvoord thinks this passage describes the regenerate person's struggle with sin. He quotes from a 1962 article of mine, in which I supported this view. But I have since changed my mind. I now see this passage as a description, seen through the eyes of a regenerate person, of an unregenerate person (e.g., an unconverted Pharisaic Jew) struggling to fight sin through the law alone, apart from the strength of the Spirit. I admit that this position is not the usual Reformed interpretation. I should add that the view of the Christian as a new person does not stand or fall with the exegesis of Romans 7:14–25 here defended.

What is the Scriptural basis for this interpretation? First, Romans 7:14–25 reflects and elaborates on the condition pictured in verse 5: "When we were controlled by the sinful nature, the sinful passions aroused by the law were at work in our bodies, so that we bore fruit for death." This verse obviously describes unregenerate persons, in contrast to the regenerate persons described in verses 4 and 6. Verse 13 reads, "In order that sin might be recognized as sin, it produced death in me through what was good." This passage describes the same type of person pictured in verse 5 (namely, an unregenerate person); note the parallels: sinful passions aroused by the law produced fruit for death (v. 5), and sin, through what was good (i.e., the law), produced death (v. 13). Verses 14 and 15, which begin the controversial passage, have three *fors* in them (see the Greek text, ASV, NASB). By means of these *fors* Paul ties in what follows with what he has just finished saying. The rest of chapter 7, therefore, elaborates on the condition of the unregenerate person described in verses 5 and 13.

Second, there is no mention of the Holy Spirit or of his strength for overcoming sin in Romans 7:14–25, but chapter 8 has at least sixteen references to the Spirit.

Third, the mood of frustration and defeat that permeates this section does not comport with the mood of victory in terms of which Paul usually describes the Christian life. The person pictured is still a captive of the law of sin (7:23), whereas the believer described in 6:17–18 is no longer a slave to sin.

Finally, Romans 7:25 reads: "I of myself serve the law of God with my mind, but with my flesh I serve the law of sin" (RSV). The words "I of myself" are emphatic in the Greek. Paul is here describing a person who tries to "go it alone," to keep God's law in his or her own strength, rather than in the strength of the Spirit. I believe, therefore, that the biblical description of the normal Christian life is found, not in Romans 7:14–25, but in Romans 6 and 8.

Response to Walvoord

Stanley M. Horton

Early Pentecostals felt that the outpouring of the Holy Spirit in the 1906 Azusa Street revival in Los Angeles with its world-wide effects indicated the imminence of Christ's return. Almost without exception they turned away from the postmillennialism of the holiness churches and became strongly premillennial. It was not long before they felt the influence of the Scofield Bible, Blackstone's *Jesus Is Coming,* and Larkin's *Dispensational Truth.* The latter became a textbook in most of our early Bible institutes. This pretribulational premillennialism became a bigger barrier between the Pentecostals and the older holiness (Methodist) groups than our interpretation of the baptism in the Holy Spirit was.

It was necessary, of course, for our writers and teachers to modify the dispensational system to fit our Arminian position and our belief that the gift and gifts of the Holy Spirit are for today. But dispensational charts became popular and are still much used in the Assemblies of God churches today, as are many of the textbooks written by dispensationalists such as John Walvoord. Dispensationalists modify their Calvinism to allow for human responsibility and response, which is one reason Pentecostals can use so many of their books.

With respect to Augustine's view that Romans 7:14–25 refers to the struggle within a Christian, there is no agreement among Pentecostal writers. Some take the view that the passage is descriptive of those under the law. Others, especially those who have had experiences of deep inner conflicts after their conversion, agree with Augustine.

Pentecostals have no disagreement about the two natures in Christ. This position is specified in section 2 of the Assemblies of God "Statement of Fundamental Truths." Section 5 goes on to state that the inward evidence of salvation is the direct witness of the Holy Spirit (Rom. 8:16) and that the outward evidence is a life of righteousness and true holiness (Eph. 4:24; Titus 2:12). Nothing is said in the statement, however, of the continuation of the old nature along with the new, although this view is commonly held. Our writers point out that, if we do not walk in the Spirit, we are walking in the flesh. They also emphasize that the call to a holy life is important because we are in a battle for God and righteousness and against sin. Those who are under the law are under condemnation and cannot enter into the battle. But under grace we are free from sin. God has justified us and released us from sin's bondage so that we can give ourselves to the fight. We must therefore stop giving our bodies over to the flesh, or to sinful desires, and must put ourselves at God's disposal, taking a positive stand for righteousness.

Pentecostals take issue with Walvoord with respect both to the doctrine of eternal security (which we believe is based on human philosophical deductions and ignores the many warnings of Scripture) and to the baptism of the Holy Spirit. We do recognize that in the four Gospels the baptism in the Spirit is always mentioned as a future work of God, but we dispute Walvoord's interpretation of 1 Corinthians 12:13. In the entire passage the Spirit is the agent giving the gifts. The baptism in this verse is thus very definitely by the Spirit into the body of Christ (at the time of regeneration) and is therefore distinct from the baptism by Christ into the Holy Spirit on the Day of Pentecost. This understanding fits well with the distinction between conversion and the baptism in the Holy Spirit found in the Book of Acts. It has been observed that the rejection of this position often leads to a downward trend that ends in the neglect of the work of the Spirit in the believer's life. As Walvoord admits, this neglect of the Holy Spirit has been all too common in Reformed theology. However, the attention given by Dunn to the Holy Spirit is weak exegetically, and he contradicts himself in places. Pentecostal scholars have been able to answer his arguments, as well as similar arguments by dispensationalists.

Most Pentecostals recognize the word *seal* has nothing to do with security. Rather, it is an outward mark indicating that we are His workmanship. In view of Ephesians 1:13, "In whom [i.e., by Christ] also after that ye believed, ye were sealed with that Holy Spirit of promise" (KJV), some Pentecostals draw attention to the fact that Christ is the one doing the sealing after the believing. Therefore, they identify it with the baptism in the Holy Spirit (as in Acts 2:4). Even Dunn admits that the aorist participle (used here of the believing, as in Acts 19:2) would ordinarily mean that the believing comes before the sealing. The context also indicates anointing and service.

Response to Walvoord

J. Robertson McQuilkin

Many Keswick teachers and the basic Keswick approach are in harmony with John Walvoord's presentation, though some would take exception to his strong insistence on two coexisting substances (natures) in the believer. It is unclear to me how the latter half of the chapter, which enunciates his doctrine of sanctification, is related to, let alone dependent on, the two-nature theory to which the first half of the chapter is devoted. Why not simply go with the last half? Or at least show the relationship between the two? If, however, we consider only the first half, dealing with the two-nature theory, I remain unconvinced by the argument, possibly because it is grounded more in theoretical discussion than in biblical exposition. But it seems harmless enough if it leads on to the doctrine of progressive sanctification in the life of the believer, which Walvoord advocates. At the same time, I must admit to some uneasiness, since many adherents of the two-nature theory do not follow his lead. There is much abuse of the notion of two natures residing within the believer by those who hold that the old nature is unredeemable and that the new nature is perfect (or is Christ Himself). Who, then, is responsible for Christian conduct? The old nature cannot grow better, nor can the new nature grow, for it is already perfect, yet the concept of development or growth is the key idea of the Christian life in apostolic teaching. As a result of this distorted teaching, a whole genre of higher-life, deeper-life teaching has developed, a genre that advocates a do-nothing, let-Jesus-do-His-thing kind of passive Christian existence. The two-nature idea need not lead in this direction, as Walvoord clearly demonstrates. But it often has led into various aberrations, so that the notion surely demands more than deduction based on an analogy with the two natures of Christ, itself another logical deduction. So important an issue surely demands direct, clear biblical teaching, not only to establish the doctrine, but to guard it from abuse.

There are other, lesser matters of concern. If there is a qualitative difference among authentic Christians between those who are filled with the Spirit and those who are not (e.g., see pp. 215–16), it would be helpful to have a more thorough biblical basis for the definition of *fill*, which is clearly a figure of speech. Though agreeing with the general tenor of the definition offered, I do not see adequate biblical evidence to limit the definition of *fill* to "control." Furthermore, I wonder exactly *how* the Spirit of God uses "the human body as His instrument" (p. 220).

Having indicated concerns, however, it should be stated again in conclusion that the doctrine of sanctification as enunciated by John Walvoord is in harmony with the Keswick approach.

NOTES

CHAPTER 1

[1] See, for example, Maxim Piette, *John Wesley in the Evolution of Protestantism* (New York: Sheed & Ward, 1937), and Martin Schmidt, *John Wesley: A Theological Biography*, 2 vols. (New York: Abingdon, 1962, 1973).

[2] Among other studies, see Albert C. Outler, "John Wesley as Theologian—Then and Now," *Methodist History* 12 (July 1974): 63–82; Kenneth E. Rowe, ed., *The Place of Wesley in the Christian Tradition* (Metuchen, N.J.: Scarecrow, 1976); Colin Williams, *John Wesley's Theology Today* (New York: Abingdon, 1960); and Mildred Bangs Wynkoop, *A Theology of Love: The Dynamic of Wesleyanism* (Kansas City: Beacon Hill, 1972).

[3] "Address to the Clergy," in *The Works of John Wesley*, ed. Thomas Jackson, 14 vols. (London: Wesley Conference Office, 1872; reprint, Kansas City: Beacon Hill, 1978), 10:484 (hereafter cited as *Works*); R. S. Brightman, "Gregory of Nyssa and John Wesley in Theological Dialogue" (Ph.D. diss., Boston University, 1969); Ted A. Campbell, "John Wesley's Conceptions and Uses of Christian Antiquity" (Ph.D. diss., Southern Methodist University, 1984).

[4] George Croft Cell, *The Rediscovery of John Wesley* (New York: Holt, 1935).

[5] John Wesley to John Clayton(?), March 24, 1739, in *Works of John Wesley*, ed. Frank Baker, 26 vols. (Oxford: Oxford University Press; Nashville: Abingdon, 1974–82), 25:616.

[6] Sermon, "The Witness of the Spirit," *Works* 5:129, 133.

[7] Sermon, "The End of Christ's Coming," *Works* 6:277.

[8] "A Plain Account of Christian Perfection as Believed and Taught by the Reverend Mr. John Wesley from the Year 1725–1777," *Works* 11:395, 417.

[9] Ibid., 415.

[10] Sermon, "Christian Perfection," *Works* 6:5–6.

[11] See Harald Lindström, *Wesley and Sanctification: A Study in the Doctrine of Salvation*. (London: Epworth, 1950; reprint, Grand Rapids: Zondervan, Francis Asbury Press, 1984), p. 12.

[12] Cell, *Rediscovery of John Wesley*, p. 341.

[13] Lindström lists other writers who support these views; see *Wesley and Sanctification*, pp. 12–13.

[14] See Albert C. Outler, "Holiness of Heart and Life," in *Wesleyan Theology: A Sourcebook*, ed. Thomas A. Langford (Durham, N.C.: Labyrinth, 1984), p. 243.

[15] *Works* 8:294–96; 11:389–91

[16] *Works* 6:64–65.

[17] Lindström, *Wesley and Sanctification*, p. 12.

[18] *Works* 6:276–77.

[19] See "Upon Our Lord's Sermon on the Mount, I," *Works* 5:247–61.

[20] "On Sin in Believers," *Works* 5:146–47.

[21] Ibid., 5:147, 151–56.

[22] "Plain Account," *Works* 11:401.

240 | Five Views on Sanctification

[23]John and Charles Wesley, *The Poetical Works*, Collected and arranged by G. Osborn, 13 vols. (London: Wesleyan Methodist Conference Office, 1868–1872), 2:321.

[24]"On Perfection," *Works* 6:413–15.

[25]"Christian Perfection," *Works* 6:5–6.

[26]"Minutes of Several Conversations," *Works* 8:328–29.

[27]"Plain Account," *Works* 11:426.

[28]Outler, "Holiness of Heart and Life," p. 243.

[29]"The End of Christ's Coming," *Works* 6:276.

[30]See references cited above in n. 3.

[31]Cell, *Rediscovery of John Wesley*, pp. 265ff.

[32]This small club was a spiritual growth group that the Wesleys, Whitefield, and a few other friends formed while they were students at Oxford University.

[33]See "The End of Christ's Coming," *Works* 6:276–77.

[34]See Lindström, *Wesley and Sanctification*, pp. 11–14.

[35]Outler, "Holiness of Heart and Life," p. 242.

[36]*Works* 8:285.

[37]In the sermon "Living Without God," Wesley describes the "Atheist," the fallen person devoid of the Spirit of God, as one who "has not the least sight of God. . . [or] any desire to have any knowledge of his ways. . . . He *tastes* nothing of the goodness of God" (*Works* 7:351). See also "The New Birth," *Works*, 6:70.

[38]"The Doctrine of Original Sin," *Works* 9:193–194.

[39]Sermon, "Original Sin," *Works* 6:63.

[40]"Sermon on the Mount, XI," *Works* 5:406.

[41]Sermon, "The New Birth," *Works* 6:66–67.

[42]"The Doctrine of Original Sin," *Works* 9:433.

[43]*Works* 7:337–43.

[44]*Works* 9:242–43; 10:190.

[45]"The Doctrine of Original Sin," *Works* 9:381.

[46]Ibid., p. 327.

[47]Ibid., p. 255; Sermon, "The Fall of Man", *Works* 6:223.

[48]"The Doctrine of Original Sin," *Works* 9:275.

[49]Sermon, "Working Out Our Own Salvation," *Works* 6:512.

[50]See Lindström, *Wesley and Sanctification*, pp. 61ff.

[51]Sermon, "Justification by Faith," *Works* 5:57; also, "The Lord Our Righteousness," *Works*, 5:237–45.

[52]Lindström, *Wesley and Sanctification*, p. 75.

[53]Journal for June 15, 1741, *Works* 1:315.

[54]"Sermon on the Mount, V," *Works* 5:311–14.

[55]Ibid.

[56]"The Original [sic], Nature, Property, and Use of the Law," *Works* 5:438.

[57]Letter to Joseph Benson, November 30, 1770, *Works* 12:415. Wesley refers for proof to Romans 8:3.

[58]"Sermon on the Mount, V" *Works* 5:311.

[59]Sermon, "The Law Established Through Faith, I," *Works* 5:450, 454; "Plain Account," *Works* 11:414–16.

[60]"A Farther Appeal to Men of Reason and Religion," *Works* 8:47.

[61]"The Law Established Through Faith, II," *Works* 5:462.

[62]Wynkoop, *Theology of Love*, p. 222.

[63]Sermon, "The Almost Christian," *Works* 5:21, 22.

[64]Sermon, "The First Fruits of the Spirit," *Works* 5:88–89.

[65]"Plain Account," *Works* 11:401.

66 Wynkoop, *Theology of Love*, p. 248.

67 Timothy L. Smith, "John Wesley and the Wholeness of Scripture," *Interpretation: A Journal of Bible and Theology* 39 (July 1985): 258.

68 See Ibid p. 260; see also n. 15 above.

69 "Plain Account," *Works* 11:408; sermon, "Christian Perfection," *Works* 6:10–11.

70 *Works* 8:297, 298.

71 Ibid., p. 284.

72 Wynkoop, *Theology of Love*, p. 320.

73 John Leland Peters, *Christian Perfection and American Methodism* (New York: Abingdon, 1956; reprint, Grand Rapids: Francis Asbury Press, 1985), and Charles E. Jones, *Perfectionist Persuasion: The Holiness Movement and American Methodism, 1867–1936* (Metuchen, N.J.: Scarecrow, 1974), thoroughly review this aspect of American Methodism.

74 For fuller development, see Melvin E. Dieter, *The Holiness Revival of the Nineteenth Century* (Metuchen, N.J.: Scarecrow, 1980); Timothy L. Smith, *Revivalism and Social Reform in Mid-nineteenth Century America* (New York: Abingdon, 1957); and idem, *Called unto Holiness: The Story of the Nazarenes, the Formative Years* (Kansas City: Nazarene, 1962).

75 See Melvin E. Dieter, "The Development of Nineteenth Century Holiness Theology," *Wesleyan Theological Journal* 20 (Spring 1985): 61–77, for more extensive development and documentation of the issues under discussion here and following.

76 The largest of these today, often representing subsequent mergers of smaller bodies, are the Salvation Army, the Church of the Nazarene, the Church of God (Anderson, Ind.), the Wesleyan Church, and the Free Methodist Church. The former three grew out of the revival; the latter two were smaller Methodist bodies that espoused the revival. The world-wide movement numbers about eight million members today.

77 See Frank Baker, "Unfolding John Wesley: A Survey of Twenty Years' Studies in Wesley's Thought," *Quarterly Review: A Scholarly Journal for Reflection on Ministry* 34 (Fall 1980): 44–58.

78 Phoebe Palmer, *The Way of Holiness* (New York: Palmer & Hughes, 1867), pp. 52ff.; idem, "The Act of Faith by Which the Blessing Is Obtained," in *Sanctification Practical: A Book for the Times*, ed. J. Boynton (New York: Foster & Palmer, 1867), pp. 115–30.

79 See Dieter, "Development of Holiness Theology," pp. 64–65.

80 Sermon, "The Repentance of Believers," *Works* 6:165.

81 See for example, E. G. Marsh, *The Old Man* (Cincinnati: Revivalist, 1930), chap. 16. The emphasis is much more moderate in Donald S. Metz, *Studies in Biblical Holiness* (Kansas City: Beacon Hill, 1971), 142–43, 173.

82 Wynkoop's *Theology of Love* represents the most thorough development of this trend. J. Kenneth Grider represents a more traditional view in his *Entire Sanctification: The Distinctive Doctrine of Wesleyanism* (Kansas City: Beacon Hill, 1980).

83 John Fletcher, "The Last Check to Antinomianism, " in *The Works of the Reverend John Fletcher, Late Vicar of Madeley*, 4 vols. (New York: Mason & Lane, 1836), 2:526.

84 See extended discussion of Fletcher's use of a Pentecostal hermeneutic in understanding entire sanctification, in Lawrence W. Wood, *Pentecostal Grace* (Grand Rapids: Zondervan, 1980), pp. 177–239; also see Dieter, "Development of Holiness Theology," pp. 66–74, and Timothy L. Smith, "How John Fletcher Became the Theologian of Wesleyan Perfectionism," *Wesleyan Theological Journal* 15:1 (Spring 1980): 66–87.

[85] Donald W. Dayton, "Asa Mahan and the Development of American Holiness Theology," *Wesleyan Theological Journal* 9, (1974): 60–69; Idem, "The Doctrine of the Baptism of the Holy Spirit: Its emergence and significance," *Wesleyan Theological Journal* 13 (Spring 1978): 114–26.

[86] See especially Fredrick Dale Brunner, *A Theology of the Holy Spirit: The Pentecostal Experience and the New Testament Witness* (Grand Rapids: Eerdmans, 1970), and James D. G. Dunn, *Baptism in the Holy Spirit* (London: SCM, 1970).

[87] The *Wesleyan Theological Journal* 14 (Spring and Fall 1979) carries the heart of the Fletcher-Wesley debate in the contemporary movement.

[88] "Plain Account," *Works* 11:394, 397, 444.

CHAPTER 2

[1] See in this connection the brief but incisive study of Christian separation by Johannes G. Vos entitled *The Separated Life: A Study of Basic Principles* (Philadelphia: Great Commission). In contrast to Christians who hold that the life of Christian separation means primarily abstinence from certain material things, Vos contends that the Bible requires a spiritual separation from conduct that is sinful in itself.

[2] John Calvin, *Institutes of the Christian Religion*, ed. John T. McNeill, trans. Ford Lewis Battles, 2 vols. (Philadelphia: Westminster, 1960), 3.1.1. On the relation between union with Christ and sanctification, see James S. Stewart, *A Man in Christ* (New York: Harper, 1935), and Lewis B. Smedes, *Union with Christ* (Grand Rapids: Eerdmans, 1983).

[3] Herman Bavinck, *Gereformeerde Dogmatiek*, 3d ed., 4 vols. (Kampen: Kok, 1918), 4:277 (my translation).

[4] On the image of God see G. C. Berkouwer, *Man: The Image of God*, trans. Dirk W. Jellema (Grand Rapids: Eerdmans, 1962), and Anthony A. Hoekema, *Created in God's Image* (Grand Rapids: Eerdmans, 1986).

[5] On the matter of following Christ's example, see G. C. Berkouwer's chapter entitled "The Imitation of Christ," in his *Faith and Sanctification*, trans. John Vriend (Grand Rapids: Eerdmans, 1952), pp. 135–60.

[6] J. H. Moulton and George Milligan, *The Vocabulary of the Greek Testament Illustrated from the Papyri* (Grand Rapids: Eerdmans, 1957), pp. 335–36.

[7] Louis Berkhof, *Systematic Theology*, rev. and enl. ed. (Grand Rapids: Eerdmans, 1941), p. 534.

[8] John Murray, *Redemption—Accomplished and Applied* (Grand Rapids: Eerdmans, 1955), pp. 184–85.

[9] Bavinck, *Gereformeerde Dogmatiek*, 4:286; Charles Hodge, *Systematic Theology*, 3 vols. (1871; reprint, Grand Rapids: Eerdmans, 1940), 3:212; Berkhof, *Systematic Theology*, p. 534.

[10] This aspect of sanctification is incisively set forth by John Murray in his chapters "Definitive Sanctification" and "The Agency in Definitive Sanctification," in *Collected Writings of John Murray*, 2 vols. (Carlisle, Pa.: Banner of Truth Trust, 1977), 2:277–93. Cf. also Chester K. Lehman, *The Holy Spirit and the Holy Life* (Scottdale, Pa.: Herald, 1959), pp. 108–20. Lehman uses the word *punctiliar* (as distinguished from *linear*) to describe definitive sanctification.

[11] Murray, *Collected Writings* 2:277.

[12] Ibid., p. 279.

[13] Ibid., p. 280.

[14] See ibid., pp. 289–93.

15 Ibid., p. 293.

16 In Greek the expression is *palaios anthrōpos* (rendered "old man" in the KJV and the ASV but in the newer versions often as "old nature" [RSV, NEB] or "old self" [RSV, JB, NASB, NIV]). Since the word *anthrōpos* means "human being" and not "male human being," the rendering "old self" is to be preferred to "old man."

17 Here again, whereas the older versions (KJV, ASV) have "new man," the newer versions have "new nature" (RSV, NEB) or "new self" (JB, NASB, NIV).

18 Herman Bavinck, *Magnalia Dei*, 2d ed. (Kampen: Kok, 1931), pp. 474–75 (my translation). Similar interpretations of the roles of the old and the new self in the believer are found in comments on Romans 6:6 in John Calvin, *The Epistle to the Romans and the Thessalonians*, trans. Ross MacKenzie (Grand Rapids: Eerdmans, 1979); Charles Hodge's comments on Ephesians 4:22 in his *Commentary on the Epistle to the Ephesians* (Grand Rapids: Eerdmans, 1950); Berkhof, *Systematic Theology*, p. 533; William Hendriksen, *New Testament Commentary on Ephesians* (Grand Rapids: Baker, 1967), pp. 213–14, n. 123; Gordon Girod, *The Way of Salvation* (Grand Rapids: Baker, 1960), pp. 137–38.

19 John Murray, *Principles of Conduct* (Grand Rapids: Eerdmans, 1957), pp. 211–12.

20 Ibid., p. 218, n. 7.

21 Presumably, the new self is "the person in his unity," or totality, ruled by the Holy Spirit. This new self, as we saw above, is being continually renewed after the pattern of the image of God.

22 Note that both Col. 3:9–10 and Eph. 4:22–24 confirm the point developed earlier, namely, that the pattern of sanctification is likeness to God.

23 Murray, *Principles of Conduct*, p. 218.

24 Note that, according to 2 Cor. 7:1, believers must still fight against defilements (RSV) or contaminations (NIV) of the spirit—refuting those Christians who teach that after conversion the human spirit becomes sinless.

25 I do not here adduce Rom. 7:13–25, since I understand this passage to be a description, seen through the eyes of a regenerate person, of the struggle found in an unregenerate person (e.g., an unconverted Pharisaic Jew) who is trying to fight sin through the law alone, apart from the strength of the Holy Spirit. See my book *The Christian Looks at Himself*, 2d ed. (Grand Rapids: Eerdmans, 1977), pp. 61–67; also Herman Ridderbos, *Paul: An Outline of His Theology*, trans. John R. De Witt (Grand Rapids: Eerdmans, 1975), pp. 126–30.

26 Murray, *Principles of Conduct*, p. 220.

27 See Hoekema, *The Christian Looks at Himself*, particularly pp. 13–76.

28 H. K. Carroll, "John Wesley," *The New Schaff-Herzog Encyclopedia of Religious Knowledge*, ed. S. M. Jackson, 12 vols. (New York: Funk & Wagnalls, 1912), 12:309.

29 Donald S. Metz, *Studies in Biblical Holiness* (Kansas City: Beacon Hill, 1971), pp. 19, 250.

30 Ibid., p. 226, quoting John Wesley.

31 Ibid., pp. 228–30, 243.

32 Though justification and sanctification must be distinguished from each other, they must never be separated. Both are essential aspects of our union with Christ.

33 The NASB rendering is preferred, since it translates *sarx* literally as "flesh," whereas the NIV here uses the paraphrase "sinful nature."

34 On this point, see F. F. Bruce, "Commentary on Colossians," in *Commentary on Ephesians and Colossians* (Grand Rapids: Eerdmans, 1957), pp. 268–69.

35 Calvin, *Institutes* 2.7.12.

[36]On this aspect of sanctification, see further Berkouwer's chapter "Sanctification and Law," in *Faith and Sanctification,* pp. 163–93.

CHAPTER 3

[1]Stanley H. Frodsham, *With Signs Following* (Springfield, Mo.: Gospel, 1946), p. 20.

[2]Frank Bartleman, *How Pentecost Came to Los Angeles* (Los Angeles: Printed by author, 1928), p. 58.

[3]Edith Blumhofer, "The Finished Work of Calvary," *Paraclete* 18:4 (Fall 1984): 21.

[4]Gary B. McGee, "A Brief History of the Modern Pentecostal Outpouring," *Paraclete* 18:2 (Spring 1984): 22.

[5]P. C. Nelson, *Bible Doctrines,* rev. ed. (Springfield, Mo.: Gospel, 1948), p. 101.

[6]Myer Pearlman, *Knowing the Doctrines of the Bible* (Springfield, Mo.: Gospel, 1937), p. 266.

[7]Ibid., pp. 253, 261, 257.

[8]Cited in Nelson, *Bible Doctrines,* p. 108.

[9]*Minutes of the Twenty-ninth General Council of the Assemblies of God,* (Springfield, Mo.: Gospel, 1961), p. 22.

[10]Pearlman, *Knowing the Doctrines,* p. 250.

[11]Nelson, *Bible Doctrines,* p. 103.

[12]Ernest Swing Williams, *Systematic Theology,* 3 vols. (Springfield, Mo.: Gospel, 1953), 2:256.

[13]G. Raymond Carlson, *Salvation: What the Bible Teaches* (Springfield, Mo.: Gospel, 1963), p. 76.

[14]Nelson, *Bible Doctrines,* p. 104.

[15]Williams, *Systematic Theology,* 2:258.

[16]Pearlman, *Knowing the Doctrines,* p. 254.

[17]Williams, *Systematic Theology,* 2:259.

[18]Ralph W. Harris, *Our Faith and Fellowship* (Springfield, Mo.: Gospel, 1963), p. 24.

[19]Stanley M. Horton, *Adult Teacher, 1970* (Springfield, Mo.: Gospel, 1969), Fourth Quarter, p. 71.

[20]Blumhofer, "Finished Work of Calvary," p. 21.

[21]Williams, *Systematic Theology,* 2:259.

[22]Stanley M. Horton, *What the Bible Says About the Holy Spirit* (Springfield, Mo.: Gospel, 1976), p. 251.

[23]Ibid., p. 253

[24]Ibid., p. 258.

[25]Ibid., p. 240.

[26]Nelson, *Bible Doctrines,* p. 52; Albert L. Hoy, "Sanctification," *Paraclete* 15:4 (Fall 1981): 5.

[27]Williams, *Systematic Theology,* 2:232–33; 3:34.

[28]William W. Menzies, "The Spirit of Holiness," *Paraclete* 2:3 (Summer 1968): 15.

[29]Pearlman, *Knowing the Doctrines,* pp. 255–56.

[30]Ibid., pp. 266–67; Kenneth Barney, "The Holy Spirit and Holiness," *Paraclete* 14:4 (Fall 1980): 2.

[31]Hoy, "Sanctification," p. 5.

[32]J. Dalton Utsey, "Romans Seven and Sanctification," *Paraclete* 18:2 (Spring 1984): 4.

[33]Hoy, *Sanctification*, p. 7.

[34]Zenas Bicket, "The Holy Spirit—Our Sanctifier," *Paraclete* 2:3 (Summer 1968): 4–5.

[35]Ibid., p. 5.

[36]Horton, *What the Bible Says*, p. 214.

[37]Anthony D. Palma, "Baptism by the Spirit," *Advance* 16 (June 1980): 16.

[38]L. Thomas Holdcroft, "Spirit Baptism," *Paraclete* 1:1 (Winter 1967): 30.

[39]*Minutes of the Thirty-eighth General Council of the Assemblies of God* (Springfield, Mo.: Assemblies of God Headquarters, 1979), p. 75.

[40]Horton, *What the Bible Says*, pp. 221–22.

[41]Harold D. Hunter, *Spirit-Baptism* (Lanham, Md.: University Press of America, 1983), p. 257.

[42]Ibid., pp. 261, 275.

[43]Williams, *Systematic Theology*, 2:264; John W. Wyckoff, "The Doctrine of Sanctification as Taught by the Assemblies of God" (M.A. thesis, Bethany Nazarene College, 1972), p. 68.

CHAPTER 4

[1]Steven Barabas, *So Great Salvation* (London: Marshall, Morgan & Scott; Grand Rapids: Eerdmans, 1952).

[2]Ibid., pp. 21, 108.

[3]Ibid., p. 84.

[4]Ibid., p. 99.

[5]Ibid., p. 104.

[6]Ibid., pp. 131–32.

[7]Ibid., pp. 132, 143–44.

[8]B. B. Warfield, *Studies in Perfectionism* (New York: Oxford, 1931), 2:559–611. As an interesting sidelight, my father, Robert C. McQuilkin, a leader in the movement known as the Victorious Life Testimony, told me that when this book was published, he went to Warfield and discussed the matter of Keswick teaching and perfectionism at length. Afterward Warfield admitted, "If I had known these things, I would not have included the last chapter in my work."

[9]Barabas, *So Great Salvation*, pp. 98ff.

[10]Ibid., p. 105.

[11]Ibid., p. 72.

[12]Ibid., p. 96.

[13]Ibid., pp. 95, 97.

[14]Charles Hodge, *Systematic Theology*, 3 vols. (New York: Scribner, 1917), 3:67. The entire treatise of faith (pp. 41–113) is superb, useful to those of any theological persuasion.

CHAPTER 5

[1]J. D. Douglas, ed., *The New Bible Dictionary* (Grand Rapids: Eerdmans, 1965), p. 869.

246 | Five Views on Sanctification

T. A. Hegre, *The Cross and Sanctification* (Minneapolis: Bethany Fellowship, 1960), pp. 95–96.

[3]Ibid., p. 96.

[4]Anthony A. Hoekema, "The Struggle Between Old and New Natures in the Converted Man," *Bulletin of the Evangelical Theological Society* 5, no. 2 (Spring 1962): 42.

[5]Ibid., pp. 42–50.

[6]Philip Schaff, ed., *A Select Library of the Nicene and Post-Nicene Fathers of the Christian Church*, 14 vols. (rep. ed., Grand Rapids: Eerdmans, 1979), 1:121.

[7]Ibid., n. 8.

[8]Charles Hodge, *Commentary on the Epistle to the Romans* (New York: Armstrong & Son, 1909), pp. 376–77.

[9]Ibid., p. 377.

[10]Schaff, *A Select Library*, 1:571.

[11]Ibid., 2:264–65.

[12]Ibid., 3:390.

[13]Charles Hodge, *Systematic Theology*, 3 vols. (New York: Scribner, 1899), 2:387, 389.

[14]Benjamin B. Warfield, *The Person and Work of Christ*, ed. Samuel C. Craig (Philadelphia: Presbyterian and Reformed, 1950), p. 211.

[15]Charles C. Ryrie, *Balancing the Christian Life* (Chicago: Moody, 1969), p. 34.

[16]Ibid., pp. 34–35.

[17]Lewis S. Chafer, *Systematic Theology*, 8 vols. (Dallas: Dallas Theological Seminary, 1947–48), 2:285.

[18]Ibid., p. 288.

[19]C. I. Scofield, ed., *The NIV Scofield Study Bible* (New York: Oxford University Press, 1967), p. 1184. While the wording in this revised edition is slightly changed from Scofield's wording in the 1917 edition, the thought is the same.

[20]David C. Needham, *Birthright* (Portland: Multnomah, 1979), p. 65.

[21]Ibid., p. 92.

[22]Scofield, *NIV Scofield Study Bible*, p. 1183.

[23]Ibid., p. 1239.

[24]Hodge, *Systematic Theology*, 3:5.

[25]For a more complete discussion, see John F. Walvoord, *The Holy Spirit* (Findley, Ohio: Dunham, 1958), pp. 128–37.

[26]I have discussed this topic further in ibid., pp. 139–50.

[27]Abraham Kuyper, *The Work of the Holy Spirit*, trans. Henri de Vries (New York: Funk & Wagnalls, 1900).

[28]James D. G. Dunn, *Baptism in the Holy Spirit* (Naperville, Ill.: Allenson, 1970), p. 112.

[29]Chafer, *Systematic Theology*, 4:92–100.

[30]For additional discussion, see Walvoord, *The Holy Spirit*, pp. 151–56; Chafer, *Systematic Theology*, 6:122–37.

[31]Further discussion appears in Walvoord, *The Holy Spirit*, pp. 189–224. For a classic study of the spiritual life, see Lewis Sperry Chafer, *He That Is Spiritual* (Grand Rapids: Zondervan, 1967), pp. 23–172.

[32]Benjamin B. Warfield, review of *He That Is Spiritual*, by Lewis Sperry Chafer, *Princeton Theological Review* 17 (1919): 322.

[33]Ibid.

SUBJECT INDEX

SCRIPTURE INDEX